by ALAN LINDGREN

POETRY

The Seeker (1986)
O Days Are Made of Riddles (1987)
The Sun Sings / WORD-PICTURES 1997 (1999)
Winter Hymns (1997-1998)
Pulsing Love and Light Eternal (1998)
Sun and Moon and Stars of Night (1998)
Summer Songs (1998)
Autumn Harvest (1998)
The Diary (1999)
Instrument of the Poetic Word (1999)
A Poet's World (1999)
Ego and Love (1999)
Night-Mysteries 2004–2005 (2005)
Sun, Sparrow, and Star / Sacred and Secular Songs / Selected Poems (2009)
Journeying with the Sun / An Evolving Imagination / A Poetry Chronology (2013)

POETRY with ESSAYS and SHORT FICTION

Balance is Freedom and Freedom is Love (2002)
By the Sunset there's a Door (2002)
The Courage of the Flame (Two Editions) (2003)
The Magic of the Stars (Two Editions) (2004) (2005)
LOVE-PICTURES 2003–2005 (2005)
The Tides of Evening (Two Editions) (2006)
Love Was All He Vowed (2006)
Imagination: The Final Poems (Two Editions) (2006) (2007)
Imagination and Insight: Selected Poems and Essays (2007)
LIGHT-LICHT: Selected Poems with Three Essays (2007)

SHORT FICTION, PLAYS, a LIBRETTO, a TREATISE and a NOVEL

Regrouping in Idea and Practice, A Treatise on Mars (2007)
Fiction and Fact: Tales, Stories, and an Essay (2007)
The Folk Tale of the Two Tom-Tom Bird Cousins (2008)
Two Folk Tales 2008 (2008)
Michael and Los Angeles /A Novel (2008)
Oliver and Nancy / A Humorous Story in Ten Chapters (2009)
Two Short Plays by Alan Lindgren (2010) (2011)
Saltiff Shore – Where Love's Requited / A Comedy in Six Acts (2010)
The Property / A Play in Three Acts (2010)
Kings & Commoners, Mouse, Magic and More / Stories and Tales (2011)
Sons and Daughters / An Operetta in Prologue and Five Acts / The Libretto (2012)

BIOGRAPHIES

Margaret Lindgren: A Biography and Picture of the Human Being (2005)
Alan's Life-Story (Two Editions) (2005)
The Life of Paul Stanley McLester (2006)
Arne Ragnar Lindgren: Man of Heart, Hand and Mind (2006)
Disa Ellen Lindgren: A Biography of a Modern Human Being (2006)

Alan Lindgren

Journeying with the Sun

An Evolving Imagination
A Poetry Chronology

℘

Sun Sings Publications
Culver City
2013

Journeying with the Sun
An Evolving Imagination
A Poetry Chronology by Alan Lindgren

Published by:
Sun Sings Publications
4144 LaFayette Place
Culver City, CA 90232-2818 U.S.A.

© 2013 by Alan Lindgren
All rights reserved. Published in the United States by Sun Sings Publications, Culver City. No part of this book may be reproduced or transmitted in any form or by any means, electronic or mechanical, including photocopying, recording or by any information storage and retrieval system without written permission from the publisher. Direct all other inquiries to the publisher.
Printed in the United States of America
Book design by Alan Lindgren

10 9 8 7 6 5 4 3 2 1

Library of Congress Control Number: 2012955568

Grateful acknowledgement is made to Mercury Press, which first published *The Sun Sings*, whose verses, poems, and poetic prose are republished in this volume.

1. Lindgren, Alan David, b. 1962—Poetry—United States.
2. Poetry—End of 20th/Beginning of 21st Centuries—United States.
3. Poetry—Chronology—Lindgren, Alan David, b. 1962. I. Title.

Lindgren, Alan.
[Poetry]
Journeying with the Sun/Alan Lindgren.–1st ed.
p.   cm.
ISBN: 978-0-9832053-8-8
2013

This volume of poetry is dedicated to the following special sun personalities and individualities: Rudolf Steiner†, whose Waldorf education introduced me to verse and poetry as a child; my dearest Christ-brother Monsieur Gérard Klockenbring†; my best and dearest friend Dr. Virginia Sease, who has taken the deepest interest in my human being, my vocation as a poet, and my poetry*; my good and very dear friend John Alexandra; my very dear friend and classmate Oliver Steinrueck; my dear courageous and sunny Dutch friend Hans Peter van Manen†, essential Christ-helper when I was a youth in Europe and most needed it; my dear Danish friend Dan Lerche-Petersen who, with candid and wise insight, and friendliness, pointed my way to Germany and therewith my destiny; Walter Brecker†, my dear sun South African friend and wise guide in Los Angeles; Greg Fawcett, my wonderful dear friend from my Pomona College days; my very dear sun friend Ida†; my gentlest dear friend Dorothy Walcer†; my dear sunny friend Mary Gilvarry; my warm clear friend Cindy Hindes; my warm kind patient and dear friend David Alden Thiele†; my dear warm open friend Dan Cook; my dear warm original friend Morley Lyle; my very dear warm friend Judy Jaeckel; my dear friendly friend Gisela Wielki, my dear warm friend Mary I know from my work; and to my very dear good, stable and patient father Arne Lindgren†, who provided the foundation for my life. It is especially dedicated to my dearest Mother Mrs. Margaret Lindgren who, of all human beings, is most special to me.

* IMPORTANT: See Note on Endorsements on Page xxx

Acknowledgements

My good thanks to my friend Pat Thompson; I am forever indebted to her for writing the beautiful Foreword to this volume. My deep gratitude to Hans Peter van Manen† for his clear interest, insight, and friendship; and for writing *Alan Lindgren's Poetry* included in this volume. I will honor him with its publication. My gratitude goes out also to Gregory Melden, my computer technician, for his assistance with computer matters without which I never would have produced this or any other volume. I extend my deepest gratitude to Dr. Virginia Sease for her steadfast friendship, support, and guidance since our first meeting on February 15, 1986; and to John Alexandra for his good friendship and friendly counsel since October of 1978. Finally, I thank my dearest and most wonderful parents, Arne† and Margaret Lindgren, who brought me into this world, raised me with feeling and love, and who continue to love and help me to this day.

POETRY, a brief sketch by Alan Lindgren

Poetry is the uniquely human art form in that imagination is the only human spiritual faculty of the three. (Inspiration and intuition are divine faculties.) In addition the medium of poetry, words, are to be found nowhere in nature, where architecture shares spaces with ravines, canyons and caves; sculpture forms with rocks, hills and mountains; painting light and color phenomena with the plant kingdom and heavens/clouds; and music sound with birdsong, animal sounds, water and the wind in common. Thus the poet has the special task to convey his experiences in the poetic Word with its special qualities (rhythms, consonantal sounds/alliteration, vowel sounds, rhymes) with his own, unique imagination. As each human being, each poet has an imagination unlike any other. In my poetry 'word-pictures' best describes my imagery. It is most remarkable that there are images in my poetry at all because I am native to Los Angeles where I have lived all but 3 ½ years of my fifty-year life and where all but a few of my poems have been composed. Los Angeles is a huge urban phenomenon. A true poet, I can live near LAX International Airport with planes going by every four to five minutes, or walk on a major street with heavy ground traffic, experiencing nature right in the midst of the city: the sun speaks to me in her clear resounding light; the sparrows win my heart all over again; the mountains in the distance portray the end of my landscape, Christ appears in the white bright billowing Christ-clouds, the dear sunset in its beautiful colors deepens the passion and crucifixion of Christ in my heart, the glorious sunrise announces a new day of God's deeds in His Creation. So I draw many of my images from nature-phenomena right here in Los Angeles where I have my poetic experiences.

The poet is an individual I and so singular. The reader for whom poetry is to mean something necessarily has an individual relationship to a poem. Thus each will have her/his favorites and derive, not only the universal content of a poem—what is objective—, but what is of a personal nature. Indeed the objective aspect of an artwork is personal for the same reasons: The artist's soul ("Individuality of expression is the beginning and end of all art." Johann Wolfgang von Goethe) and the beholder or reader's soul make it so. In this spirit I ask that you seek to discover what lies in each poem, while enjoying the qualities of the poems, which speak to you personally. In this manner you may take joy or sorrow in an individual poem, and you may also find what is special about my poetry. Now enjoy the poems, my experiences I share with you here.

Alan Lindgren
Culver City, June 15, 2012/Los Angeles, February 3, 2013

Table of Contents

Foreword by Pat Thompson, A.A. xxv
Preface xxvi
Introduction xxix
* IMPORTANT: See *Note on Endorsements* xxx
Passage from Hans Peter van Manen's work xxxi
Introduction to *The Sun Sings* by Virginia Sease, Ph.D. 69
Alan Lindgren's Poetry by Hans Peter van Manen, Ph.D. 103

Journeying with the Sun
The Poems, Excerpts from correspondence and
other Insights into the Poems

Chapter One. 1986–1987:
The Discovery of My Vocation

PART ONE. August – December 1986: THE SEEKER,
Verses of a Seeker After Christ

The Seeker 36
To Be a Poet 37
Mountain Climbing 38
By the Sunset there's a Door 39
The Sky is Free to Me 40
Lost in the Darkness I Wander 41
Might I Not Resume Life Once More? 42
The War 43
Take a Look at Your Soul 45
The Uniting 46

PART TWO. January – March 1987: O DAYS ARE MADE
OF RIDDLES, Toward the Threshold of the Spirit:
Poems in the Light

I Have a Weakness and a Strength 48
O Zartes Kind! 49
O Gentle Child! 50
Ich Habe Zwei Brüder 51
I Have Two Brothers 51

Table of Contents

Licht 52
Light 53
Outlook 54
Problem-Solving 55
I Have Left My Home 56
O Days Are Made of Riddles 57
Bewußt-Sein 58
Conscious-Being 58

Chapter Two. 1994–1995: Early Sun and Other Poetry

A long time ago 60

From a card from Virginia Sease, Ph.D., from Dornach, Switzerland, written late 1995 or (early?) 1996 60

The Rainbow and the Plant 61
Evening Song 61
Words 62
Sun of My Heart 62

From a card from Virginia Sease, Ph.D., from Dornach, written October 30, 1997 63

Chapter Three. The Sun Sings WORD-PICTURES 1997

Introduction by Virginia Sease, Ph.D. 69

O Mother Poetry! 70

Verses Especially for Children

Little sparrow up above 73
Wind and rain and hail and snow 73
On this summer afternoon 73
Thou beamest forth, O glorious Sun 74
The sun is golden in the sky 74
Brilliant peach across the sky 74
Summer sunsets rich in hue 75
After the night of forgetting and sleep 75
A Child's Grace at Mealtime 76

Table of Contents

The Four Gifts 76
Solid earth beneath our feet 77
Language is a wonderful thing 78
The arts are the sweetest things I know 78
America – a word with thee! 79
I see the mountains in the distance 80
I saw a heavenly landscape above 80
Maria fair 81
O Christmas Night! 81

Poems and Prose for Adults

Beauty is a wondrous thing 85
Fields of clouds rolled 86
Blue ocean of sky 87
The glorious majesty of the mighty sun 88
Der Sonne Licht 88
It swirls. 89
O Night! 90
Autumn with the breezes and the rain 91
Rhythms deep 92
The Gift of a Very Small Child 93
O Kind! 94
O Child! 94
A Christmas Meditation 95
The human hand 96
The light of the heart 96
A poem lives in rhythms 97
The tree. 98
Soul-eyes of my brother 99
I saw a Christ-cloud in the sky 100
Ocean depths of happy rest 101, 102

Alan Lindgren's Poetry by Hans Peter van Manen, Ph.D. 103

Chapter Four. 1997–2001 Developing a 'Style of Myself'

PART ONE. Thanksgiving 1997 in Atlanta

The Spirits of the Night 108

Table of Contents

Sensing and Sounding the Voices of Choirs 108
The Fountain 108

From a letter from Hans Peter van Manen, Ph.D., written in
The Hague, Netherlands, December 21, 1998 110

PART TWO. 1997–1998 Winter Hymns

My Little Bird So Fair 110, 111
Hark, Do You Hear? 111
I Only Scraped My Knees 112
A Winter's Hymn 113
January Morn 114
The Wedding 115
My Songs 116
Mother Rhythm 117
Unfathomable Time 118

PART THREE. 19 January – 20 February 1998 in Inglewood

The Revelation 120
Above the meadow there's the sunlight 120
Ich würde Bücher schreiben 120, 121
Pappa my father in broad daylight 121
Sun so precious 121
In der Dunkelheit 121
Das himmlische Licht 121, 122

From a letter from Virginia Sease, Ph.D., February 12, 1998 122

Peace 122

PART FOUR. 1998 Spring, Summer Songs & Autumn

From a greeting card from Dorothy Walcer written in Los Angeles,
June or July, 1998 124

Breath 124
Two Poems Composed on St. John's (1998)
    The Wasteland 125
    We Rejoice 125
The Forest 126
And now the night draws near 127

Table of Contents

Six Summer Poems
    Dancing Elves 127
    Seasons of Sunrise 127, 128
    Writing 128
    The Few 128, 129
    Bonnie Lass 129
    Forgiveness 130

From a letter from Virginia Sease, Ph.D., written in
Stuttgart, Germany, December 6, 1998 131

A Song Beside My Door 131
The Birds in Song Presiding 132

PART FIVE. June 1999 Instrument of the Poetic Word

Five Color Poems
    Red 134
    Purple 134
    Blue 135
    Green 135
    Yellow 136

PART SIX. June – July 1999 A Poet's World

A Dream 138
Artistic Sensibility 138
Spirit-Land 138
Ein Liebessturm 139
Die Menschen 139
Die Farben 139
Die Liebe 139
Die Menschheit 139
A Pink 140
A Pleasant Green 140
O Blue of Water 140
O Brown of Earth 141
A Grey 141
A Yellow 141
Behold: the Red 141
A Purple Cloth 142

Table of Contents

PART SEVEN. July 1999 – November 2001 Ego and Love

A Time To Reminisce 144
The inner I is such a thing 144
Die Mahlzeit Christi 144, 145
Sometime share a feeling 145, 146
Dying 146
When Sky and Earth are Joined 146
My First Room 147
Da war ein Mensch 147
Accentuate a revenue 147, 148
A measured step 148
Glory of rivers and glory of seas 149

Chapter Five. 2001–2002: Celebrating Nature and Humanity

The Moon is Rising in My Mind 152, 153
The Rain is Ritual and Wreath 153
What the Mountain Means To Me 154
Fünf Deutsche Gedichte*
   1. Zwei Welten 155
   2. Gottes Segen 155, 156
   3. Eines 156
   4. Die Welt 156, 157
   5. Dein Leben 157
A Vision of Love 158, 159
For Virginia Sease 159
Of Flowers and Weeds 159, 160
The Shores 160
Schöne Nacht 160, 161
Wonders of the Night 161
Merry 162
Hellsehen* 162, 163
Reborn 163, 164
Freund* 164, 165
Aglow 165, 166
Peasant Poetry* 166
Beyond the Sea 166, 167

Table of Contents

Courage 167, 168
I Like the Plant Do Weave 168, 169
Evening Prayer 169, 170
Three Songs of Silence*
    1. November 170, 171
    2. Hope 171, 172
    3. Poet's Gold 172, 173
People: Be Wise 173, 174
Frieden 174, 175
The Magic of the Night* 175-177
Heaven* 177, 178

Chapter Six. August 2002–April 2004: Ballads and Sonnets

Lad Alan Glad – A Ballad 180
A Noble Lass in Days of Yore – A Ballad 181
The Imagination – A Ballad 182
Sonnet number 4 – Susan Young 183
Sonnet number 5 – Svetlana Chmeleva 183
Sonner number 6 – Camilla Lahn-Johannessen 184
Sonnet number 9 184
The Angel Played by Virginia Sease – A Ballad 185, 186
Fair Queen in Majesty – A Ballad 186
The Gentleman's Hat – A Ballad 186-188
Camilla Fair – A Ballad 188, 189
The War – A Ballad 189, 190
The Life of a Seeker – A Ballad 190-192
Fairest Rose – A Ballad 192, 193
Sonnet number 14 – The Christ-clouds 193
Sonnet number 16 – Promise 193, 194
Grief – A Sonnet 194
Sonnet number 20 – Water 194, 195
Sonnet number 21 – Winter 195
Sonnet number 22 – The Human Soul 195, 196
Shakespeare, the Sonnet Master – A Sonnet 196
Love – A Sonnet 196, 197
My Sunny Fair Companion – A Sonnet 197

Table of Contents

From a letter from Virginia Sease, Ph.D., summer, 2004 200

Chapter Seven. 2003–2004: The Magic of the Stars
New Poems

Unique 200
Mary's Kiss 201, 202
Shepherds' Gifts 203
Good News 204
Dream 205, 206
Christmas Glories 206
Pilgrim Song 207
Syllables 208, 209
Creation – A Poem of Celebration 209-213
Riddles of the Rose 214
Cupid's Bow 215, 216
Mornings 217, 218
Sing Birds Towards Easter 218-220
Christ, the Gardener 221, 222
Inner Landscapes 223
Fair Venus 224, 225

Chapter Eight. 2003–2006:
The Magic of the Stars, Love & Lyricism,
Songs & Elegies, Mysteries and Other Themes

My Tree 228, 229
Every Memory 229, 230
Two Poems of February 22, 2003
   1. Thinking 230
   2. Feeling 231
Red Rose and I 231
Soul Yellow 231, 232
Chris 232
Rosebush Green and Red 233-238
Morning Song 238, 239
Green 239, 240
Yellow 240, 241

Table of Contents

Blue	241-243
Red	243, 244
Wirklichkeits Glück	245, 246
Lieben und Ruhen und Schlafen und Träumen*	246, 247
A Poet's Dream-Reality	247-249
Fünf August Abendgedichte	
1. Hans Peter van Manen	249
2. Gedanken	249
3. Abend Andacht	250
4. Sonnenuntergang	250
5. Liebesgeburt	250, 251
Einsamkeit	251, 252
Tendenzen	252, 253
The Song of Winter	253, 254
The Mountains	254, 255
I Sing*	255-257
When Soldiers Die*	257, 258
On Pilgrimages*	258, 259
Song of Mother's Child*	259, 260
The Perfect Whole*	260, 261
Love Remember	261-263
Poetry Reality	263, 264
Höret! Die Sonne – Für Gérard Klockenbring	264, 265
Night is a Candle's Dream	265, 266
The Magic Kingdom	266, 267
Seek To Know a Cloudless Day	267, 268
America – A Song for Thee	268, 269
The Last Day of Summer	270
Feelings Are Special	270, 271
Rejuvenating Light	272, 273
An Angelean Autumnal Sun	273
Sincerity*	273-275
Einsamkeit und Licht	275
Die Liebe*	275, 276
The Landscape	276
Knabe Jesu*	276, 277
The Shadows and the Light*	278
Poetry – A Poem*	278, 279
The Beach on December 26, 2004	279, 280

Table of Contents

Tiefrote Rose, Gérard Klockenbring	280, 281
Why, Friend? – A Poem to Jeff Watson and to All Who Are of Too Light a Sensibility	281, 282
Dr. Martin Luther King, Jr. – A Tribute*	282, 283
Dignify the Mountain-Land	283
Silence, or Time*	284
The Mystery of Death and Love	284, 285
TOUCH	285, 286
Love and the Rain	286-288
Evenings	288-290
Taste, or Apprentice to Sais*	291
When I Fold My Laundry	291, 292
Passion Wednesday	292-294
Easter Morning, 2005	294-296
The Mysterious Place*	296
The Winter Snows Have Fallen	297, 298
TECHNIK*	298, 299
Drei kleine Juni Naturgedichte	
1. O kleine Honigbiene	299
2. Gelbweiße Rose	299, 300
3. Die Ameisen	300
Christ	300, 301
In Merriment	301
God is Good*	301, 302
When I Write the World Happens*	302, 303
Nachtandacht	303, 304
Henrietta – What You Mean To Me*	304-306
Colors*	306-308
The Beautiful Woman and the Christ	309-311
Wisdom of the Stars*	311, 312
A Song to Music*	312, 313
Johnny George	314, 315
A Boy – A Poem Dedicated to Virginia Sease*	315, 316
Good Sevenfold Man!	316, 317
Where Are the Olden Days?	317, 318
Verses*	318
Morning*	319
To Nature	319, 320
Morning Sun	320

Table of Contents

Triumph	320
Peace (2)	321
Autumn	321, 322
Sun of Evening	322, 323
Peace is a Tree!	323, 324
Prophecy	324, 325
The Rose – To Virginia Sease	325, 326
I Know in Me Myself Dwells Christ	326, 327
Michaélic Thoughts	327
Deeds of the Light*	327, 328
Stimmen	328, 329
Songs of Love and Romance	
Immersion	329
1. Trace	329
2. Love	330
3. The Colors	330
4. The Night Sky	330, 331
5. The Romance	331
Women and Men	331, 332
The Holy Child	332, 333
Nachtgesang*	333-335
The Newspaper and the Crown	335, 336
Human Beings Change	336, 337
In the Woods	337, 338
Christ's Call	338
Language	339-341
Inner Spaces Changing Blue*	341
Christ in Peach-Clouds	342
Gründonnerstag	342, 343
Zwei April Nachostern Sonnenuntergang Gedichte	
1. Die Möven	343
2. Ein Mövenlied	343, 344
The Daisies	344
May Song	345, 346
Love Was All He Vowed	346-349
Transcendence—To Don Perryman	349, 350
St. John's, Christmas	350, 351
Gardens	351
Kenelma	352, 353

Table of Contents

Suchet* 353
A Verse 353
Imagination—For John 354
Love Is Like Water 354, 355
The Roses—For Virginia Sease 355-357
The Sea* 357, 358
Dream—For Linda 358, 359
The Little Sparrows—To Margaret 359, 360
The Vineyards—For Isolde 361, 362
The Prince—For Don Perryman 362-364
The Birth 364

Chapter Nine. 2007–2008: Christ, Nature, Poet and Poetry

Beauty is Clouds, Sometimes 366, 367
Sailors 367, 368
Today Was Yesterday 368-370
Christ 370
Memories 370, 371
To the Questioning Scientist 371, 372
Congenial to the Wind 372
Time Passes Broad Things 372
What Is? 373
Earth 374, 375
Elephants 375-377
My Love Is 377-379
Serenity—A Poem of Easter Monday Evening 379, 380
Men of the Sun 380, 381
When Dreams Adorn the Heavens 381, 382
The Little Snapdragon* 382, 383
Diadem 383, 384
Sweet Time* 384, 385
Honeybees* 385, 386
Mystery 387, 388
Genius 388-390
Trampolines 390
Three Poems of Tuesday, late afternoon, September 18, 2007
    I. Leaves 390, 391

Table of Contents

II. Memory 391
III. The Thoughts of Light 391, 392
Die Lieder 392
Love 392, 393
I Always Noticed 393-395
The Chair, the Table and the Tableware 395, 396
Times To 396-398

Chapter Ten. 2008–2009: The Holy Trinity and God

God* 400
Kim 400-402
The Garden 402-406
Holy Dreams 406, 407
Grace 408
Ist die Kunst 409
Mehr "Ist" 409, 410
Good Friday 410
I Saw a Song 410, 411
Beyond An Age 411
Friendship 411, 412
Evergreen 413, 414
Chorus 414, 415
The Math* 415, 416
The Suicide 416-418
Inside the Library* 418, 419

From a card from Virginia Sease, Ph.D., written in Dornach,
April 13, 2009 420

Cosmic Christ—To Evelyn Francis Capel 420, 421
Peach 421-424
Everywhere 424

From a card from Virginia Sease, Ph.D., written in Dornach,
May 22, 2009 424

Sophia 424-427
Pictures of Places and Faces 427-430
Accompany 430-432

Journeying with the Sun   The Poetry of Alan Lindgren   xix

Table of Contents

Vision Kindness 432-434
Monk Poetry* 434-437

Chapter Eleven. 2009–2013*:
All Previously Unpublished Poems

Children 440, 441
A Christmas Night 441, 442
From a letter from Virginia Sease, Ph.D., written in Dornach,
August 22, 2010 443
America! Soul of My Heart 443-445
Rose of Heaven 445-447
I Am the Passage 447, 448
Pearl 448-450
Where Wisdom is a Verse for the Dead 450-452
Sounds of Evening 453
Interrnalize These Thoughts 453-455
Johnny 455, 446
Menschenbruder 456, 457
Human Brother 457
Love and The Meal 457-459
The Little Shoe 459, 460
Birth 460, 461
Painted Patterns 461, 462
Light 462-464
Know God 464, 465
Truth 465
Dreaming 465, 466
The Park 466, 467
Fonder 467, 468
Measure 468
Herbstanbeginn nach Weihnachten schauend
  I. Sensibelsein 469
  II. Sonne 469
Radiance 470, 471
Destiny 471, 472
The Eternal Present 472, 473
The Banyan Tree – To Richard Levin 473, 474

Table of Contents

Children (2)	474, 475
Advent, or Chanticleer	475, 476
Christmas Eve and the Meaning of All Humankind	476, 477
Hand—To Sherry	478, 479
Temple	480
Peace (3)	480-482
Mysteries	482, 483
Home	483
Christus – An Frederik van Eeden	484
Auferstehung – An Hans Peter van Manen	484, 485
From a card from Virginia Sease (for August 5, 2012)	486
Sterben, oder Sonnenuntergang	486
Evening	487
Ein Morgenlied	487, 488
ASK	488
Journey	489, 490
Seeing a Beautiful Sunset	490
Venus and My Child, the Poet	490, 491
Sentience Soul, Mind Soul, Consciousness Soul	491, 492

Three Songs of December 2, 2012
- I. Song of Summer 492
- II. Peaceful 492, 493
- III. See 493, 494

A Child of Light—To Cindy Hindes 494, 495

Chapter Twelve. Deutsche Gedichte
(German Poems: A Review) 1987, 1997–2012

TEIL EINS (PART ONE). 1987

O Zartes Kind!	500
Ich Habe Zwei Brüder	500
Licht	501
Bewußt-Sein	502

TEIL ZWEI (PART TWO). 1997–2000; 2002

Der Sonne Licht	504
O Kind!	504

Table of Contents

Ich würde Bücher schreiben 505
In der Dunkelheit 505
Das himmlische Licht 505
Ein Liebessturm 506
Die Menschen 506
Die Farben 506
Die Liebe 506
Die Menschheit 506
Die Mahlzeit Christi 507, 508
Da war ein Mensch 508
Fünf Deutsche Gedichte*
   1. Zwei Welten 508, 509
   2. Gottes Segen 509
   3. Eines 509
   4. Die Welt 510
   5. Dein Leben 510, 511
Schöne Nacht 511, 512
Hellsehen* 512
Freund* 513
Frieden 513, 514

TEIL DREI (PART THREE). 2003–2007

Wirklichkeits Glück 516, 517
Lieben und Ruhen und Schlafen und Träumen* 517, 518
Fünf August Abendgedichte
   1. Hans Peter van Manen 518
   2. Gedanken 518
   3. Abend Andacht 519
   4. Sonnenuntergang 519
   5. Liebesgeburt 519, 520
Einsamkeit 520, 521
Tendenzen 521, 522
Höret! Die Sonne – Für Gérard Klockenbring 522, 523
Einsamkeit und Licht 523
Die Liebe* 524
Knabe Jesu* 524, 525
Tiefrote Rose, Gérard Klockenbring 525, 526
TECHNIK* 526, 527

Table of Contents

Drei kleine Juni Naturgedichte
   1. O kleine Honigbiene 527
   2. Gelbweiße Rose 527, 528
   3. Die Ameisen 528
Nachtandacht 528, 529
Stimmen 529
Nachtgesang* 530, 531
Gründonnerstag 531
Zwei April Nachostern Sonnenuntergang Gedichte
   1. Die Möven 532
   2. Ein Mövenlied 532
Suchet* 533
Die Lieder 533, 534

TEIL VIER (PART FOUR). 2008; 2011–2012

Ist die Kunst 536
Mehr "Ist" 536, 537
Menschenbruder* 537
Herbstanbeginn nach Weihnachten schauend
   I. Sensibelsein* 537, 538
   II. Sonne* 538
Christus – An Frederik van Eeden* 538, 539
Auferstehung – An Hans Peter van Manen* 539, 540
Sterben, oder Sonnenuntergang* 540, 541
Ein Morgenlied* 541, 542

About the Poet 543, 544

* Poems published for the first time in this volume. They number 100.

(NOTE: The 60 German poems appear twice in the main text and thus in the Table of Contents: interspersed among the poems when they were composed, then again separately in Chapter Twelve.)

Foreword

Alan Lindgren continues to amaze me as I read the manuscript for his newest volume, *Journeying with the Sun*. His ability to observe people and his love of the seasons and nature is evident throughout.

As you read the verses from the earlier part of Alan's career as a poet and on into the latter part, you sense the progression of his evolving imagination.

I found *The Seeker* (Chapter One. Part One) to be a good introduction to Alan's desire and aspiration to convey his experiences in the verse form of literature.

In conclusion *Peace* (Chapter Eleven: *Peace (3)* and *Peaceful*) gives me a sense of Alan's fulfillment and accomplishment as a poet. The abundant poetry including and between these chapters and poems published here make up Alan's vocational task: sharing many of his poetic experiences with others.

Find sixty German poems by Alan Lindgren for readers of this language in a separate chapter at the end (Chapter Twelve). These poems first appear throughout the other chapters (Chapters One to Eleven) among all of the poems according to when they were composed.

Pat Thompson, A.A.
Culver City, California
February 4, 2013

Preface

In coming out with this first edition of *Journeying with the Sun / An Evolving Imagination / A Poetry Chronology of Alan Lindgren*, I am fulfilling a long-time dream, namely, bringing together my finest poems from all my years as a poet in a chronology. Hence I have chosen the subtitle to this book. As I write this Preface, the publication of this book remains yet a dream, for I have just recently published my most major volume, the large *Sun, Sparrow, and Star / Sacred and Secular Songs / Selected Poems* (335 poems, one essay), and my upcoming plans are to publish two short plays and a book of short fiction before embarking on bringing out this volume.* Several constraints stand in the way: time and work and, most significantly, raising the funds, for which I have no savvy or natural faculty, and I am not a rich or business man. *Au contraire*, although I invest everything that I have into my publishing, I have really very little to work with. And so it is no little feat that I have been publishing major and minor works since 1997 after writing my first volume, *The Sun Sings / WORD-PICTURES 1997* (Copyright 1999 by Alan Lindgren, Mercury Press: Chestnut Ridge, NY). They number in the dozens, as of this writing 38 to be exact. **

But none of my previous works attempts to present my poems in a chronology, although in some of my modest projects I published my poetry from a given time-period, usually less than a year, in the sequence in which the poems were composed. Here, however, is a major work, one that encompasses my sixteen-year career as a poet, and in it I set out to accomplish what I had never done.***

The above-mentioned volume, *The Sun Sings / WORD-PICTURES 1997*, is republished here in its entirety, and for the second time. (The first time was in my anthology *By the Sunset there's a Door / Poetry, Prose and Essays Celebrating Nature and Humanity* (Copyright 2002 by Alan Lindgren, Sun Sings Publications: Culver City, CA).) This is a most special work, and I ask that you read these verses, poems and poetic prose with feeling and love for their beautiful qualities and much attention to what they convey, and the *Verses Especially for Children* to the children in your life.

At the time of this writing, this nation and our entire globe are facing great crises, actually one great crisis that is manifesting in many different crises. This is a spiritual crisis that is apparent in: the global climate in its many unusual and extreme weather events and all natural disasters that have been occurring more and more frequently and with increased intensity over the past 30 years or so; childhood's fragile ecology, where the children are placed at the mercy of adults who expose them to virtual and other artificial sensations, when they require

Preface

good nutrition, sound sleep, regularity in the daily routine, abundant physical play and self-engagement in their natural fantasy-life, good human teachers and adults to guide them, and nature- and artistic-musical experiences for their growing souls; social strife witnessed in endemic mental illness and severe addiction problems, and crime because of poor or absent education and want of job training and placement; tremendous poverty, hunger and homelessness from disparity where a small materialistic minority enjoy more than their share for material comforts and conveniences, and the hoarding of money and possessions, at the cost of human welfare, where billions want for enough to eat, potable water to drink, a roof over their heads, clothing to warm and complement them, and a decent education; senseless, atrocious, perhaps unpardonable wars, all of which are bad and cause untold harm and tragedy for infrastructures and countless stricken souls; 'fat' governments that need to be slimmed down to the task of legislation; the global economy as it ails entire, manifesting in different locations as do parts of a single body and whole; the single system Lie in which every one is incorporated as a unit of information or piece of data for processing, without regards their quality/ies; and the cultural sphere that exhibits all manner of surrealistic, naturalistic, unmusical, inartistic, unpoetical, abstractionist and blatantly ugly expressions in a cacophonic chaotic condition of experimentation in which both creative and uncreative people are active today. We have made the paradigm shift, and we stand in the 21st century, but in crisis, and this great crisis is expressed in every sphere of human activity.

Here and there, signs for progress appear and offer themselves to us. There are 'pockets' of goodness, kindness, warmth, love, understanding, compassion and attention wherever there are people. Truth is present as well, though it is denied and under full attack, unassailable because it is inalterably positive and matter-of-fact, an immovable and weighty spiritual rock, and the foundation for the future Glory of Mankind. In the Arts are countless gems of beauty that show themselves, invisible to the popular stream such that the larger public is unaware of them, but they are numerous, individual, wonderful, true to the spirit, healing and a blessing to all who can receive from their source. This source is singular, even as the works are extremely diverse, and its singularity arises from the essentiality of their source, which is the Christ. Many are touched.

It is the Christ who is present wherever Goodness finds a dwelling in human hearts. It is the Christ who is the spirit of the Truth that neither changes nor budges, even as it gains in presence and might. The Christ is our common source of Beauty and Love today and forevermore. Even as we are blown by the cold winds of today's spiritual storms, Christ the Sun and Christ Venus is appearing

Preface

in His Goodness, Truth and Beauty in the persons and gifts of human beings blessed with His Grace. We may also experience Christ in the beauty of God's Creation and human co-Creation of a living character. God have mercy on our souls; may we show mercy on one another.

This volume is a modest but real contribution to 21st Century culture. I am a minor poet of the late 20th and early 21st centuries and a special one: genuine, unique, original, irreplaceable. You will not find the poems in this volume elsewhere with the exception of those in other books of mine. There are 60 poems in the beautiful language of German Romanticism interspersed among the others. These are the only poems to appear twice as they are to found again separately in Chapter Twelve, the final chapter, which is devoted to my German poetry. The manner in which the poems are organized is unprecedented: in the chronological arrangement that characterizes this groundbreaking work. All but three of my poems were composed in the Los Angeles Basin of the Southland. (See Chapter Four. Part One. Thanksgiving 1997 in Atlanta)

As we bravely strive and steer our little ships across the ocean of life in these demanding and confusing times, let us pause with wonder each day to experience the healing forces working and weaving in creativity: God's Creation (Nature) and human co-Creation (the Arts). In this thought and soul-mood, enjoy this chronology of my poetry as you participate in *Journeying with the Sun*.

Alan Lindgren
Los Angeles
November 30–December 2, 2009
February 4, 2013

*The book of short plays, *TWO SHORT PLAYS* (2010, 2011), two other books of one play each (2010), the book of short fiction, *Kings & Commoners, Mouse, Magic and More / Stories and Tales* (2011), and the libretto to an operetta, *Sons and Daughters* (2012), are in print.

**This volume makes 46 books by the author.

***My career as a poet (winter 1994-1995 through 4 February 2013) spans 18 years. This excludes my earliest poems composed August 1986-March 1987, most of which are republished here, when I knew I was a poet.

Introduction

This volume includes much of my poetry of interest. It by no means contains all my worthy poems. It is published primarily so the reader can read the poems selected for this volume in their composition time-sequence. *Journeying with the Sun* contains 441 different poems. The 60 German poems appear twice, a second time in the closing chapter. 100 poems are published for the first time.

This affords the reader an excellent sense for the progression of the poet's evolving imagination and vocational task, whereby his poetic life is seen to unfold as he finds and makes his way. It is not only a sensitive indicator of his soul life as he has undergone many outer and inner changes throughout the years 1995–2013; it is a real revelation of his inner source in the unique word-pictures or imagery of his poems over time. Thus time is the measure of this collection, time in the pulse-beat of the seasons, and in word and sound. My evolving imagination is made apparent in the sequential ordering of the poems. The actual time frame is August 1986 – March 1987 and December 1994 – February 2013. The poems are diverse and are best spoken. They will only be fully experienced by the art form of creative speech. Please read the passage regarding the etheric, imagination and the soul and spirit world that I translated from the German from Hans Peter van Manen's work *Wiederkunft und Heimsuchung* on page xxxi.

In addition to the poems selected for this volume, excerpts from personal letters and cards to the poet that concern his poetic life and poetry are included. These passages found in key places among the poems—before a (group of) poem/s of a given time-period with which they have to do—are not endorsements of any kind. (See **IMPORTANT: Note on Endorsements**, next page) They are excerpts taken from personal correspondence that may be of interest to the reader because of their pertinence to the poetry. These excerpts were and are neither written, used nor published for recommendations, neither have they anything to do with Forewords to books of mine or of others. They are included for their content regards the poetry, something invaluable to the reader for their objectivity, rather than the fact that they were written to me. Because they are true, these statements are positive, affirmative, specific and factual without adornment or glorification. In this respect they are indifferent to me; they do not represent me to anyone else. It is in this light that they are offered to the reader. Take special note of these passages as they appear chronologically among the poems with an attentive and open interest to what they convey, and enjoy the poems themselves, for they are what this book is all about.

Alan Lindgren
Los Angeles
November, 2009
December, 2012

IMPORTANT: Note on Endorsements

Virginia Sease in no way endorses this volume or any poems in it. *Journeying with the Sun* is published independently of the General Anthroposophical Society at the Goetheanum in Dornach, Switzerland, which the poet recognizes.

No one on the Vorstand (Executive Council) of the General Anthroposophical Society at the Goetheanum has endorsed/made a contribution to the publication of this volume. The Introduction to "The Sun Sings" by Virginia Sease, Ph.D., is not a Foreword. It appears in its original destination in this volume in its entirety. Excerpts, cards and letters from Virginia Sease, Hans Peter van Manen† and Dorothy Walcer† are not endorsements of any kind. *Alan Lindgren's Poetry* by Hans Peter van Manen is an independent reflection on my poetry from *The Sun Sings 1997* through 2003. It is not an endorsement but consists in factual statements by this profound Dutch historian, educator and author. Every word from these sources is published because the thoughts are indicative of the poems and demonstrate insight into the poetry and its poet and are **not** endorsements.

The words on my poetry excerpted from cards and letters to me from Virginia Sease, who is my best and dearest friend, are personally dear to me, but I include them among the poems published here because of their objective aspects, rather than any subjective tone or qualities. Everything, which comes from her, is true.

As with fidelity to facts it is a virtue of Virginia Sease that she remains entirely truthful at all times, under all circumstances. Only devotion to the truth is impartial, bestowing spiritual greatness on its practitioner. Like statements of fact it is inalterable and cannot be influenced because it is indifferent. Those who adhere only to what is true are ever positive; they recognize solely truth.

Rather than common faultfinding based on weaknesses, she elects to place before the audience/reader what is worthy, true and therefore positive in some one, situation or work. But this is what the noble spirit does. She attends to the virtues wherever they are present. Lesser men ignore or do not see what is praiseworthy. They see wrong and blame, while the gifted see gifts and genius.

Certainly much is left unsaid. Sometimes no word is the best or only way to communicate. Then what is written or said has all the more weight. Every work touched by grace such as this has special significance. Sense this if you may.

Should you be interested in the work of Virginia Sease you need only read her published lectures and writings. These publications have not only endorsement of the Executive Council. She has been a Vorstand member since 1984. Virginia Sease is a special, great Sun personality and individuality, an American, woman and rare human being, whose life is dedicated to the work of Rudolf Steiner, and who represents Anthroposophy to the members of the Society and to the world.

From the work of Hans Peter van Manen (1931-2009) in my English translation:

The etheric world is the transition between the spatial sensory world and the soul world. The entire—etheric and soul world together—is called the imaginative world or the world of imaginations, in one of the terms used by Rudolf Steiner. Such an imagination is a symbolic picture, which is formed out of an inner perception. This inner perception can be a usual sensing or a feeling. But it can also be the conscious perception of a spiritual reality or of a spiritual being. This sensing is clothed in a picture. Whoever perceives this picture often has the certain impression that it contains a message; however, if it has to do with a genuine imagination, the content of this message isn't usually clear right away. It is unspecific. The imaginative picture has shape and color and is sometimes in movement.

The student of the spirit offers constructed inner pictures (symbolic images) used in meditation to the spiritual world. Then it can happen they take on independent life. This means that etheric forces begin to penetrate the picture so that it becomes visible for spiritual beings. Those spiritual beings are meant who populate the soul world and the spiritual world. So imagination stands at the border to reality. To put it more precisely, it is a fleeting manifestation between thinking activity, creative imaginativeness and spiritual reality. [1]

…..

Imagination and inspiration also play a central role in the emergence of an artwork, here viewed in the framework of the poetic arts. But the poet doesn't necessarily construct the image. Frequently, his imagination has an inspired character: It comes to him suddenly. Often the poetic image is transparent for the reader; the message shines through it directly. Seen from this standpoint it is thinkable—spiritual scientifically-speaking—that poetry can be viewed as a mirror of the imaginative world. All artists use etheric forces in their work, whether they know it or not. The poet must be able to give his thoughts and imagery a living form; otherwise they remain abstract and dead. Exactly as with an imagination or picture in meditation, when a genuine poem comes into existence, it is a visible reality in the soul and spirit world. This is also the case with certain special prose stories, not only fairy tales, but also novels.[2] *Creativity is also beneficial for the angels!* (Virginia Sease)

1. Hans Peter van Manen, *Wiederkunft und Heimsuchung* (Verlag am Goetheanum: Dornach, 2011), Chapter 6, p. 53
2. Ibid., p. 54

CHAPTER ONE

1986 – 1987

THE DISCOVERY OF MY VOCATION

CHAPTER ONE

PART ONE: THE SEEKER

August – December 1986

Verses of a Seeker after Christ

Chapter One. The Discovery of My Vocation

The Seeker

I wanted to be a poet to some degree
To speak poetically as naturally as running free
To go places in my poetry and look there

The human world doth need exploring
To go into dark places illuminating them
Shedding light in the depths
Bringing hope and assurance to the depths
Overcoming the darkness

Such was my quest, barely begun
Yet I had begun, and wanted to go further
Further to the root of things

Bringing to bear upon the world
My mark of human work
Enlightening dark corners
Till they were friendly places
And we, free to go there

To move about and look around
Deepening understanding
Of our world, of its depths

This was my quest
Might I not resume once more
Light in hand
The mining of our earth for gems?

Part One. 1986 The Seeker, Verses of a Seeker After Christ

To Be a Poet

To be a poet
Is to meditate
Upon life's meaning
Upon one's relationship
To life and love

Upon one's inner yearnings
One's gravest wishes
Upon one's true self
Upon one's deepest loves

It is to sing all these
In poetic rhythms and rhymes
In poetic dances and words
To tunes of moods
And tones of feelings

To be love's singer
Is to be a poet.

Chapter One. The Discovery of My Vocation

Mountain Climbing

Before me a way up
Goes a path high up
Climbing rock over rubble
Through streams and o'er pebbles

The path it is a steep one
And sometimes also a narrow one
To where does it lead
This winding snake indeed?

Well, climb the climber higher
Until you reach the spire
The tip-top of the mountain of hope
Without the aid of burro or rope

There awaits the true aspirant
Freed from the lowly tyrant
The loftiest of views
Gentle light and colors of every hue.

Peace is bestowed upon him
Who ascends the mountain dim
Love surrounds the brave climber
Who now surveys the forest timber.

He is the valiant Human Being
Who right royally does the seeing
Atop the Mountain so high
In the eve when God is nigh.

Part One. 1986 The Seeker, Verses of a Seeker After Christ

By the Sunset there's a Door

By the sunset there's a door
A door to life as never before
Life that's full and filled with love
Both below and above

By the sunset there's this door
It's a-blazing as before
Blazing with life for me and you
Life so full of good things, too

Bless the sunset, bless the door
Bless the peace as never before
Life that's full, life that's green
Life worth living, that's what I mean.

Chapter One. The Discovery of My Vocation

The Sky is Free to Me

I want to be free to be me;

I want freedom as big as the sky –
freedom from negativity;

I am good person in me – a soul that feels
and is free.

The big white clouds in the big blue sky
show freedom to me;

The clouds are big and white and filled
with light;

The hue is as true as azure blue;

Why the deep, dark blue sea of sky?

Angels of light, white clouds, big and
bright;

Bright white light – angel clouds in flight;

Freedom of soul reflected in the sky whole;

True love borne aloft on angel wings of
light – a bright sight.

Part One. 1986 The Seeker, Verses of a Seeker After Christ

Lost in the Darkness I Wander

Lost in the darkness I wander
Searching for the Light
Shadows of the unseeable
Flicker dimly before my sight

I am in the depths
Of my own soul a-walking
Certain only that within myself
There lies warmth a-waiting

How dark appears my soul to me!
How drab every tree
The most sombering of experiences
The dark side of my soul is to me

One day into the future
My hope there it stands
A light will illuminate these blackened walls
Thus freeing a darkened land…and

That man who resides therein
He may then wander free
Shedding light in the depths
For all mankind to see.

Chapter One. The Discovery of My Vocation

Might I Not Resume Life Once More?

Might I not resume life once more?
Life with light so pure
Then I could be more sure

Of my true purpose thru the years
Of my life's meaning which, so dear
I cling to in all this confusion
Trying to make spaces in profusion

That I might breathe in some fresh air
And be again a boy so fair
With goals, ideals and motives noble
With love and good will to make me stable

A Christmas wish reborn each day
This is what I mean to say:

To be alive with joy for living
To be so happy with thanksgiving
To be my true self in word and deed
A free individual the truth to read;

I pray for a future with struggle again
Where I can enter life among other men
A man reborn out of ashes of old
Here lies my wish, what more can be told?

Part One. 1986 The Seeker, Verses of a Seeker After Christ

The War

You have been subjected to war,
which continues as before.
The bloodshed is grim
and the lighting is dim.

The fighting takes its toll
upon the human soul.
When the enemy stalks,
which way shall I walk?

A prisoner taken,
to what shall I awaken?
My freedom is lost,
in nightmares I toss.

The darkness overwhelms me,
the shadows fly by swiftly.
I have been hit
and nearly lost my wit.

The blood spills out furiously
as I look at it curiously.
I hallucinate madly
and droop down sadly.

I have neither insurance
nor any mental endurance.
My anguish I silence
though my head is most tense.

My thinking is whirling
inside, while it's swirling.
To memories I cling
of love and warm feeling,
as I sink in the dust
my head filled with distrust,

Chapter One. The Discovery of My Vocation

I pray that this war
won't go on any more,
that peace can be found
and planted in the ground.

I'll be waiting each day
for the good news to say:
Love is come again.
Amen.

Part One. 1986 The Seeker, Verses of a Seeker After Christ

Take a Look at Your Soul

Take a look at your soul
Your eyes upon your goal

Shedding tears of relief
That come from way down deep

Get in touch with deep feelings
Come down from the cold ceiling

Be a human again
Crying gently among men.

Chapter One. The Discovery of My Vocation

The Uniting

I wish for Christ to come to me
MySelf be there to greet Him
MySelf to come together enough
To be here when He comes
To greet Him when He comes looking
for me.

I wish for Christ to come for me
To find a heart intact in me
A heart of Self who I am
For Christ to find when He comes to
find me.

Then we will find each other both
When Christ comes to me.

Alan Lindgren will stand up to meet
Him
Alan Lindgren will arise to greet Him.

And Christ and I will embrace each
other warmly
When Christ finds me a waiting.

Culver City, California
August – December 1986

CHAPTER ONE

PART TWO: O DAYS ARE MADE OF RIDDLES

January – March 1987

Toward the Threshold of the Spirit

Poems in the Light

Dedicated to my wonderful Mother,
Mrs. Margaret Lindgren, with whom I have always been close, and whose presence in my life beginning August 1986 has the dearest significance to me and to my heart

Chapter One. The Discovery of My Vocation

I Have a Weakness and a Strength

My weakness is forgetting
What I have already learned
While my strength it is recalling
What it is that I forgot

I should remember the importance
That I do so well forget
For it's then that I remind myself
To come back to where I ought.

Part Two. 1987 O Days Are Made of Riddles, Poems in the Light

O Zartes Kind!

O zartes Kind!
Welch' Wunder, Schönheit
Augen groß und wäßrig
Körper weich und sanft
Durchleuchtende Haut

Empfindsames Wesen
Alles Wirkliche empfindest Du
Welch' Leben und Licht
Der Himmel Dir so nahe
Dein Schützengel
Der liebe Gott wirkt durch Dich

Wir wollen Dein Entfalten
Miterleben
Und Dir, Menschenkinde,
Wollen wir unsre schönste Liebe
schenken
Daß Du weißt
Du bist auf Erden willkommen.

Chapter One. The Discovery of My Vocation

O Gentle Child!

O gentle Child!
Such Wonder, Beauty
Eyes large and water-like
Body soft and mild
Glowing skin

Sensitive Being
All that is real do You feel
What life and light
Heaven is so close to You
Your guardian angel
Our dear God works through You

We want to experience with You
Your unfolding growth
And we want to give to You,
Child of Humanity,
Our purest, most beautiful love
That You may know
You are welcome upon the Earth.

Part Two. 1987 O Days Are Made of Riddles, Poems in the Light

When reading this poem aloud, watch
your hands as they present themselves,
both individually and together clasped.

Ich Habe Zwei Brüder

Ich habe zwei Brüder
Die rechte Hand und die linke Hand
Sie wirken zusammen
Sie leben zusammen
Sie schaffen zusammen
Weil sie zusammenge<u>hör</u>en, ja
Ich habe zwei Brüder
Meine rechte Hand and meine linke
Hand.

I Have Two Brothers

I have two brothers
The right hand and the left hand
They work together
They live together
They create together
Because they be<u>long</u> together, yes
I have two brothers
My right hand and my left hand.

Chapter One. The Discovery of My Vocation

Licht

1.
Ich bin stumm vor Dir
Du sprichst zu mir
Du erscheinst meinen Augen
Dein Licht – aus Finsterschatten,
Wolkengrauen
Durchleuchtende helle Klarheit
Reines Licht –
Ich habe nur einzuatmen
Kein Mund – die Vögel aber singen
Dein reines Licht aussprechend
Klare Töne hervorbringend
aus den Lüften
Durch die Lüften
Deiner Licht-Taten entsprechender
Gesang.

2.
Ich verweile dort
Unter Himmelgeschichten
Zwischen Wolken, Vögeln
Tiefen Blauen, Sonnenmächten
Ein Kampf über mir, um mich herum
Und ich öffne mich vor großem Wunder
Der Offenbarungen des Lichtes –
Meine Augen aufgewacht
Und dann die Ohren
Bis ich (so erfüllt von lichtvoller,
klarer, freiender Luft)
In das enge Menschenhaus heimkehre
Weiter wundernd, staunend
Die Reinheit, Schönheit, Klarheit
des Lichtes.

Part Two. 1987 O Days Are Made of Riddles, Poems in the Light

Light

1.
I am still before You
You speak to me
You appear before my eyes
Your Light – from dark shadows,
darkened clouds
In brightest clarity shining through
Pure Light –
I can only inward breathe
Speechless – while the birds do sing
Sounding Your pure Light
Calling forth clear tones from out of
the air
Through the air
Songs composed to Your Deeds
of Light.

2.
I linger here
Among Heaven's Happenings
Between clouds and birdsong
Sky's deep blue and Sun's bright Light
A battle in Freedom above me – around me
And I open myself in huge awe
To the Revelations of the Light –
My eyes awakened
And then my ears
Until I (so filled with light-filled,
clear, freeing air)
Retire back into my little human house
Still in awe and deepest wonder
Of the Purity, Beauty and Clarity
of the Light.

Chapter One. The Discovery of My Vocation

Outlook

I concern myself
In inner landscapes
Removed from reality
I lose myself in that world
Knowing no reward is there
I grow cold and weak
In worlds of illusory temptations
Until I see myself
Lying there – a self-made victim
Surrounded by a pale host of wild
malcreatures
Who – unlike myself – they know
no self-control
And I see this emptiness where
I lie
And I say
I will stand up into true worlds
And I get myself upright
And I go on.

Part Two. 1987 O Days Are Made of Riddles, Poems in the Light

Problem-Solving

There I sit enveloped
All enrapped in searching thought
My eyes look out tragically
Answers outside me there are not

I've been here before
And a solution led me out
Still in the mean time I must go on
Until I can forget to pout

Gradually it comes upon me
And sinking deeper in
The re-solution for me is
It's a smile upon my chin

Which growing ever broader
My big belly rumbling awake
It breaks out in open laughter
And my whole body does it shake!

O solutions are hard lessons
Which we all do have to learn
But the magic of resolutions
Is the humor ourselves to discern.

Chapter One. The Discovery of My Vocation

I Have Left My Home

I have left my home
My home I make where I am
I look for you
Yet you are there

I miss you
My dearest brother
To think I thought I had no brother!

How many are we here
Sharing this world together

Now when I am lost
Wandering the streets of life alone
Yearning for heaven and fullness inside
I do know where to turn

And you are there.

Part Two. 1987 O Days Are Made of Riddles, Poems in the Light

O Days are Made of Riddles

Sometimes I remove myself
And go out by myself
And walking, thinking, feeling things
While I am motionless

And then I find I've come to where
I turn myself around
I move myself then back again
And back again I come.

O days are made of riddles
In which we are perturbed
Then evenings we come back again
Our home we have well earned

I know it is important
These days to struggle through
That when we do come back again
I know I'm here with You.

Chapter One. The Discovery of My Vocation

Bewußt-Sein

Du siehst weder-noch
Das Gute noch das Böse
Doch spürst Du, beide Geiste

Ich sehe entweder-oder
Und spüre jedoch
Die Anwesenheit des anderen

So kann ich – in jeder Gegenwart –
Klar entscheiden
Das Gute in mir, in Dir
Zu bejahen.

Conscious-Being

You see neither-nor
The Good nor the Evil
Still do you sense, both Spirits

I see either-or
And therewith do I sense
The presence of the other

So am I able, in each present moment
To clearly choose
The Good in me, in you
To affirm.

Culver City, California
January – March 1987

CHAPTER TWO

1994 – 1995

EARLY SUN AND OTHER POETRY

Chapter Two. Early Sun and Other Poetry

A long time ago there lived a peasant on a farm. His daily life included the carrying out of many chores. Milking the cows, churning the butter, making cheeses and feeding the farm animals occupied some of his time. In the spring he was often to be seen out in the fields sowing the grain and planting the vegetables. But when he had any free time he loved to walk along an old earthen road as his ancestors had before him, softly singing sweet tunes to himself, especially at the end of the day. Then he would stop walking and gaze for a long time at the heavens, watching the colors change in the sky while the sun set and the first stars appeared. After looking at the stars for a good while, he would slowly turn back and walk down the old road to the farm where a meal of bread and cheese and hot tea awaited him. As the next day he would be rising very early, so he retired early to bed after saying a prayer of thanksgiving. He slept well every night as he worked hard during the day, lying on his bed of straw next to the cows who kept him warm, even in winter.

Los Angeles
December 2004

From a letter from Virginia Sease, Ph.D., late 1995 or (early?) 1996:

>Thank you for brightening my day with your Sun poems.

(This statement of appreciation refers to the numerous Sun poems that I composed almost weekly from early 1995 to April 1997 that I mailed to Virginia Sease as my sole experiences untouched by the rough times I knew at this time. I did not retain copies of most of these poems, and those I did—aside from the special "Sun of My Heart" found on page 62—I did not select for this volume because my more mature Sun poems were composed from April 1997 on, found especially in my volume "The Sun Sings" (see Chapter Three, pages 73-75; 85-89). All my poems composed early 1995 to April 1997 were my poetry "apprenticeship", when I gained perfect ease in composition through much practice. In April 1997 I moved, and my inner experiences transformed to always clear and sunny, so good and kind to me, reflected in "The Sun Sings" verse, poetry and poetic prose. All of my Sun poems are dedicated to and inspired by the sun. This entire volume is so named—*Journeying with the Sun*—, because of all things in Nature, in Creation, the sun is dearest to me and to my heart.)

Chapter Two. 1994 – 1995 Early Sun and Other Poetry

The Rainbow and the Plant

The earth is dense, the air is fine
And in between the water winds

The earth is dark, the sun is bright
And in between shines rainbow's delight

The plant is rooted in the earth
The sun to fruit gives seeds their birth

And in between grow stalk and leaf
Find in metamorphosis relief

Up above are plant-like clouds
Ever changing sky-light shrouds

Bless the earth and bless the sun
And all that's in their dominion.

Evening Song

The day was warm, it's cooled down
And nighttime nears with evening sounds

The day was bright with sunlight pure
Now evening shadows cool the earth

Bless the night and bless the day
Moon and starlight, sun's loving rays

Tomorrow with the morning sun
A new day starts for everyone.

Chapter Two. Early Sun and Other Poetry

Words

Words are like magic, they give us the means
To tell what we're thinking and feeling in green
In blue and in yellow, in orange and red
In purple and nuances which can then be read

They open the doors of the mind and the heart
Sharing the gems of experience we impart
They do so in rhythms, with consonant and vowel
In thought-trains and feeling and will of the soul.

Sun of My Heart

Sun of the day and sun of my heart
Sun of my eyes with each day we start

Thou art so precious, yes thou art so dear
When the clouds part and thine orb shines so clear

Brightening the day and warming my heart
Greeting my soul, may we never ever part

May thou shine in my sleep and smile in my dreams
My own faithful sun and thy glorious beams.

Los Angeles
1995

From a card from Virginia Sease from Dornach, Switzerland, written in German, referring to the poems for "The Sun Sings" (see Chapter Three, below):

30. Oktober 1997

Lieber Alan,
     Da die Karte deutsch ist, schreibe
ich auch ein paar Grußworte auf
deutsch. Anbei sind die Kopiere Ihrer
sehr schönen Gedichte. Alles Gute für die
Zusammenstellung.
…..   Mit vielen herzlichen Grüßen
          Ihre   Virginia Sease

CHAPTER THREE

The Sun Sings

WORD-PICTURES

by Alan Lindgren

1997

Chapter Three. The Sun Sings WORD-PICTURES 1997

Die Sonne tönt nach alter Weise
In Brudersphären Wettgesang,
Und ihre vorgeschriebne Reise
Vollendet sie mit Donnergang.

Ihr Anblick gibt den Engeln Stärke,
Wenn keiner sie ergründen mag;
Die unbegreiflich hohen Werke
Sind herrlich wie am ersten Tag.

Prologue to *Faust, Part I*
by Johann Wolfgang von Goethe

This collection of poetry is dedicated to Dr. Virginia Sease, my dearest friend, to Monsieur Gérard Klockenbring†, my dearest brother, and to all the children of the world, past, present and future.

Acknowledgements

I would like to thank my Mother, Mrs. Margaret Lindgren, for her unceasing support over the years; and my dear friend, John Alexandra, for his encouragement and guidance, and for his editing and typesetting.

The Sun Sings

Introduction

The poetry in this volume represents but a fragment of Alan Lindgren's creative work in the last two years. The poems spring forth both from his rich life of soul and from his ability to observe people and nature-phenomena in a penetrating manner. Even through the title, the reader will notice that the human being's relationship to the sun occupies a central place among the thematic overtures sounded in this collection. Whereas many people today tend to disregard the sun, unless it becomes unbearably warm or the sun is hidden by cloudy, rainy weather for many days, Alan Lindgren invites us to sense how the physical sun is also the messenger of the spiritual world. In poetic form this realization also leads to an underlying, yet all-pervasive expression of gratitude. These qualities, plus many charming rhythms and word sequences, make the verses for children especially welcome. As a child, the author attended a Waldorf School and thus experienced personally the deep enrichment through poetry, especially when recited, as a normal part of the education process.

The adult will find aesthetic-spiritual nourishment in the poetry and prose section of this little volume. Here one can experience the pulse-beat of the course of the seasons and the call to the human being to connect the spirit within, to the holy Trinity and to the mighty Time-Spirit of our age, Michael. These "word-pictures" confirm that the author has touched his own innate, creative wellspring. We may thank him for sharing his experiences with others.

Virginia Sease, Ph.D.
Goetheanum, Switzerland
January, 1998

Chapter Three. The Sun Sings WORD-PICTURES 1997

O Mother Poetry!
Thou who blesses us so richly
Making our experiences whole
and complete
Uniting sense with thought
Giving us Word-Pictures to paint
A panorama of nature and Man
Of things lowly and things high
Earthly and divine
We raise our hearts to thee most
joyfully
In this song of praise,
Mother Poetry!

The Sun Sings

Verses Especially

for Children

Chapter Three. The Sun Sings, Verses Especially for Children

Little sparrow up above
Singing his sweet song of love
Little sparrow on the ground
Eating small crumbs he has found
Little sparrow come to me
And I will love you tenderly.

****

Wind and rain and hail and snow
Birds and beasts and things that grow
Mountains and rocks and gems below
Seas and lakes and rivers that flow
O how I love the things of God
Nature and life and breath and blood!

****

On this summer afternoon
I thought I saw an ancient rune
Written down in times of old
On a stone forgotten told

Then I looked up into the air
And saw the sun shining so fair
It warmed my heart and did me good
On the spot right where I stood

O Sun! I thank thee for thy love
Shining to earth from heaven above.

Chapter Three. The Sun Sings WORD-PICTURES 1997

Thou beamest forth, O glorious Sun
With loving light for everyone
While birds do wing upon the breeze
Aloft on air banks with great ease

O Sun, thou warmest our hearts dear
With thy light shining so clear
We send our love and thanks to thee
Each day as we thy wonders see.

****

The sun is golden in the sky
In the eve when God is nigh
Shining brilliant, radiant beams
Through the air her light doth stream
Her disc a shimmering orb of might
Warming hearts full loving bright.

****

Brilliant peach across the sky
In the eve when God is nigh
Fanning out to rose and pink
As the sun dips down to drink

Orange-golden now they turn
And a red can one discern
All in a sky of pale blue
Are these colors rich in hue.

Chapter Three. The Sun Sings, Verses Especially for Children

Summer sunsets rich in hue
Yellow, orange and red too
In a clouded sky of blue
Painted by the sun's light true

At the close of a long day
When we've basked in her warm rays
Now a glorious night draws near
In which the heavenly stars appear
And the silver moon so clear
Reflecting the gold sun's light dear.

****

After the night of forgetting and sleep
When we return to Thee God and the deep
We awake to the morn and the light of the day
To bask in the warmth of the sun's golden rays

It is like winter, the night and the dark
And the summer, the day and the free meadowlark
We are thankful to Thee, almighty God dear
For the rhythms of night and day and of the year.

Chapter Three. The Sun Sings WORD-PICTURES 1997

A Child's Grace at Mealtime

Father and Mother
Sister and Brother
We are a family of heaven and earth

Painting a picture
Roaming the pastures
Dining together
At God's holy table.

We are so thankful
For the abundance
Of the Lord's blessings
Bestowed upon us.

The Four Gifts

Love is the gift of the Child at heart
With love each life does take its fresh start.

Esteem is the gift of the Man in us all
With which we have courage and boldness withal.

Compassion's the gift of Middle Age trials
For the suffering of others with a tender smile.

Interest's the gift of Old Age which hears
And speaks with the wisdom of many long years.

Chapter Three. The Sun Sings, Verses Especially for Children

Solid earth beneath our feet
Ground for growing corn or wheat
Soil, stones and metals hard
Sing the songs of the gnomes' bard

Fluid water of the seas
Of the plants and of the trees
Sap of life, of rivers flow
Undines do thy waters know.

Air and light expanding there
In the heavens O so fair
Animals breathe for life
Birds upon the wing, sylphs.

Sun and fire up above
Thy spirit is of warmth and love
Man's element Prometheus won
Salamanders every one.

Chapter Three. The Sun Sings WORD-PICTURES 1997

Language is a wonderful thing
Where meaning and sound together sing
Vowel and tone – intonation ring
Consonants mark ends and beginnings.

Rhythms pulse in a life-blood flow
Marching and moving in wonders below
Rich in texture and color are words
Phrases and verses in seconds and thirds

Language is a wonderful thing
Where meaning and sound together do sing.

****

The arts are the sweetest things I know
Which like beautiful flowers do grow
In the sunshine and the air
With the rainfall and with care
In the soil of the ground
With the minerals which there abound

Beginning with small seeds
Sprouting among weeds
In due course they unfold their leaves
From a stem like little trees
Until the bud and blossom come
In the warmth of the great sun

How colorful are they
These flowers of the day!

Chapter Three. The Sun Sings, Verses Especially for Children

America – a word with thee!
A land so young, who ardently
Boldly lives and lives so bold
Proud among other nations old

Rich in life and variety
Land of the brave and of the free
Peoples of all walks and ways
Do come to live out here their days

All folks and races are found here
Foods and landscapes, places where
Men and women work far and wide
Children play as old have died

America – my country new
Land of many, never few.

Chapter Three. The Sun Sings WORD-PICTURES 1997

I see the mountains in the distance
Far away they show
On the horizon, gently rising
They appear to grow

Nearer trees and buildings stand
And birds do fly above
The landscape is a broad adventure
The sun shines upon with love.

****

I saw a heavenly landscape above
All made of clouds and sky
Interwoven with the light
Of the sun up high

The clouds were gray, the sky blue
And it was broad and fine
And birds did freely fly up there
Where the sun did shine.

Chapter Three. The Sun Sings, Verses Especially for Children

Maria fair
Maria mine
Maria mother
Of all mankind.
Thou art so precious
This Christmastime
I sing for thee
This little rhyme.

****

O Christmas Night!
Two thousand years ago
Through the heavens
A star did go
O'er Bethlehem
O'er a stall
Where in a manger
Within four walls

There lay a babe
The King of Kings
Above which did
The angels sing.
About the manger
Ox and ass did rest
Keeping the babe
Warm with their breath

'Round the Child
Sat Joseph kind
And his wife
Maria fine
Then there came
Three shepherds dear
With their gifts
Of love and cheer.

The Sun Sings

Poems and Prose

for Adults

Chapter Three. The Sun Sings, Poems and Prose for Adults

Beauty is a wondrous thing
As when we hear birds' music sing

As billowy clouds up in the sky
Or sunsets painted – God is nigh.

As great cathedrals, sculptures sweet
And poets' words our hearts entreat

But the most beautiful I find
Is the Sun of all mankind.

Chapter Three. The Sun Sings WORD-PICTURES 1997

Fields of clouds rolled, floating over a vast sea of sky. The clouds parted, opening wide a great blue ocean above. Shining there in its midst was the mighty, burning gem of the sun radiant bright. Splitting, spilling forth from its perfect roundness was the splendid loving light of the day sky, resplendent in its greatness of broad, bright, pulsing brilliance. Flinging far and wide its lustrous love, the sun shone unabashedly in mighty, merry magnificence to the grand pleasure of God's creation, heaven and earth. Each day anew it takes its great course, questing through the wondrous dome of ocean-sky from sunrise through high noon to color-chords of sunset. Faithful beacon of God's mighty love, our thanks and love we send to Thee above.

Chapter Three. The Sun Sings, Poems and Prose for Adults

Blue ocean of sky, vast and deep. White flames of clouds fleeting, wispy sweep. Magnificent sun, orb of might, bright with radiant light, reaching to the widest widths of the day sky, beyond horizons, casting brilliant glances upon all creation: in the heavens above, where birds upon the wing do sing, to the earth below, where stones repose and beasts and men do go. And trees blowing in the breezy air, spreading leaves green and fair: all nature sings to thee, O Sun!

Pulsing, love-warmth of the sun
Our sentient hearts are wholly won
Virtuous light
Bright streaming sight

Christ-Sun to Thee
We send our love
From here on earth
To heaven above.

Chapter Three. The Sun Sings WORD-PICTURES 1997

The glorious majesty of the mighty sun before sunset
Shining disc 'midst clouds bright and warm
Behold her love spreads forth in evening mood
While breezes blow o'er the earth
Beaming wondrous bright with strength and might
A dear and precious sight.

****

Der Sonne Licht strömt von oben her
Durch den Himmeln zu uns auf Erden

In Abendstimmung gnadevoll
Wir preisen Gott mit Lobgesang

Die Seele hat sich aufgetan
Nun bereitet sie sich für Schlafes Ruh'

O danke Gott für diesen Sommer Tag
Und segne uns für diese stille Nacht.

Chapter Three. The Sun Sings, Poems and Prose for Adults

It swirls. It swirls to eternity. The light permeates the curling, swirling clouds as they spiral upwards to its center, to its wellspring source, until they, transparent, become the face, the countenance of the sun in all its brilliance. The sun is fathomless, a shimmering counter-orb of negative space, of pure love, a disc of never-ending, inexhaustible love from which there ceaselessly streams bright loving light. The light shines making morn, noon, and evening, illuminating and warming all while it shines, spilling forth color and splendor as it weaves through leaves, petals, pulsing radiant through clouds, glistening through dew-drops into one great chorus, a rainbow from heaven to earth. And when the sun has finally set, the grand night opens her vast gates and starry pools of thousand suns in a secret celebration where only the moon reflects in silver upon the golden day of the sun's light.

Chapter Three. The Sun Sings WORD-PICTURES 1997

O Night!

Full of a thousand—nay
A thousand, thousand stars
Shimmering, some faintly, some brightly

I gaze in thy deep heavenly pools
Even as I sleep

Not only with mine eyes
But with my very body and soul
Bathing in thy firmament

My thirst is quenched
In a million wondrous ways

Naked am I here
With thee – thy Child

Thy myriad suns do make me free
I among them

O Night!

Chapter Three. The Sun Sings, Poems and Prose for Adults

Autumn with the breezes and the rain
Nights grow longer, days are on the wane
Light is clearer that thinking keener lives
Dying happens as life begins to give

Men are called upon to be brave and strong
All through this season of the autumn long
Michaél, Archangel of this time of year
In this crisp, awakening air so clear.

Chapter Three. The Sun Sings WORD-PICTURES 1997

Rhythms deep
       of conversation
              of gesture

Of an older woman
      with a young boy
           understanding
She speaks
      —concern in her movement
                    in her voice
He listens
      —still and open
Rhythms of the heart
And timeless
      Time transpires
She gesturing, speaking
Then moving, they part.

Chapter Three. The Sun Sings, Poems and Prose for Adults

The Gift of A Very Small Child

The friendly, smiling face
And waving hand
His tiny outstretched hand

—He grasps my two fingers
—His squeeze
His smile all the while

And then faces
Faces of all ages
Young and old

Timeless faces
Gentle faces appear
While the air does blow.

Chapter Three. The Sun Sings WORD-PICTURES 1997

O Kind!
Schauend
       lächelnd
              grüßend
Mit Augen
       Mund
              und Hand
Dein Geschenk ist
Offenheit
       und Wunder
              und Liebe
Durch dich
       grüßt uns
              der Vater-Gott.

****

O Child!
Looking
       smiling
              greeting
With eyes
       mouth
              and hand
Thy gift is
Openness
       and wonder
              and love
Through thee
       greets us
              the Father-God.

Chapter Three. The Sun Sings, Poems and Prose for Adults

A Christmas Meditation

The Sun shines
Shines greatly in love
Lovingly in streams
Streaming bright

Streaming bright
Streaming warm
Warm rays to earth
Where there is birth

Birth of a Child
A Child of Light
Light in the Night
Bright in the Night

Bright in the Night
Warm in the Night
Warm in the Cold
Is His great Light.

Chapter Three. The Sun Sings WORD-PICTURES 1997

The human hand is strong and sure
The human heart is sweet and pure
The human head is filled with light
Wise and ever streaming bright
The human land is all these three
A land where many wonders be.

****

The light of the heart
Is the light of the eyes
The strength of the heart
Is the strength of the wise

Moving in limbs
In wonders below
The rhythm doth beckon
The rhythm doth flow

The warmth of the heart
Weaves through head and hand
Bestowing love's blessings
In this beautiful land.

Chapter Three. The Sun Sings, Poems and Prose for Adults

A poem lives in rhythms
A poem lives in rhymes
Flowing forth in verses
Flowing forth in time

It speaks in thoughts and feelings
With words expressing things
The poet wants to tell of
The poet wants to sing

With consonants and vowels
With language rich in sound
A poem paints a picture
With colors which resound.

Chapter Three. The Sun Sings WORD-PICTURES 1997

The tree. The tree stood tall and massive in the forest, roots deep in the earth, branches outreaching in the sky. Clouds drizzled rain in the misty, post-Atlantean, Irish landscape. The sun came out, and a rainbow appeared in the heavens with its beauteous colors. A squirrel picked up a nut on a tree branch, glancing this way and that, his tail fanning in furry waves. A boy of 16 years walked dreaming through the forest, his eyes bright and full of wonder. He fell asleep on the moss of the forest floor. When he awoke, it was night, and through the tree's branches there shimmered countless stars. The boy climbed the great tree all the way to the top from where he could see the stars uninhibited and the great white moon. Beneath him all was dark and still, above bright and sparkling with the music of light of the night. The air was fresh and cool; the clouds had gone. It was a clear, autumn night.

Chapter Three. The Sun Sings, Poems and Prose for Adults

Soul-eyes of my brother
Thou art the hall
In which the Christ
Is sitting at the table

I see him there
His shining Light
Come greeting me
So warmly

O Christ-brother
Brother-friend
In this moment
Do we sup together

O Christ-brother
Brother-friend
In this moment
Are we joined together.

Chapter Three. The Sun Sings WORD-PICTURES 1997

I saw a Christ-cloud in the sky
In the autumn day so high
It shone up there so pure and white
With the sun's heavenly light

O Christ, Thou comes to us here
Appearing in the heavens so clear
In the clouds among the blue
Great and billowing most true.

Chapter Three. The Sun Sings, Poems and Prose for Adults

Ocean depths of happy rest
Stones sink through thee on their quest
For the bottom floor below
Schools of fish thy currents know

On the surface boats and ships
Ride the waves their crests and dips
From the deck of the sailboat
Do I make this awesome note:

In the middle of the sea
The horizon's grand curve – do you see?
Water seeks to form a sphere
Many lessons make this clear

Drops of dew upon the leaves
Raindrops falling through the trees
When it's hot on the ocean grand
The sun makes felt her mighty hand

Evaporating water up
Into the reverse heavenly cup
Where clouds do form in different ways
After air currents and sun's rays

Then often over land blow they
To precipitate both night and day
Often taking different forms
Sometimes giant thunderstorms

Sometimes hailing balls of ice
Pounding down like great big dice
Sometimes coming down as snow
Hexagonal crystal patterns show

Each one detailed and unique
The answer to this mystery seek
Sometimes in the early morn
The morning dew o'er all is born

Chapter Three. The Sun Sings WORD-PICTURES 1997

And if it is cold enough
Frost appears, this magic stuff
A special miracle is when
A great bridge from earth to heaven

Appears when while it still does rain
Upon which the sun does shine
The rainbow with its colors seven
A fortunate sign to us is given.

Inglewood, California
April – December 1997

Alan Lindgren's Poetry

Reading the poetry of Alan Lindgren can cause a gradually rising amazement. He started with 'simple' sunny verses, sunny in more than one respect. They reflect a mood of cheerfulness and of gratitude towards the celestial body, in which he recognizes the picture and the real source of morality, divine and human. With the naivete that still can be the mark of youthfulness he stepped into the tradition that has been shaped by such great spirits as the grand Persian prophet Zarathustra, the Egyptian Pharaoh Akhnaten, the last heathen Roman emperor Julian the Apostate and Saint Francis of Assisi. That is not meant as an indication of the level of his art but simply of the direction in which the origin of his inspiration can be found: the spiritual essence of the Sun who became man in Christ. The freshness of his poems mirrors the mood of a sunny morning.

Each morning is the birth of a new day. It can also appear as a rebirth after a dark night of probation. Lindgren's poetry is the fruit of such a rebirth. That is not only visible in the religious themes and pictures in his songs, it is very much alive in the charming combination of light-footed rhythms and reflections of an elegiac kind. The most striking example that comes to my mind of this combination are some of the war poems of the English poet Siegfried Sassoon, who outlived the battles in northern France 1914-1918 and out of that Inferno created the most humanely serene verses. Another guiding star in that direction is Nelly Sachs, of German Jewish birth, who survived the Holocaust as a human being and as a lyric poetess. It may be wise to keep in mind that poetical creation appears not only as a fruit but also as a source of inward probation. In that realm one can still find the most adequate counsel in Rainer Maria Rilke's "Briefe an einen jungen Dichter."

Hans Peter van Manen, Ph.D.
Poros, Greece
November, 2002

CHAPTER FOUR

Thanksgiving 1997 – November 2001

DEVELOPING

A 'STYLE OF MYSELF'

CHAPTER FOUR

PART ONE

Thanksgiving 1997

in Atlanta

Chapter Four. Developing a 'Style of Myself'

Part One. Thanksgiving 1997 in Atlanta

The Spirits of the Night

The cool autumn of the Southeast comes
With leaves which fall to the ground
The air is crisp and fresh
The evening stirs around
And if one listens closely
One can hear the spirits of the night
Come nearing us to welcome in
The Christmas with the Light.

Sensing and Sounding the Voices of Choirs

The morning light dawns
Awakening the earth
Colors arise
Here there is birth
Of a new day
In this world of ours
Sensing and sounding
The voices of choirs.

The Fountain

Little water
Little brook
Gurgling, singing
O'er cranny and nook
How I love Thee
Little one
Thy bright spirits
How they run!

Atlanta
Thanksgiving 1997

CHAPTER FOUR

PART TWO

1997 - 1998

Winter Hymns

December 1997 – February 1998

Chapter Four. Developing a 'Style of Myself'

From a letter from Hans Peter van Manen, Ph.D., written in The Hague, Holland, December 21, 1998:

….

….I wanted to congratulate you to the fact that you found a spiritual home in Poetry. You steadily work and find your way towards a style of yourself. You don't bother a bit about current forms of desperate or cynical or completely irrational expressions; you chose a cheerful, sobre, lyrical way of expressing yourself. You sing in words and your songs are a way of saying 'Yes' to life. With much appreciation I read your last two bundles 'word pictures': Winter Hymns and Summer Songs…..

….

My Little Bird So Fair

Once upon a sad, sad day
A bird wept, if you may
She cried and mourned
She was forlorn
But why she would not say.

I rounded up the golden light
Of the sun so pure and bright
And sent it to the sad, sad bird
With a gentle and kind word.

Then that bird stirred from out her depths
She fluttered, plumed and off she swept
Into the sky, into the air
Happy and carefree as where

As where the other birds chirped 'round
And glory did abound
O glory did abound
Upon that little bird.

Part Two. 1997 – 1998 Winter Hymns

Now she is fair and most content
She does not weep, she does not grieve
For her sorrows are relieved
My dear and happy bird.

She sings her songs
All filled with glee
She sings her songs most merrily
My little bird so fair.

Hark, Do You Hear?

Hark, do you hear?
An angel, an angel is upon the wing
Do you hear, do you hear her sing?

The Christ is born, is still a babe
In Maria's arms so tenderly
Cradled, rocking, O so gently

God has come to us poor men
To us poor souls in our sin
He smiles, Christ Jesus, the sweetest smile

Our hearts are warmed, warmed by His Light
And now there is peace on earth
Peace ever since His birth
Of this Child so fair

Harken, all ye citizens
Of earth and heaven
Ye sinners, too, harken now

The time is near
The time has come
The time is now at hand.

Chapter Four. Developing a 'Style of Myself'

I Only Scraped My Knees

I fell a thousand feet from on a precipice
But only scraped my knees, the stones I missed
Landing in a golden meadow turned
Flowering as bedecked with sun
And sun rose up again on high

I washed my bloodied knees deep in the cool waters
Of a pool no man had ever seen before
And all was fresh, only the ouch
Upon my knees still clinging to the wounds.

There sprang a deer from out the forest glade
Pausing in the riverbed to wade
Then off she danced to merry tunes most sweet
A summer scene of solitude retreat

My knees still ache and sore but scrapes do heal
And I at thousand feet would never squeal
For the Lord protected me most sure
Lest I fall to my death, but I endure

And I still live to tell my story here as well
And the meadow is as sweet as any knell
So I go on and pray my Lord me safe to keep
Each night to bed I go to sleep.

Part Two. 1997 – 1998 Winter Hymns

A Winter's Hymn

I am a man who speaks of blood and rivers flowing through my veins
Of life and Nature, my soul's horses do I hold by the reins
A man of bone and muscle, flesh and skin
Who sings a poet's song, a winter's hymn.

I am a man who bold doth brave the currents of life
Somewhat alone as I will never have a wife
A man of courage and conviction
Who speaks his mind disregarding reputation.

But I am a man who dearly loves all things of beauty
Things tender, mild, sweet, so gently
As a rose, a red, red rose just beginning to open up
Her delicate and fragrant blossom cup,

And I love stones, all kinds and shapes and sizes
And birds who sing their melodies most pure
I am a man who praises God's vast Nature
Filled with tiny wonders as with grandeur.

Chapter Four. Developing a 'Style of Myself'

January Morn

The morning is ours, my friend, is ours!
I saw it as I went out after breakfast
Into the cool fresh air of dawn
Upon this January morn.

All freckled with an insect's feelers
All warmed by a lion's breast
All feathered by a sparrow's wing
How sweet it is, the morning freshness
And here I pause to laugh aloud and sing.

O morning bedecked with dew
Gentle as a baby's breath
Soft as a deer's footprints
Light as a butterfly's wings
All upon the glorious dawn is here.

O morning!
The praise goes to thee, O Sun
Almighty, dearest, highest One
Who warmest our hearts to life
After the deep dark of sleep
Who enlightens our world to color
And fills our day with joy.

All praise to thee, O Sun
Thou art the everlasting One
O holy God, the Sun
The dear and noble One
Who shines each day glorious love
From the heavens up above
Amen, amen.

Part Two. 1997 – 1998 Winter Hymns

The Wedding

Wouldst thou draft mine engagement
to a woman I never knew
To betroth me to her, as I grew?

O no, I cry, O no!
Single I am and shall remain
All thanks, just the same
My body is mine to keep
And if I choose to weep
So be it.

And if I choose to laugh
Alongside a giraffe
Then who'll stop me?

And the great elephants
And the tiny ants
They're my friends too.

O Nature, thou'rt my wife
I'll cuddle thee all my life
Our children shall be the winds
Shall be without the sins
Their father has known.

O let's have a wedding
Just you and I
In a gorgeous valley
Among some tall mountains

The birds shall sing for us
Just thou and I.

Chapter Four. Developing a 'Style of Myself'

My Songs

I once was a peasant, O so poor
I only knew a bit of folklore
I once was a man so rich
I knew not how to dig a ditch
Such was my galore.

And now I am just me
A poet merrily
Sometimes quite earnest
Sometimes filled o'er with jests
All filled with glee.

So I do sing my songs
All through the days long
And if they rhyme that's great
But if they don't, it's not wrong.

A poet is so free
Just himself to be
To share his thoughts
From me to thee.

So please don't take offence
For I have no defense
The words they just come out
And I hope that they make sense.

Part Two. 1997 – 1998 Winter Hymns

Mother Rhythm

Rhythm, thou Mother of my pulsing blood
Who checks the outpour, checks the flood
Who quietly keeps all peace and calm
Who grants the poor beggars their warm alms

Yes, rhythm flow ever onward stream of life I know
Ever goodness cheering us on bestow
All good things of life do come through Thee
Enabling us to think thoughts which set us free

Raising us up above the animal's drives
Whether or not we choose to be husbands and wives
'Tis rhythm beckons us along not slothful be
Nor too quick when merry we are with glee

O Rhythm, Mother of a thousand years
Thy pulsing love beats always ever near.

Chapter Four. Developing a 'Style of Myself'

Unfathomable Time

The chilly winter morning invites in the new day
A dawn filled with hope and the sun's gentle rays
The breezes blow fondly but also cold here
And we pray so that Springtime were evermore near.

But as the day grows up into a man bold
We feel the warmth coming in not yet old
O Sun, thou'rt kind in these winter hours
All we are wanting for is little flowers.

But time is something unfathomable and true
Seasons come and go, we pass them through
Yet eternity stays with us always
Never changing through the changing days.

But I thank Thee God for this In and Out
Breathing of the days and seasons about
It were so much the sameness were every day
About the selfsame ordinary way.

Yes we are blessed.

Inglewood, California
December 1997 – February 1998

CHAPTER FOUR

PART THREE

19 January – 20 February 1998

in Inglewood

Chapter Four. Developing a 'Style of Myself'

The Revelation

A man, not young, not old, was walking along a street, not in any particular direction. He passed by shops, by coffee houses, by trees and flowerbeds, roses in bloom, and neatly trimmed lawns. Then he chanced upon a woman, older in years, walking her dog. "Good day," she said, but he said not a word, only kept on a-walking. Then he chanced upon a homeless man, who asked him for some change, a dollar if he could spare, but he only shook his head and went on. But then he saw a young mother holding her baby but two years old, and that child did smile at him, all grinning and all waving in the breeze. And you know that man, his cold heart melted there, and he too smiled, and blew the child a kiss.

January 19, 1998

Above the meadow there's the sunlight
Ever so true, ever so bright
It reigns supreme in heaven's above
With the might of God's own love
In hearts of men here on earth
Awakening joy, awakening birth.

February 8, 1998

Ich würde Bücher schreiben
Von Worten bunt und treffend
Über Dingen schön und zart
Die meine Seele bewegen.

Ich würde Bücher schreiben
Von Welten tief und breit
Mit Herzenswärme drinnen
Pulsierend in der Zeit.

Part Three. 19 January – 20 February 1998 in Inglewood

Ich bin ein Dichter grüßend
Die ganze Welt so groß
Ich möchte Lieder singen
Aus meinem Seelenschoß.

17. Februar 1998

Pappa my father in broad daylight
Pappa my father in shimm'ring starlight
Filling my soul with Thy warm beams
Sending me comfort in my dreams
Giving new substance to these rhymes
Eternity tempo and measure in time
Sense of direction, whither I go
Sense of purpose, what I do know
Pulse-beat of breath and pulse-beat of blood
A place here of life with my God.

February 18, 1998

Sun so precious, Sun so dear
With Thy rhythms throughout the year
Pulsing with warmth, with Thy might
Evenly coursing, radiant bright
Thine is a special and glorious sight
Beautiful, splendid, inspiring light.

February 20, 1998

In der Dunkelheit, vergesse nicht das Licht
In Finsternisse, der Sonne Angesicht
Die strömt so warm, die leuchtet hell
Die ist des Lebens Liebesquell'
O Sonne schön, O Sonne mein
Zum Weltenschein, bringst Du Dasein.

Das himmlische Licht strömt weit und breit
Mit einer ewigen, erfreulichen Schönheit
Von der Sonne mit Wärme und Mut

Chapter Four. Developing a 'Style of Myself'

Es leuchtet klar und tut uns gut
Aus einer Quelle strahlt das Licht her
Eine Quelle der Liebe, der Morgenstern.

20. Februar 1998
Inglewood, Kalifornien

From a letter from Virginia Sease, Ph.D., written in Dornach, Switzerland, February 12, 1998:

….Your poems indicate
that you are going through a darker period. This is often connected with the mid-point in one's incarnation—between the 33rd and 38th year approximately, but, of course, it varies according to the individual. Remember, as you can express it so well and in such great nuance—the sun is still there despite the clouds.

(I was in my 36th year—35 ½ on February 5, 1998—when the letter from which this passage is excerpted was written.)

Peace

I write a song of love and pain
And of a quiet, soothing rain
It rains so gently on the fields
Softly falling, the grass yields
To the breezes blowing by
Skirting mountains, mountains high
But in the valley down below
All is peaceful, this I know.

Inglewood, California
End February, 1998

CHAPTER FOUR

PART FOUR

Spring 1998

Summer Songs 1998

Autumn 1998

Chapter Four. Developing a 'Style of Myself'

From a greeting card from Dorothy Walcer written in Los Angeles, June or July, 1998:

>   Thank you so much for the beautiful poems.
>   They are so upbeat and full of imagery.
>   I appreciate how hard you must have
>   worked to make them so vivid.

Breath

Here, a man is thinking
Quietly
Here, a man is breathing
Peacefully
Would I could see
His thoughts
Feel his breath
Softly as a snowflake
Rising,
      falling upon the bough
Of an evergreen
      in mid-winter's
Peaceful night
   of silent slumber
        in silhouette.

Los Angeles
End winter or springtime 1998

Part Four. 1998 Spring Summer Songs Autumn

Two Poems Composed on St. John's (1998)

The Wasteland

I saw a wasteland in the night
Human Beings in the blight
A World-Struggle crisis in
A World-Wasteland blown by winds
Above the stars blazed beacon bright
Men who died becoming light
For the living on our earth
Engaged now in this painful birth
Men and women on the plain
Of our earth with blood stains
Of the brave who sacrifice
Daily with this dear, dear price
Courageous for humanity
Each single one free may be
The challenge met by the few
Encouraging us to follow through
Resolved now we each one may stand
For a future Holy Land.

We Rejoice

I saw the golden sun on high
Way up in the summer sky
It shone so warm, so beacon bright
With its glorious, loving light
For all creation it did shine
Radiant splendor, might divine
For stones and plants upon the ground
Animals and Man, whose heart resounds
In one great unison true voice
Praising the Sun do we rejoice.

Los Angeles
June 24, 1998 (St. John's)

Chapter Four. Developing a 'Style of Myself'

The Forest

Although it was summer, deep in the shade of the forest all was cool. I sat down on the soft green moss and carefully laid out my precious shells from the sea. I had been collecting them every summer since I was a little boy. I love their shapes, their surfaces and colors. I knew that they had been homes to sea-creatures, like the empty snail shell is to the snail. Again with care, I gathered together my seashells in my special box. Now I began exploring the forest for mushrooms and berries.

I knew which were poisonous to avoid and which were edible, and I loved the small blueberries, which grew there on small, low-to-the-ground bushes. Coming upon a whole area filled with blueberries, I took out a sack I had been carrying with me and began picking the sweet berries, working quietly on until the bag was three-quarters full. Then I went to another part of the forest where I found some kantarellar, orange mushrooms, edible and delicious when sautéed in butter, picked a number of them, putting them into the sack with the blueberries, and began my way back out of the forest, walking on the soft, plush, green moss.

Los Angeles
July 1998

Part Four. 1998 Spring Summer Songs Autumn

And now the night draws near, majestic moon
He soon will shining rise on high in the dark sky
And thousand stars light up above the heavens as well
Their sparkling spirit-stories us to tell
While we among them in the timeless time of sleep
May mingle body and spirit in the vast pool
Bathing in the fresh and divine cool
Our hearts and souls a-fire for love
Community
The living and the dead united
joyously
In one great resounding human-angelic
Family
A celebration of
    Man and God and Being
We our voices raise on high to Thee
        Great Father-Spirit.

Los Angeles
July 1998

Six Summer Poems (1998)

Dancing Elves

Love is where the words live
Love is where the sounds give
New meaning to the words themselves
Like faeries, pixies, dancing elves.

Seasons of Sunrise

Seasons of sunrise, dawning of days
Making each morning with sun-golden rays
Open us outward prepared by the night
Gone are the planets, the sky of starlight
Grand stand the men anew on the earth

Chapter Four. Developing a 'Style of Myself'

Fresh for the first steps, this time of new birth
The babe cries aloud, away from the womb
At the start of its life's long road to the tomb
Bold breaks the sun, majestic in might
Accompanied by birdsong, this outpour of light
Fresh in its power, as on the first day
The sun on its course, sure making its way.

Writing

A poet not recalcitrant
To do his work, not put in print
Only in ink upon the page
Where it did show off with its age
Writing of his hand, not chance
The words they seemed, they seemed to dance
With a certain rhythmic flair
Bold, yet buoyant, and something fair
Expressing with the content-thought
Something else for which he'd sought.

The Few

A poet thought a thought one day
What shall I think, what shall I say?
Here I stand upon this earth
Which is now giving, giving birth
In a most modern techno-age
Information on a page

How painful must this birthing be
Those in the heavens clearly can see
Yet men and women down here below
Unaware seem not to know
Engaged in virtual fantasies
Dehumanizing, feel not ease

When pausing stop consider this
High-tech world, the soul they miss
All is refined but imitation

Part Four. 1998 Spring Summer Songs Autumn

Without life, humanization
Still on they go with ne'er a pause
Selling their souls – pleasure's the cause

The price so high, think not to pay
See the whole world goes too this way
A Godless world more and more
If Godless then, what is in store?

The burden for all humankind
So few carry, who seek to find
In daily life, in friends and nature
The eternal-divine – they are our teachers
Our future hope, examples living
And engaged in receiving-giving

They humanize wherever they are
And when they die they become stars
In the homeland of the spirit
Where with good beings of great merit
They help us here in our sore need
To make offerings of our deeds.

Bonnie Lass

Bye bye, Bonnie Lass
The breeze blowing o'er the grass
When will I ever see Thee again?
Thy long golden locks
Dangling down when I'd knock
On the window, Thy glass window pane

O come back, Bonnie dear
Thy blue eyes shining clear
Both in sunshine and in the rain
Thy graceful little feet
Dancing ever sweet
My heart longs for Thee Bonnie again.

Chapter Four. Developing a 'Style of Myself'

Forgiveness

I carved a world deep in stone
A place where I did sit alone
I let the Light shine in my world
To keep me warm while I was curled

Up in a blanket on the ground
Feeling quite sad, for I had found
No one else there inside my stone
In which I sat, I sat alone

My name I etched upon its walls
And while I wrote I heard a call:
Was it a bird, a wolf, the wind?
Who called to me? I knew I'd sinned

I ached within, my conscience called
And an echo I heard withal
As though my soul had grown so large
As if all Nature had been my charge

That when I felt a certain way
Nature, she too, was heard to say
My thoughts, my mood right back to me
Alone no more, as you can see

So I stood up and stepped outside
Of my stone home, as if I'd died
And left my body behind in there
Free to go forth any-, elsewhere

I saw the trees, the clouds above
The sunlight pouring down as love
I breathed in deep, fresh gulps of air
I was in Nature, Nature most fair
The breezes blew all over me
It felt so good, so good to be.

Los Angeles
Summer 1998

Part Four. 1998 Spring Summer Songs Autumn

From a letter from Virginia Sease, Ph.D., written in Stuttgart, Germany, December 6, 1998:

> ....The poem which you read over the telephone arrived several days later and it is very beautiful. "Pictures in words" really describes your artistry. In regard to your nature images I am always especially attentive to the fact that they spring from your poet's soul because in the naturalistic setting of a city like Los Angeles such images generally are non-existent.
> ....

(This refers to other poems but applies to all of my nature poetry)

A Song Beside My Door

A round-about, a where-with-all
A comely, timely true
When sycophants, and elephants
Come fully into view
As I lay there in reticence
All quietly listening to
A great and holy gathering
Of singing birds near to
My window there, my bedside where
My world stretched before
A natural, a symphony
A song beside my door.

Chapter Four. Developing a 'Style of Myself'

The Birds in Song Presiding

I lay there drummeled on my bed
In memories residing
When outside of my something room
The birds in song presiding
Did shower me with all their joy
Their heart-felt song unmeasured
A joyful flock, a gladsome tone
A pure and treasured pleasure
How do I love those cheery sweet
Little God-made wee-ones
How they do overflow with praise
To God and Light and Sun.

Los Angeles
November 1998

CHAPTER FOUR

PART FIVE

June 1999

Instrument of the Poetic Word

Chapter Four. Developing a 'Style of Myself'

Five Color Poems

Red

Flaming Red so brave and bold
Of all colors oldest old
Glowing warmth does take its start
Color Red begins with heart

Red comes ever to the fore
Rising up from the ground floor
Evident, is always seen
Holds its own in midst of Green

Courage stands up unafraid
By itself, no outer aid
In the face of pain and fear
Red emerges strong and clear.

Purple

Purple magic Christly be
Color human sovereignty
Princesses all reigning free
In the nights of mystery

Purple mountains rising tall
Awesome wonder, all else small
Glory, honor, purple heart
Idealism finds its start

Purple poised upright and sure
Loyal, faithful, ever pure
Lover earth of heart and mound
Venus dreaming all around.

Part Five. June 1999 Instrument of the Poetic Word

Blue

Meditation, deep blue sky
Growing deeper into high
On the earth a tender flower
Smiling face in nighttime hour

Star-light shining platinum blue
Ever-speaking, crystal hue
God Divine of heavens blue
Of all colors truest true

Cool, refreshing air-sky pool
Eternity of spatial rule
Vast and all-encompassing
Inner peace does blue us bring.

Green

Middle balance color green
Soul-restoring, welcome scene
Grazing pastures, grassy fields
Tender blades to raindrops yield

Liquid green sea harmony
Springtime shoots, foliage on trees
Carpet plush, forest green moss
Human Figure on the Cross

Green of Life and green of Death
Inhale-exhale God, His Breath
Plant kingdom, vegetable growth
Contract-expand of stem-leaf both

Green is neither dark nor light
Neither blue nor yellow bright
Between the two is green place found
Harmonizing pleasant ground.

Chapter Four. Developing a 'Style of Myself'

Yellow

Yellow beams of golden rays
Noontime is the warmth of day
Cheerful color, smiling gay
Bringing joy is yellow's way

Glad and warm is the sun's light
Beaming brilliantly and bright
Expanding outwardly with might
Such a splendid sunny sight

Soul-life streams from thee, O Sun
Loving light for every one
Gleaming, shining radiant clear
Changing moods throughout the year

Sun- and soul-light pouring here
Widths of space, soul-depths appear
Splitting into colors seven
Rainbow bridge from earth to heaven.

Los Angeles
June 1999
Revised January 10, 2013

CHAPTER FOUR

PART SIX

June – July 1999

A Poet's World

Chapter Four. Developing a 'Style of Myself'

A Dream

An inkling of, a twinkling of a shimmer, glimmer faint
And large and luminous bright lights fair color-pictures paint
And in a deep and darkened sleep drips water in a well
And sounds of distant singing birds, and ringing, clinging bells
Until in moments solitude, a solitary note
Upon a stream, as in a dream, sweet gentle feelings float.

Artistic Sensibility

Artistic sensibility grows fonder by the hour
As tender as small drops of dew upon a golden flower
And shining bright through rose-flamed clouds, the sun of dusk all red
Sinks slowly down into her sleep, horizon's ocean-bed.

Spirit-Land

Listen to the color-chords of sunset flaming red
And yellow, orange, golden-rose, as children go to bed
The prayers of evening fill the sky, and moods of dusk they speak
And planets, moon and stars appear above the mountain-peak
And if your wonder lifts you up above the dying earth
Among the stars you shall then bathe, in Spirit-Land your birth.

Part Six. June – July 1999 A Poet's World

Ein Liebessturm

Ich möchte gerne schlafen, tief in Dunkelheit
Mit Träumen und mit Glaube, getrostet Herrlichkeit
Ich atme ein die Lüften, und aus mein Lebensblut
Ein Liebessturm des Herbstes, mit Farben und mit Mut.

Die Menschen

Es gibt im Leben vieles was mir offenbart
Die Menschen, ihre Arten, die Wege ihrer Fahrt
Wir treffen uns bei Tage und träumen Nächte süß
Zusammen während Schlafe: ein Menschenbrüdergruß.

Die Farben

Die Farben mannigfaltig der Seele schwimmen frei
Im Ätherleibeswasser fließen allerlei
Sie mischen sich wo Lichter strahlen sonnenklar
In Fluten strömend einfach Leben ganz und gar.

Die Liebe

Die Mitte der Erfahrung ist Schmerz und Freude Herz
Seelisch Fühlen-Tiefen, für Wahrheit leidend Schmerz
Ein ständig ein und aus, ein Atmen rhythmisch lebt
Und von dem Herze Liebe haucht und lacht und schwebt.

Die Menschheit

Wir wissen Sachen üblich, die Schwächen unsrer Zeit
Die Oberfläche Lebens, Gefahren Gesamtheit
Tiefer lebt Gewissen, pulsiert die Liebe treu
Und vorwärts geht die Menschheit mit Morgenkraft ganz neu.

Chapter Four. Developing a 'Style of Myself'

A Pink

There was a pink which smiled at me
I could not think more happily
That pink appeared for me to see
That pink endeared itself to me
And now I can see nothing else
Were I a man or but an elf
For that dear pink my heart did win
And now I think, it made me grin.

A Pleasant Green

A pleasant green became the ground
On which my comfort I did found
It soothed and blessed my tired mind
And transformed into thoughts most kind
It eased my pain, a solace, peace
I found I needed its release
And when I search with all my soul
'Tis green doth heal and make me whole.

O Blue of Water

O blue of water, blue of awe
And blue of ever, divine law
Of depth and peace, profundity
Which further than the eye can see
Encompasses entire space
The heavens grand, small flowers' face
Blue is the biggest thing of all
As large as God, both wide and tall.

Part Six. June – July 1999 A Poet's World

O Brown of Earth

O brown of earth all rich and moist
You speak with simple, peasant voice
Of life which in the darkness dwells
And of coarse virtue feeling tells
Which nurtures growth above the ground
A world of roots and insects found
You drink deep draughts of melted snow
And the wet rains seep down below.

A Grey

There was a grey without a trace
Of rainbow glory, sunlit grace
A grey all washed and hazy blend
A mist, a mire, a distant end
I could not point, nor clarify
Nor find an answer to my why.

A Yellow

A yellow jumped and sang out loud
Dispersing dark and rainy clouds
It soared and swung; it danced and laughed
Exclaiming life, a winged giraffe
Which talked incessantly and smiled
A bubbly, cheerful, happy child.

Behold, the Red

Behold, the Red commands the stage:
"Look at me now, I never age
"I am the One, who brave and strong
"Has come to serve, to right all wrongs
"Focus on me; I'll be your guide
"I never cry; I never hide
"I show no fear, endure all pain
"Am ever clear, sunshine or rain."

Chapter Four. Developing a 'Style of Myself'

A Purple Cloth

There stood reposed, and calm and sure
With quiet strength, which shall endure
A purple cloth, noble and dear
Of priceless worth throughout the year
With noble blood and sovereignty
Steadfast and true, a prince' decree
Whose magic works both deep and strong
And stands with grace, slender and long.

Los Angeles
June – July 1999

CHAPTER FOUR

PART SEVEN

July 1999 – November 2001

Ego and Love

Chapter Four. Developing a 'Style of Myself'

A Time To Reminisce

Time to feel, reminisce, poignant, dear and serene
Like a maiden or a lady or a fine, gentle queen
Who feels all for her country, for the Folk and the Land
In the food and the drink and the castle great and grand
She surveys all of Nature, all the forests and the streams
And the people, simple peasants, bathe in warm,
                                         sundrenched dreams.

The inner I is such a thing
As only joy and sadness bring
As thunder, lightning, rain and sleet
As sunlit clouds and rainbows meet
As earthquakes, famines, floods and waves
As pain and fear and death men brave
For life in Christ like blood is red
Is with the living and the dead
And smiles loving tender there
Compassion feeling everywhere.

July 27, 1999

Die Mahlzeit Christi

Ich fühle wie da draußen, die Ich-Sucht gefährlich droht
Ich fühle in meiner Innenwelt, die Liebe brennt und glüht
Ich denke stark Gedanken, vom Chaos ungestört
Das Denkenslicht sich strahlet, die Töne hab' ich 'hört

Die Töne fröhlich Christi, die Töne klingen laut
Die Farben heil'ges Feuer, ich habe sie geschaut
Ich will mein Herz und Seele, mit Geist durchtränken warm
Und Mut und Freiheit langen, wie nahe und wie fern.

Die Welt bringt mir kein Frieden, Getümmel herrscht in ihr
Die Unruh' der Gespenster, gehören nicht zu mir

Part Seven. July 1999 – November 2001 Ego and Love

Die Liebe stirbt am Tage, und lebt die Nächte auf
Wir brauchen stark die Glaube, und leiden dieses Haus

Unsre Erdenwohnung, der Leibestempel und
Der Seele Freud' und Schmerzen, in Rhythmen Jahr und Stund'
Der Geist des Menschen quellet, aus Gottesgründen tief
Und segnet Herz und Seele, Er ruft uns und Er rief

Seit zwei Tausend Jahren, erweckend Menschen lieb
Er wird immer treu bleiben, Er bleibt wie auch Er blieb
Der Eine, der Geliebte, der Menschensohn, das Kind
Der hilft uns wann es regnet, im Sonnenschein, im Wind

Der Jesu-Knabe liebet, Seine Brüder hier
Sein Herz ist süß und rein, Sein Auge leuchtet klar
Er will uns immer helfen, beten wir darum
Wir brauchen Seine Hilfe, sowie Sein Heiligtum

Nun herrscht im Himmel droben, der Vater-Gott im Geist
Er sandte uns Seinen Sohn, Ewigkeit in Zeit
Er mag die Krankheit heilen, die Toten aufersteh'n
Er wird zu jedem kommen, damit wir vorwärtsgeh'n

Wenn an die Tür es klopfet, und Christus will herein
Essen wir das heil'ge Brot, und trinken süßen Wein
Das ist die Mahlzeit Christi, damit wir leben fort
Des Lebens Sinn, Bedeutung, das Licht, das Herz, das Wort.

August 1999
Los Angeles

Sometime share a feeling
In grounds of heart and soul
For no other reason
For no further goal
Feelings they are special
Stirring warm with love
Like the clouds at sunset
And a pure white dove

Chapter Four. Developing a 'Style of Myself'

Like the springtime flowers
And like food and drink
Beneath the snows of winter
Reddish rosy-pink.

Los Angeles
September 14, 1999

Dying

So sad, a drop, a falling leaf
Yet see in golden hue,

An autumn die, falling to earth
The sighing breezes blow.

A gust, a swirl, a circling dance
See spirals, now the leaves,

Fall there, on fire, a-fighting fierce
Yellow, orange, red.

When Sky and Earth are Joined

A brisk and cool morning
With moisture in the air

Above in heavens cloudy
The sunlight brightens fair

How lovely is the morning
When sky and earth are joined

As clouds and fog come down here
Fine sense and spirit tuned.

Torrance, California
Autumn 1999

Part Seven. July 1999 – November 2001 Ego and Love

My First Room

Tell me tender tales of woe
In the oceans far below
Buried in the sands of time
With the shells and rocks and lime
I feel currents of the sea
Little fishes touching me
Painted coral, waters warm
Long years ago I here was born
In my Mother's gentle womb
I discovered my first room
Safe inside this world so deep
I found nurturing me keep
In the darkness beating sound
Two hearts pulsing there be found.

Van Nuys, California
2000 (summer?)

Da war ein Mensch, der saß und meint'
Er war mit andern ganz vereint
Und dies' Gedanke bracht' ihm Trost
Sein Herz erwärmt, er trank mit "Prost"
Dann ging er hin, und sang ein Lied
Das überbrückt' all' Unterschied
Und nun gemeinsam in der Welt
Er freute sich, sein Weg erhellt.

Culver City, California
20. November 2000

Accentuate a revenue
Of every shade, of every hue
The golden sheathes, the fair green blades
The roses red, the blue which fades
And I immerse my soul, my all
Until I hear a voice me call
Me call to think all crystal clear

Chapter Four. Developing a 'Style of Myself'

And then a rainbow does appear
And then I know that colors speak
Through every day, through every week

They speak in tones, in shades and hues
In reds and greens, yellows and blues
For us to share their language lore
Until we reach some distant shore
Where time bestows in rhythms deep
The meaning of eternal sleep

Now there remains for us to ford
A river ferry for to board
To cross in magic twilight hours
A threshold ushered in with flowers
The colors of the sunset fade
And we have entered secret glades

Where in the vast celestial dome
Our Father welcomes us to home
That starry world, eternal love
The symbol of a snow-white dove
Of Christmas Night, tender and mild
The spirit-birth, the Spirit Child.

November 16, 2001

A measured step, a word, a phrase
As pastures green where cows do graze
Where up above in the sky blue
Great clouds of white do billow true
And the gold sun streams with her light
Yellow golden beams so bright
And in a garden colorful
One rose of red is wonderful.

November 17, 2001

Part Seven. July 1999 – November 2001 Ego and Love

Glory of rivers and glory of seas
Mountains and forests and grasses and trees
Currents, tides rising and waves crashing loud
Cliff-rocks and sunshine and rainbows and clouds
Animals playing in fresh springtime air
Birds singing, flying with nary a care
Glorious Sun-disc, mighty orb gold
Silvery Moon shining clear wisdom old
And our dear Earth dying, aging now come
Come let us gather, Earth becomes a sun!

November 17, 2001
Van Nuys, California

CHAPTER FIVE

2001 – 2002

CELEBRATING

NATURE AND HUMANITY

Chapter Five. 2001 – 2002 Celebrating Nature and Humanity

The Moon is Rising in My Mind

The Moon is rising in my mind
Trailing streaks and moving showers
In the tides and growth of plants
Before the blossoming of flowers

The Moon appears before my soul
Round and perfect, clear and whole
In a silver mode of thought
Reflection answers my North Pole.

The Moon does acquiesce and seem
All my questions to redeem
In his unifying stream
Clearer than the clearest dream

The Moon is ancient with my Sun
Causing rhythms to implore
Waves of oceans to cast out
Foam refreshing fine before

The Moon is one and only the
Special silhouetting sea
Sending sudden certainly
Motions making rhythmically

The Moon recalls the Sun for me
In his ponderings I see
All the science Stonehenge be
Druids keeping company

The Moon is motion, measure, mist
Ages bygone seem to ask
Do remember crescent curves
Tending alway to my task

The Moon through every cycle of
Waxing, waning sentient here

Chapter Five. 2001 – 2002 Celebrating Nature and Humanity

Feel his timeless ever-pull
In our souls returning near

Like some beacon messenger
The Moon our constant visitor
Accompanies our monthly modes
Like some Roman Senator.

Seated in the sky so still
Stretch imaginations some
Nightingales inspiring all
Minstrels serenading strum.

The Rain is Ritual and Wreath

The rain descending drop by drop
Refreshes all my opened pores
Like little musical etudes
Whose melodies my mind implores

The rain requires responsiveness
And rushing restfully repeats
The sound of timpani and touch
In soothing special bursts of beats.

The rain reveals in rhythms rules
Of heaven's holy happenings
To drink its draughts the earth allows
Her friend the water entering

The rain is ritual and wreath
Adorning plant and home and street
Is sacred water heart to heart
Its footsteps feeling toes and feet

The rain repeats in pleasing play
Upon this wet and rainy day
I love to listen to its song
Inside in my own inner way.

Chapter Five. 2001 – 2002 Celebrating Nature and Humanity

What the Mountain Means To Me

A mountain stands before my mind
Majestic crowning citadel
In lordly landscape all to me
Impervious to infidel

A mountain stands and gestures up
Meeting sky and cloud and star
An arm of earth in strength and hand
Clear though in the distance far.

A mountain meets the sunlight clear
Tremendous in his solid way
A presence for the gods to walk
Like children with the rocks do play.

A mountain stands in silence great
Powerful yet quiet, calm
Stretching upward toward the sky
Like an open, trusting palm.

Mountain, do you know your worth?
Surely you unchallenged stand
Amidst the hills and valleys, plains
Rise on high, ye mighty land.

A mountain prays by night, by day
In an understanding way
People lift their eyes to see
What assurance has to say.

What the mountain means to me
Forested by wood and tree
Speaking for humanity
In stillness and nobility.

Los Angeles
November 24, 2001

Chapter Five. 2001 – 2002 Celebrating Nature and Humanity

Fünf Deutsche Gedichte vom 15. Februar 2002

1. Zwei Welten

Ich werde sprechen
Du aber redest
Ich werde schreiben
Du machst Notizen
Ich werde denken
Du aber spinnest

Ich werde atmen
Du fliegst schnell über
Ich geh' in Rhythmen
Du kannst dich nicht ruhen
Ich möchte schlafen
Du nimmst nur Pausen

Ich muss klar wachen
Du träumst die Tage
Wir sind zusammen
Erwachs'ne und Kinder
Zwei ganz verschied'ne
Anschauungswelten.

2. Gottes Segen

Wir Menschen meinen
Alles schnell
Vorübergehend, unruhig
Rastlose Energie

Doch die Liebe
Schweigend pulsiert
Friede bringend
Ihr Gottes Segen

Wie ein Regenbogen
Nach dem Sturme des Lebens

Chapter Five. 2001 – 2002 Celebrating Nature and Humanity

Bei der Wiedererscheinung
Der Sonne, ihres Lichtes

Die Sonne uns erwärmend
Das wir fühlen
Das Güte wohltuend
Christi.

3. Eines

Vor kurzem
Als ich Dir vorbei fuhr
Sah ich in Deinen Augen
Das klare Christus-Licht

Wir waren für einen Moment
Eines
Christus, Du und ich

Gemeinsam durch unsren Herrn
Durch unsren Bruder Christus
Einig.

4. Die Welt

Die Welt
So groß
Ergibt uns
Kleine Schönheiten
Wenn wir sie bemerken

Blumen, Vögel, Bäume
Und große Landschaften
Irdische Ebene, Bergen
Himmlische Weiten, Sonnen-Taten
Dämmerungen, Sonnenuntergänge

Licht-Taten
Farben-Gemälde
Bunte Herrlichkeiten

Chapter Five. 2001 – 2002 Celebrating Nature and Humanity

Erfreuliche Stimmungen
Die uns zum Lächeln bringen
Und unsren Herzen erwärmen

Stille Momente
Am Abend für Andacht
Und Nachdenken
Für Atmen
Und Fühlen
Tiefen.

5. Dein Leben

Ich bin
So spricht das Herz
Höre dieses Wort

Ich bin
So fühle ich mir selber
Ich und in mir
Mein treuer Christus

Christus
Vergebe mir
Meine Schulden

Ich bin
Ein Sündiger
Ich bin
Daran schuldig

Deine Luft
Atme ich
Dein Blut
Erwärmt mich
Dein Leben
Hält mich am Leben.

Culver City, Kalifornien
15. Februar 2002

Chapter Five. 2001 – 2002 Celebrating Nature and Humanity

A Vision of Love

Who knows why we men, we women
Why we humans must live, suffer, and die?
Just what did God have in mind
When He created us
To live out our days
Our hopes and dreams
On this battlefield of mercy

Of heart and mind
Of holy reverence and simplicity
Of complex karmic relationships
And the web of destiny
In which each one of us
Is a thread?

This is some tapestry
God – Christ – the Lord of Karma
Who weaves masterfully
A beautiful Persian rug
Out of all the colorful strands
Into a world-picture-pattern
Beyond my knowing

Mystery runs through the loom
His Light in our souls
Creating beautiful colors from our darkness
And in the center – the motif
Stands the Lamb
And the Cross

Can you see
The Easter Resurrection
Free above the carpet radiant bright?
Christ has woven
Does weave
Will weave until
All the darkness is brought to Light

Chapter Five. 2001 – 2002 Celebrating Nature and Humanity

And this magnificent rug becomes
A vision of love

March 26, 2002

For Dr. Virginia Sease

A flock of small birds in swift flight at sunset
Their movements in formation
Here, then there

Appearing as a revelation
Revealing soul to my vision
Then disappearing as they go beyond my view

And in the background sunset mood's color vista
Claims my heart with the love
Of Christ Jesus' Passion and Crucifixion

Until, at dusk's departing death
The day ends sun's deeds done
And night at twilight does draw near in darkened sky
And moon and stars appear.

March 28, 2002

Of Flowers and Weeds

I speak of flowers sweet, and weeds,
The beauty here, there interest reads;

The daisy smiles its little face,
The clover hidden in its grace;

The daffodil, pure perfect choice,
The peasant dandelion's voice;

If both are yellow, one's the queen,
The second commoner is seen.

Chapter Five. 2001 – 2002 Celebrating Nature and Humanity

We always love the blossoms fair
Of flowers colorful of air,

But I suggest the different weeds
Secretly my interest heeds.

The Shores

Remember what the shores give,
Upon which lapping waves live;
They wash upon the sands of time,
In rhythmic melodies and rhymes,

The shores of ministry of birds,
Of shells and seaweed, poets' words,
Of solitary figures lean
Who walking thoughtfully do dream
Of memories, and then they see,
Among the clouds the sun's glory.

March 29, 2002

Schöne Nacht

O schöne Nacht
Du bist erwacht
Und bleibst auf ewig treu

Vergessen nun
Des Tages Tun
Und Lichtes Scham und Scheu

In dieser Welt
- die Sternenzelt
Still, geheimnisvoll

Um mich herum
- mein Mund ist stumm
Klingt Sternen Dur und Moll

Chapter Five. 2001 – 2002 Celebrating Nature and Humanity

In Dunkelheit
Und Raumes Weit'
Erscheint das ew'ge Licht

Die Sonne singt
Der Vater bringt
Uns Christi Angesicht.

29. März 2002

Wonders of the Night

I mention here
- my mind is clear
The wonders of the night

Behind us lies
The sunlit skies
All blushing in the light

And in the deep
In secret sleep
Of darkness there do dwell

The spirits of
Eternal love
All in the starry well

And there among
Forever young
The dead we bathe and breathe

The cosmic song
Resounding strong
New Life does us bequeath.

March 29, 2002

Chapter Five. 2001 – 2002 Celebrating Nature and Humanity

Merry

A poem of
Eternal love
Of music and the Light
In sweetest
Reveries I dwell
In memories of Night

And then I hear
The songs of birds
Who in the flight of air
Release my
Captive spirit-mind
And free from me all care

They chirp with sentient
Thrilling throats
The merriest of hearts
And with their
Singing morning love
My every day does start.

April 5, 2002

Hellsehen

Hellsehen
Sonne Schönheit
Lieber Christus

Himmelskrone
Herrlich strahlend
Wunderbar

Unsre Liebe
Dankbar schenken
Herz erfüllt

Chapter Five. 2001 – 2002 Celebrating Nature and Humanity

Nach Dir
Frühlingsfreude
Mit den Vögeln

Bis zur Sonne
Zu den Sternen
Kosmisch ist Dein
Ew'ges Leben

Mit der Erde
Ist der Atem
Ausgeatmet

Das wir unsres
Selbst in Dir
In Deinem Leben
Finden.

5. April 2002

Reborn

I open up within my mind
A space where light does shine
My inner freedom, thinking's realm
Awakens clear and fine

And colors glow before my soul
The courage of the flame
In rose and red, in pink appears
The flower of my name

And in the sunset's dying mood
I see Christ's suffering
His Passion speaks, His Cross and Death
His Holy Offering

The flames of dying, burning thoughts
The fiery, pulsing Word

Chapter Five. 2001 – 2002 Celebrating Nature and Humanity

Ascends in love, and heavenward
Begins to fly, a bird

The Thought of Christ appears to me
I grasp it in the Light
And shining there all radiance
A-glowing fair and bright

Reveals from out of tragedy
From sorrow's heavy load
Through death's deep passage spirit-birth
A true and sacred road

The road of agony and pain
Becomes the purest joy
And then there in the feeble man
Of old becomes the boy

A little child of innocence
Of pure and goodness heart
And as a child is born through death
And heaven is the start

This child smiles, his cares relieved
His sorrows have become
The happiness and cheer of youth
A new and reborn son.

April 8, 2002

Freund

Sag mir Bescheid
Das mein Kummer und Leid
Vorübergehend ist

Nimmst Du mein' Hand
Aufs Meer und aufs Land
Das ich weiß Du mein Freund bist

Chapter Five. 2001 – 2002 Celebrating Nature and Humanity

Wehe all' Grau
Nur Purpur und Blau
Nur Grün, Gelb und Rot sind gut

Farben sind bunt
Sie geben sich kund
Beim Licht, Wasser, Wolken und Blut

Sing mir ein Lied
Dann darfst Du Mitglied
Unter Vögel und Sänger sein

Dann bleibst Du treu
Und auf ewig neu
Du mein Freund und ich auch Dein.

27. Juni 2002

Aglow

Some afterglow
A memory
Of sunsets by the shore

The veil of evening
Transports time
And opens Night's portal door

We are again
As little ones
Small children kneeling pray

In gratitude
And reverence
For yet another day

As one by one
The curtains close
And we to bed retire

Chapter Five. 2001 – 2002 Celebrating Nature and Humanity

To die in glory
Holy Night
Aglow in spirit-fire.

July 26, 2002

Peasant Poetry

A call for peasant poetry
In plough and porridge poverty
Beneath a simple doorway there
An earthen floor, a wooden stair

A candle burns, a single flame
Casts gentle light, while outside rain
Beats rhythmically like little drums
The children eating morsel crumbs

And soup of broth which mother made
By humble earnings father paid
The family huddled in the cold
About the hearth where stories told

Of farmers' sons and daughters wed
And ailing cousins sick in bed
Of fields and forests, how the land
Reveals its secrets to the hand

Of him who tills and toils by day
And works with cows and corn and hay
And now the children tired begin
To fall asleep, it's night again.

August 1, 2002

Beyond the Sea

Essentially – a footed note
A steep stone path – in hat and coat
A pilgrimage – through mist and wind

Chapter Five. 2001 – 2002 Celebrating Nature and Humanity

My breathing hard – through bush and bend

I could not see – the fog so thick
My mind a swirl, my stomach sick
So carefully, each step, each word
Only the sounds of horn and bird

To guide me there up to the shore
To take my leave of land and lore
This one last stretch of poetry
These final words before the sea

To sink and fly among the sails
Of outbound ships, of winds and gales
While down below where currents deep
My energies would steal and keep

Me from the sun, from warmth and light
Where I would dance and soar in flight
Only beyond horizon there
I let my voice rebound so clear

In echoing, and then at last
To disappear before my past
And now I see one seagull high
In freedom go before I die.

August 18, 2002

Courage

Flaming sunset orange-gold
As in valiant days of old
Speak to me of courage, love
Soul descending from above

Incarnation, Passiontide
Crucifixion when Christ died
Soon will I in Spirit-Light

Chapter Five. 2001 – 2002 Celebrating Nature and Humanity

Join the dead in starry night

Ask forgiveness that I sleep
In the secret dark night deep
For another dawning day
With new hope in sun's clear rays

Now in autumn we draw near
To the winter Child so dear
May St. Michaél help us
To prepare for pure Christmas
From the dying, aging earth
To experience Spirit-birth.

October 1, 2002

I Like the Plant Do Weave

I sought to draw from warmth and light
The colors beautiful of sight
I sought to pull from darkness cold
The strength and clarity of old

I sought to keep my dreams so pure
Imagination-pictures sure
I sought to hold upright my thoughts
Intuition-words clear taught

Between these two extremes live I
Neither below nor up in sky
Neither a cosmic being free
Nor earth-bound like the roots of tree
But human on the surface there
Like water between earth and air

I look above and see the light
I feel below earth's deep, dark night
And I do breathe in inner breath
And find life's meaning there where death

Chapter Five. 2001 – 2002 Celebrating Nature and Humanity

Does strike by day upon my mind
Where life abundant would make blind

Where leaf does balance there I grow
Before the blossoms colors show
And up above the gnarled roots
I sprout and send my new green shoots

I am not mineral, not stone
Nor heavenly bird away has flown
But like the plant I breathe and weave
My inner harmonies perceive

Between the mighty sun and earth
To human feelings give I birth
And therein find my inner worth
With joys and sorrows, pain and mirth.

October 7, 2002

Evening Prayer

Ever-dying evening into night
The shroud of dusk befalls us 'fore starlight
The cloak of sunset colors richly breathe
The sacrifice our Saviour in the eve

The evening we are speaking and we taste
The sacrament of holiness and faith
Within the dying colors lights a flame
In which there blazes every human name

We live with courage, ask for Christ's pure aid,
In everything behind us we have made
Begins to shine as candles in the night
The birth of mystery and love and light

O grant me peace this evening that I sleep
Forgiven in the realm of spirit-deep

Chapter Five. 2001 – 2002 Celebrating Nature and Humanity

Receive my soul, my body left in bed
That I may join the spirits of the dead

The twilight soon transports us from the day's
Bright radiant sunbeam, warm and streaming rays
Into the sepulcher of hearts inside
Our Source and Saviour Jesu Christ, our Guide

Receive me Lord, I pray, and take my soul
Into Thy world of stars in cosmos whole
That in Thy Glory Sun of Night I may
Discover once again my inner way

O pardon me and help me as I seek
Thy inner Light before Thee I be meek
And enter into night's abundant love
My spirit free to fly as a pure dove.

October 31, 2002

Three Songs of Silence

1. November

The magic of the summer disappeared,
Like precious gold quite suddenly quick stolen
By evening's shadow-hand and crusty beard,
The gentleman of autumn's purse now swollen

Replaced by dusty linen-clumps in size
Quite similar in shape without the shine,
Deceiving to the unobservant eyes,
Yet worlds apart to him discerning fine

"What happened," asks the year, "my day now done,
I was so wealthy, in abundant form,
So richly blessed by noontime's glorious sun,
That all the world felt pleased and good and warm?

Chapter Five. 2001 – 2002 Celebrating Nature and Humanity

November tells me different things have come,
And dying reaches into every place;
My room once filled with joy now sounds a drum
Which hollow beats its rhythms into space"

Yet deep within is knowledge of the earth;
December this dull music bottomless
Might turn to hear the song of sweetest birth,
Though autumn left the coffers penniless

When choirs sing of gladness in the night,
When ox and ass the Child with breath warm keep,
While angels praise the Sun's triumphant Light,
The world by peace be blessed in quiet sleep.

2. Hope

Time is ticking in my tapping teeth,
And yet I lack the rhythm of the blood;
The steadiness of breathing down beneath,
Slows nearly stopping by the weight of wood

Inner forest timber stretches out,
Like large blue avalanching mountain slopes;
The branches crack, the roots do sprawl about;
I tumble, yet I still retain my hope.

And at the valley bottom there I lie;
My hands are warm, the rushing is behind;
Above I see the beautiful blue sky;
A single twig is all that's left to find.

A little bird has flown beyond the peak;
High above the clouds repeats my mind,
To look for forest timber, trees to seek,
But only snow abundant is to find.

I want to stand yet sit there still, amazed
That I survived catastrophe my head;

Chapter Five. 2001 – 2002 Celebrating Nature and Humanity

I know that I am troubled, also dazed,
And almost wish to be among the dead.

Whenever I my feeling cease within,
The ticking of the time returns once more;
My clattering teeth remind me of my chin;
The cold I'm feeling knocks upon my door.

3. Poet's Gold

Quiet, I hear nothing but the dogs,
Deaf to voice, to tone, to thought and word,
Encapsulated in a chamber fog,
Lost to every favorite singing bird

The cars I know are rushing in the night,
And sleep betrays the tiredness I feel,
Blinded like the beggar after sight,
Wandering, the darkness all too real

The streets lie cold and humanless before
My avenues of silences alone,
Enwrapped like cabbage rolls asking for more,
As greedy as a weighty graveyard stone

The ants keep walking like pickpockets poor;
They never seem to have enough of me;
They bite my thoughts, small pieces on the floor,
Each time I glimpse who I do long to be

Without a moment's freedom to become
The answer to the question of the hour,
I nibble every hard and stale crumb,
And miss the beauty of the passing flower

The men are working; I care not for them;
I have my own agenda they would steal;
My rhythms hold my wealth like precious gems;
Before them I am writing as I kneel

Chapter Five. 2001 – 2002 Celebrating Nature and Humanity

And every opportunity is real;
The children know this well and find the way,
Imagining a world they do feel,
As true as any word can mean by day

And forward is the touch I ever hold;
I give it with a squeeze in handshake good,
Like a coin my words are cast in poet's gold,
I know when read they will be understood.

November 13, 2002

People: Be Wise.

People: be wise.
In your present decisions,
In your responsibility
Or irresponsibility today
You future lies.

People: be wise.
Do not do what comes
So easily to you
Choose your road to walk
To make your progress prize

People: be wise.
Take time to pause
For quiet inner calm,
And from such moments clear
Tomorrows plans revise.

People: be wise.
Listen to the hour.
Feel the inner love
In pulse of blood and breath
Learn to sink and rise.

People: be wise.

Chapter Five. 2001 – 2002 Celebrating Nature and Humanity

Live each day in full,
And sleep each night serene,
So that tomorrow brings
New hope in the blue skies

People: be wise.
Grow strong by challenges
And keep good company.
Help your brother there
Who grows, who ails, who dies.

People: be wise.
Share, give and receive.
Enter with your love,
And good will exercise.

People: be wise.
Make every moment count,
Make every day worthwhile.
Create a better world.
People: be wise.

Los Angeles
November 15, 2002

Frieden

Komm kleines Kind
Mit mir – und wir
Werden gehen zu Fuß zu den Fluß
Wo wir werden reden mit Fäden.

Wenn dunkel es funkeln
Die Sterne gerne
Bis Morgen Sorgen.

O Pracht der Nacht!
Erwacht mit Macht;
Mein Leben wird Streben,
Mein Tod führt zum Gott

Chapter Five. 2001 – 2002 Celebrating Nature and Humanity

Sein Angesicht von Licht ist
Linder für Seine Kinder,
Ganz Glanz;
In Seinen Händen enden
Die Bücher Geistsucher.

Nimm mein Sinn;
Führe mich zum Traum Baum.
In des Grafes Schlafes
Sinke zur Linke

Mein Geist reist,
Mein Leib bleibt
Zum Glück zurück,
Meine Seele am Landrand
Den Strand fand

Höre die Chöre
Singen, sie bringen
Frieden hernieden.

21. November 2002

The Magic of the Night

A morning song whispered to me
As tenderly as leaf and shoots
Of verdant green, of grassy fields
Before the summer and the noon

And as I dreamt of yesterday,
I felt this song had went its way,
And then I knew 'twas eventide,
That night had come to me inside.

And after all this morning verse,
I prayed for winter's Christmas birth,
That I might sleep and be renewed
By nightly inner quietude

Chapter Five. 2001 – 2002 Celebrating Nature and Humanity

And so I dwell on inner moods,
I linger there where spirit broods;
And if I find within my child,
Then you may know that I be mild.

And every single tiny word
Is sung to music of a bird;
And this my song, and this my note
Lives simply here and not remote

And here I am, and here I write,
And here I children would invite,
Into my heart, into my love,
Until I fly to heav'n above,

Where this my love descended from,
To take abode in earth's own womb;
May I prepare my heart's dark earth
For such a child of spirit-birth

Until the hour of midnight still
May I press onward with my will;
Now it grows late and all the men
Have gone away to bed again

The spirits of the night emerge,
While inside melodies do surge;
Such is the music of the night,
The darkness shines with inner light.

The dead do live in starry lands,
While God shapes creatures with His Hands;
We only see them picture-like
After their spirit-archetype

Now may I join in spirit-spheres,
Reality in me appears;
In me might find all peace and light,
In me the warmth of inner might

Chapter Five. 2001 – 2002 Celebrating Nature and Humanity

In me the quiet strength to test
My challenges, until I rest.
Now may I rest, until once more
I must awake through sunrise' door

But first the magic of the night
Does bid me come, does me invite.

November 23, 2002

Heaven

A morning thread was woven long
And lilted lovingly in song;
It danced like little buzzing bees
And blew like whispers through the trees.

And when I followed lightly through
This spinning silken thread to view,
I found another land unknown,
Yet it was my eternal home.

It differed from the earth and ground,
It left all separation bound
By spatial and temporal laws
And disappeared the human flaws

This world eternal vast and true
Saw inner light with warmth imbued,
Heard sounding tone and forming speech
By intermingling beings each

One spirit-beings, angels pure,
And everywhere the Christ most sure
Was working spirit-active there;
Activity was everywhere.

And when I chanced to pass my gaze
To earth below and human ways,

Chapter Five. 2001 – 2002 Celebrating Nature and Humanity

Appeared to me great wastelands vast,
Both north and south and east and west

With little lights where humans free
Were sharing love activity;
The earth herself began to shine,
Becoming sun of Christ divine

And then I knew I must return,
Responsibilities to earn,
To play my part where fellow men
Contribute every day again.

Because the Future beckoned me
I must keep human company;
But now I know, though I forget,
My only home before I met

My body and the earth and stones,
Before my clothes were flesh and bones,
Is heaven's spirit-land above,
With spirit-sun and light and love.

Los Angeles
November 24, 2002

CHAPTER SIX

August 2002 – April 2004

BALLADS AND SONNETS

Chapter Six. August 2002 – April 2004 Ballads and Sonnets

Lad Alan Glad – A Ballad

One fair and sunny springtime morn
A wonder special did appear
To Alan, lad in heart and glad,
Revealed a lady magic rare

She wore a golden ring and pearl,
Her golden hair shone radiant bright;
Her voice rang golden pure and clear,
Her fair blue eyes smiled golden light.

Lad Alan stood there still, amazed;
He could not speak, his lips were mute,
Could only listen like a child
When Lady's voice sang like a lute.

But she, this lady rare and fine,
Spoke all the louder, candidly,
Rejoicing, thrilling with her voice,
Great gladness spreading openly

Her name soon spread on waves and wind,
On Alan's lips did come to rest,
And stirring now within his heart
Gail Sherwood, Lady Guest.

Whene'er she spoke to neighbors there,
She rang her hands and voice with life,
Her lips in passion quivering;
No man could claim her as his wife.

All the world revealed to her,
Each man and woman, none could hide;
And truth awakened in their hearts;
And harmony did there abide.

August 22, 2002

Chapter Six. August 2002 – April 2004 Ballads and Sonnets

A Noble Lass in Days of Yore

Yon bonnie sea, yon bonnie shore
Brought one young man to home and kin;
A noble lass in days of yore
Impressed him as a royal queen

Her carriage straight, her skin so fair,
Her brown eyes bold, her curly hair,
Her presence changed the atmosphere,
Surrounding her with freshest air

And she was gracious, she sat tall
As royalty on throne and call
Her beauty rarer than them all
Transformed a room into a hall

With purity untouchable
Inspired she all boys and men,
As truth so near, attainable,
Yet also out of reach again.

Her simplest garments appeared to be
Like golden robes with silken veil,
So pure and chaste this lady be,
A servant of the Holy Grail

Her name was French, befitting queens
Who highest honors well deserved;
Heavens red rose on earthly green,
Nicôle Divine, she reigned and served.

Her elegance beyond compare,
And radiant, her shining eyes,
As though around her in the air
Clear sunlight brightened all the skies.

August 23, 2002

Chapter Six. August 2002 – April 2004 Ballads and Sonnets

The Imagination – A Ballad

A timelessness without beginning, end,
Imagination in my memory,
While driving with my very dearest friend
Along a highway of eternity

She drives the car at an unchanging speed,
The highway is New England in the fall
(Now picture everything which you here read
As I this story timeless do here tell).

She sitting at the wheel whole entering
With soul and heart into all everything,
Which I excited am experiencing
And telling her all childlike bringing

My words concern themselves now only
With solely one subject matter entirely,
And what is this topic, namely?
A woman by the name of Dorothy Schlie

My dearest friend (whose name I'll soon reveal)
Is nearly bursting o'er excitedly,
Because most joyful she does for me feel,
And also very overwhelmingly

Yet she remains in all this happiness
Herself, and drives us onward steadily;
And who could feel such inner boundlessness,
While still maintaining perfect harmony?

This dearest friend of mine in all the world
(In German Ph.D., not Portuguese),
Both lady gracious, wise and little girl,
Is the American Virginia Sease.

August 24, 2002

Chapter Six. August 2002 – April 2004 Ballads and Sonnets

Sonnet number 4 – Susan Young

December, nineteen ninety-seven year,
When Christmas was approaching very near,
A beautiful unhappy woman dear
Appeared to me, her blue eyes shining clear;
Those eyes like crystal skies were radiant bright
Each time I looked upon them in the night,
They smiled and greeting me with their pure light
Inspired my heart to poetry of sight;
'Twas love most special for at once I knew,
As soul mates we'd finally each other found;
How close we were, old love became anew,
And our abundant feelings spread around.
    Her name to me as dear as flowers sprung
    In springtime, sweet and lovely Susan Young.

August 24, 2002

Sonnet number 5 – Svetlana Chmeleva

A sweet and lovely little girl eighteen,
To me more beautiful in all the world
(In all the many places I had been)
Than every single other pretty girl;
She smiled with lips enchanting to my heart,
Her pouting was endearing as her laugh,
Her blush was like the roses' springtime start;
She walked as gracefully as young giraffe.
Her figure slender and enticing both,
Her eyes of brown looked sadly from her soul;
She dreamed her days, a model and a myth,
Her humor like a pony with his tail
    Svetlana was to me a bird so rare,
    A sorrowful flamingo debonair.

August 24, 2002

Chapter Six. August 2002 – April 2004 Ballads and Sonnets

Sonnet number 6 – Camilla Lahn-Johannessen

A small and charming girl of seventeen
With pale soft skin, red lips and blue pool eyes,
Looked out to see if I her face had seen;
And strong she was for a young girl her size.
Both heaviness and lightness in her soul,
Her brown hair hanging parted on the side,
Her smile and voice uneven, musical,
Rare beauty hers, her young heart in her stride,
Her head oft leaning tilted with a look,
Her little laugh delighted in small things,
Like water dancing lightly in a brook,
A magic nymph plays fun freshwater springs
    Camilla was Norwegian, never tired,
        A mountain goat above the fjord inspired.

August 24, 2002
Revised January/February, 2013

Sonnet number 9 by Alan Lindgren

The Light of morning with the early dawn
Does brighten all the world from sleep of night;
The children 'waken happy, old folk yawn,
And open to the day their eyes in sight.
What is this gift the sun bestows each day?
Her radiance streaming spreads a sky of blue,
'Tis colors 'ppear when by her loving rays,
The rainbow bridges heav'n and earth in hues.
Most glad the animals from slumber rise,
The roses and the daffodils do smile,
The squirrels look about, the birds in skies,
And boys and girls express themselves with style.
    O red divine of dawn and green of earth,
        And sovereign purple, yellow sunlight birth.

August 28, 2002

Chapter Six. August 2002 – April 2004 Ballads and Sonnets

The Angel Played by Virginia Sease – A Ballad

One long and winding day among the fields,
I sought to learn about the air and light,
The blades of grass to breezes did they yield,
The sun had risen faithfully in might.

'Twas then I noticed walking slowly by
A figure in solemnity with grace,
She quietly unnoticed by the whys
And wherefores of the common human race

A timelessness eternal in her pace,
An even measure in her stepping true,
Her bearing wrapped in concentration's face,
A purity surrounding her to view

I knew her name, yet never'd heard her speak,
Until the role of angel in the play,
Of Paradise in winter showed her cheek,
And she most specially her words did say.

And when the cast about the room did go,
And singing all the songs great love did show,
I heard her Tone resounding, this I know,
Deep within the heart, above, below

She played the angel with of truth the sword,
Tremendous strength and shining purity,
A messenger from God almighty, Lord,
All gracious in nobility was she.

She spoke with wisdom and authority,
As only one who, lofty in ideals,
Embodies in essential quality,
The certainty of inner Christ-like zeal

And so this lady rare upheld for all,
The highest in her presence, good and true,

Chapter Six. August 2002 – April 2004 Ballads and Sonnets

A teacher at my school, Highland Hall,
Virginia Sease with dignity imbued.

August 31, 2002

Fair Queen in Majesty – A Ballad

She is the fairest of the fair,
In purity both lovely, rare,
Her beauty quite beyond compare,
Her radiance golden in the air

She is the Glory of the day,
In faithfulness her coursing way,
And mighty are her beaming rays,
Her substance love with which we pray

Who is this beautiful, bright queen?
Heav'ns red rose o'er earthly green,
Whose daily deeds are clearly seen
In all the colors in between

She is the reigning majesty
Of the longest dynasty,
Through all the ages artistry,
The Sun of our humanity.

September 2, 2002

The Gentleman's Hat – A Ballad

Three docks lay in the mist,
'Twas night when ships set sail;
Three girls three sailors kissed,
The winds grew to a gale.

The moon shone full and round,
The harbor brightly lit;
A lonesome baying hound
Cried out like she'd been hit

Chapter Six. August 2002 – April 2004 Ballads and Sonnets

The waters stirred around,
The tide was high and all
The soldiers on the ground
Gave out an echo call

The rain began to pour,
A sorrow seemed to stand,
Like prisoners before
The guardsman's cruel hand

Inside the inn the maid
Sang loud and lustily,
While a piano played,
Old men drank heartily.

Behind the bar a rat
Stole breadcrumbs from the floor,
A gent put on his hat,
And exited the door

He left behind a note,
To Mary of the town,
Inside her pocket coat,
A man of great renown

The words were spelled quite plain:
Meet me behind the gate
At noon, sunshine or rain,
Nor be ye minutes late.

But after he'd gone out
Into the dark of night,
He turned the corner 'bout,
And disappeared from sight

Never again was seen,
His face a memory,
His name became a dream,
Like garden greenery

Chapter Six. August 2002 – April 2004 Ballads and Sonnets

Sweet Mary went to sea,
A sailor married she,
Sweet Mary found a key,
And it belonged to he

She opened up the gate,
One rainy, gloomy day,
But she was all too late,
Was she, sweet Mary Mae.

She saw only a cat
And on the stepping stone,
The gentleman's fine hat,
There sitting quite alone.

What was his famous name?
The soldiers know it well,
The sailors and the dames,
All everyone can tell.

A man of goodly girth
Was he, and wealthy, too,
The richest man on earth
Was Jonathon Laroo.

September 5, 2002

Camilla Fair – A Ballad

Fair Camilla, fair maiden mine,
I would we married be,
For never in all Europe grand
Did shine one more lovely

Fair Camilla, fair maiden mine,
I am in love with thee,
In thy small footsteps Norway climbs
The mountain fjord country

Chapter Six. August 2002 – April 2004 Ballads and Sonnets

Fair Camilla, fair maiden mine,
Would I had thy lips red
With my own kissed and we, lovers,
Another joined in bed

Fair Camilla, fair maiden mine,
Would I had touched thy skin,
Ne'er was there purer white more soft
In all my kith and kin

Fair Camilla, fair maiden mine,
Would I could hold thy hand
Sure then together we would be
On true Norwegian land

Fair Camilla, fair maiden mine,
Would thou to me appear,
'Twas long ago in Bergen town
That I thy voice did hear.

September 5, 2002

The War – A Ballad

A twisted barb, a thicket thorn,
O rue the day when I was born!
Caught up in jeopardy and torn
'Tween hot and cold all tired, worn.

My only hopes dashed by the waves,
Sent down below into their graves;
My mind an emblem of a war
I thought I'd fought and won before.

My stratagems and secrets hid,
My enemy within the grid,
Whilst I maneuver like a cat
Beneath a fence of this and that

Chapter Six. August 2002 – April 2004 Ballads and Sonnets

I make my way and storm the bay,
With bullets all around the fray,
Nor do I see for all is grey,
Upon this dank and dismal day

My lip is scowling in a pinch,
I make my way by bit, by inch,
And when I feel another blow,
Then on I fight and on I go.

I shall not stop nor satisfy
My questioning, the reason why;
I only know this war's my own
And feel the blood in tooth and bone.

And fight I must, and fight I will,
I'll dig a ditch and climb a hill,
I'll push myself and pull the foe,
I'll tossle here and to and fro.

I stumble crazed by pain and fear,
I cough the bloodied atmosphere;
But at the end I'll conquer and
Emerge a victor on the land.

September 6, 2002

The Life of a Seeker - A Ballad

A child was born in fantasy,
A land of dream reality;
Its parents taught it courtesy;
It lived in pure simplicity.

When it was ready for the school,
It bravely strode into the room
To learn the lessons with a rule
Until the bell did ring at noon

Chapter Six. August 2002 – April 2004 Ballads and Sonnets

Its teacher was a goodly man
Whom all the children dearly held;
Each morning they did shake his hand;
Respectfully they learned right well.

And as the child grew in love
Through all the grades did lightly pass,
It graduated high above,
The shining star of all the class

In high school changed into a youth
Of deepened sense, ideals knew;
The feeling for the lofty truth
Opening up a higher view

Before the youth became a man
He traveled far and distant lands;
He felt within a change, began
To seek and strive, heart, mind and hand.

This seeking grew in inner strength,
A journey lifelong meaningful;
He struggled painfully at length
For something dear and wonderful

He worked and gained experience;
He entered college, studied there;
He joined the larger audience,
Yet he was somehow more aware.

And so he schooled himself each day,
And life and college taught him well,
Until he, ready, made his way
Up to the turning point, his goal

Conscious now, in manhood he,
His seeking clear, in company
Of fellow human beings, three
His brother-friend and Christ and he

Chapter Six. August 2002 – April 2004 Ballads and Sonnets

And as he struggled, darkness fell,
And in the darkness strength emerged
In his own words his life to tell,
While his best friend him onward urged.

And so this man and seeker brave,
As Poet his true I did seek,
Within his soul's dark inner cave
The Light did show him to be meek.

This battle won, he further strode
Until he crossed triumphantly;
The threshold was his joyous ode,
And love did flow abundantly.

And still he seeks, and still he writes,
And still he journeys day and night
Between the depths and highest heights
To find the quiet inner Light.

September 11, 2002

Fairest Rose – A Ballad

Do you see the gracious rose,
How she stands and bows and grows?
Elegant adorns this place,
Poised and strong with courage, grace

Red she is, my smile and love,
Crowning glory from above;
Warm she is and self-assured,
Christ of heaven is her Word.

Fairest in the garden she,
Blesséd is her company;
All aspire to reach her state,
Pure perfection, emulate.

Chapter Six. August 2002 – April 2004 Ballads and Sonnets

Love her scent and color deep,
Cherish her into my sleep;
Memories of glory days,
Of the golden summer rays

Rose, fair rose, thou queen behold,
Bravely are thy virtues told;
Thy good strength doth steadfast hold,
As unchanging red, red gold.

September 17, 2002

Sonnet number 14 – The Christ-Clouds

High up above in purity of sight
(And billowing most glorious and true),
All radiant with sun's heavenly light,
Where everything is fresh and clean and new;
'Tis there Thou art, majestic, snowy white,
Appearing on an autumn morning fair,
Abundant clouds of love and Christed bright,
Our thoughts enlivened are by light and air.
We thank Thee Christ, this wonder of the sky,
Of magic, awe and beauty openly,
Reveals to us on earth Thy presence nigh,
Thy glory and Thy grandeur verily
    Such splendor is uplifting to men's souls
    Is spoken as some huge and divine vowels.

September 29, 2002

Sonnet number 16 – Promise

An orphanage forlorn of girls and boys
As sorry rags discarded in a bin
Dreamed visions of imaginary joys
And on their dirty faces sweetest grins
If these forgotten waifs had not the power
To see in mental pictures scenes of light
Then all the mean and lowly weeds ne'er flowered

Chapter Six. August 2002 – April 2004 Ballads and Sonnets

Nor followed night of greyness morning bright
But God did grant the humblest of men
The faith of courage and the hope of morn
And from the child adult mature becomes
And out death's ashes new life sprouts reborn
    Forget not those who live in misery
    In their condition gifts of promise see.

April 21, 2003

Grief – A Sonnet

Now rudely treated by a band of thieves,
My heart mishandled as some poor plaything,
My soul in sorrow now but sadly grieves,
And sorrowful my tune poetic sings;
When men do laugh and scorn what rightful true,
When as a little child defenseless cries,
My heart does follow on this bluish hue,
I weep for breath and gulping air do sigh;
Such men and women cruel poke at fun,
They derive pleasure from the other's sorrow,
Instead of well rejoicing in the sun,
And faith and love and hope cherish the morrow;
    Alone in poetry I keep my share
    And comforted in verse my heart is there.

June 5, 2003
Los Angeles

Sonnet number 20 – Water

Tire not of drinking water of the well,
Such fluid satisfies only the hour,
When sure again thou thirsty comes to tell,
And sure enough display a wilted flower;
For water of this world temporal lives
And satisfies but temporary need,
When what the soul desires here not gives,
Relief replenishing her thirst to heed;

Chapter Six. August 2002 – April 2004 Ballads and Sonnets

Each time thou drinks the earthly water fresh,
Believes to quench thy direly pressing thirst,
But deeper still untouched by mortal wash,
Remains but thirsting as upon the first;
    Eternal water only satisfies;
        Only from Christ, the other one belies.

Culver City
December 5/6, 2003
Revised Los Angeles
January 5/12, 2013

Sonnet number 21 – Winter

Each winter frost and freezing cold does chill,
All warm of blood move to the fires inside;
The barren trees outside upon the hill
Paint wintry death, this season's cold abide;
The families do gather 'round the hearth,
To warm themselves they rub their face and hands;
Outside unfriendly lies the lifeless earth,
The mountain forests and snow-covered lands;
And old becomes this landscape vast and white,
With cold's hoarfrost in silence whispering;
The heart longs for the summer's golden light,
Whose warmth in memory cheers welcoming.
    Remember in the midnight hour each year,
    The sun is born anew to warm us here.

December 5/6, 2003

Sonnet number 22 – The Human Soul

Indwells the human soul both depth and light,
And in her compass strength and gentleness;
She is the subject of the lover's sight,
Her beauty lovelier than manliness;
She dreams a dream of fondness all her own,
And suffers daily true reality,
And in her heart she lives her life alone,

Chapter Six. August 2002 – April 2004 Ballads and Sonnets

Both joy and pain does know intimately;
Her feeling is as tender as a dove;
In warmth she cherishes her feelings there;
Her kingdom is the sphere of special love;
Her fragrance like a rose does waft so fair.
      There gazing from her chamber us does greet,
      Perceiving do we Christ our brother meet.

Culver City
December 6, 2003

Shakespeare, the Sonnet Master – A Sonnet

'Tis Shakespeare, who alone high master of
The sonnet, others after him show pale,
For he, with skilled craft in his pen of love,
Outdoes them all by far o'er hill and dale;
He who, above the others, well-assured,
Does sketch full masterful his sonnets there,
Most artful he demonstrates with the Word,
Such none beside him dare with him compare;
This Shakespeare, solid in intelligence,
With ease of greatness carves his sonnets true,
Whose wit combines with thought of soundest sense
When at the helm he steers his course there through.
      I humbly bow and take my hat off, man,
      Thou Shakespeare hast the gift ten
            thousand men.

Palmdale, California
January 22/23, 2004

Love – A Sonnet

Thou, love, untouched by winter's ageing hand,
In purity dost dwell in places light,
A mountain-spot of undefiled land,
A star which brightly shines in star-filled night;
Thou art my music of an afternoon,
My source of being well on Easter morn,

Chapter Six. August 2002 – April 2004 Ballads and Sonnets

My sweet, harmonious, lovely song and tune,
As new as Christmas newly come and born;
Thou art to me a golden lamp of light
Which golden shines and golden makes all things,
By virtue of thy golden thoughts and sight
And fingers decked with golden jewelry rings.
    Without thee life of mine would meaningless
    I owe to thee my every happiness.

April 11, 2004

My Sunny Fair Companion – A Sonnet

Know I, a world barren of thee, friend,
Would echo as a wasteland echoes twice,
In emptiness would echo hollow, end
A desert or a swamp of sordid rice;
But God has sent to me into this place,
For solace and encouragement and love,
He deemed it fitting for our human race
To bring among our numbers one above;
Thou art this lovely, brave, good heart and soul,
My music, sunny fair companion and
My love so fair to round this world whole,
To fashion mountains, sunsets o'er the land
    Thou art the beauty of my inmost heart,
    And twice the beauty of my soul and art.

April 16, 2004
Los Angeles

CHAPTER SEVEN

2003 – 2004

THE MAGIC OF THE STARS

NEW POEMS

Chapter Seven. 2003 – 2004 The Magic of the Stars New Poems

From a letter from Virginia Sease, Ph.D., summer, 2004:

I sense a deepening in your poetic imagery which is most special.

Unique

Each single one unique but is
Himself alone in specialness,
Creates his own one-of-a-kind
In giftedness, heart, hand and mind
(We do but share, in humble ways,
Our humanness our livelong days,

But to our work we give our stamp:
Creative be our inner lamp);

Now may we each ourselves pure find
In I myself my nature bind;
Into these things (I give them life)
Creation's work (Nature's my wife);
My children are what I bestow
From love above to earth below;

I take the light; I weave it there
Into the golden, glowing air,
To send beyond this several space,
Beyond this time, this earthen place,
That what I've made becomes a joy
Eternally, my little boy;

Now do your thing; make your delight;
Create what never came to light,
And do most rare a work your own,
Then call it what, a singing stone;
Your gift I praise: 'tis but God's grace;
We don quite human heaven's face.

Culver City, California
October 23, 2003

Chapter Seven. 2003 – 2004 The Magic of the Stars New Poems

Mary's Kiss

The spell is broken, freedom's out
The spirits move freely about
And love's a many splendored thing
All dancing in a faerie ring.

So many artists gaily weave
Their tapestries, that we believe
In wonder, magic, mystery
In love's abiding artistry.

Now be so good and be so kind
To linger in my humankind
That's where I find my poetry
A-flowing golden radiantly.

My river is creatively
A drop of Christ essentially
Which mingling in the atmosphere
Becomes a light this autumn clear.

This light encounters darkness, see
How colors come to shine, to be!
My colors are my rainbow love
My thankfulness to God above.

He has reached down from heaven's heights
And deigned to bring our earth His Light
Now do we solemnly prepare
Our hearts a place His Son to bear.

This Christmastime like Mary, we
Devoted with humility
Receive the Child, humanity
Our Christ, the Saviour comes to be.

If we have sinned, forgive us please
That pardoned we our karma seize

Chapter Seven. 2003 – 2004 The Magic of the Stars New Poems

And may go forth renewed once more
For Christ bestows time's richness' store.

He makes the moment new to give
Us meaning that we centered live
Within our hearts in tenderness
Both joy and pain, a mother's kiss.

El Segundo, California
October 30, 2003

Chapter Seven. 2003 – 2004 The Magic of the Stars New Poems

Shepherds' Gifts

Little letters on a page
Make music to the Poet's ear
His pen is penning poetry
Poetry's own song is here.

Little footsteps in the hall
Children running – father's here
Children joyous Christmas cheer
Christmas music in the ear.

Christmas circles; Christmas light
Christmas wreathes and candlelight
Christmas music; Christmas cheer
Christmas birth is in my sight.

Christ is coming, but a Babe
But an Infant Child mild
Christ is Jesu tenderly
Mary's tending the Christ-Child.

Mary sings a plaintive song
Mary simple, pure, serene
Mary is a gentle soul
Mary is a faerie-queen.

See the shepherds bring their gifts
For the Child in innocence
Wool and flask of milk they bring
And a lamb this Lamb announce.

November 22, 2003

Chapter Seven. 2003 – 2004 The Magic of the Stars New Poems

Good News

Tender is the gift so holy
In the winter melancholy
Of the birth of love descending
Heaven's angels to earth bending.

Hear the music angel choirs
Son of God ignites hearts' fires
Christ is born a Babe, a Child
Infant love so sweet and mild

Joy awakens, feel the wonder
Shepherds in the fields yonder
Come to worship at the manger
Jesu Christ, good news harbinger.

Mary greets the shepherds bringing
Gifts of love, ox and ass lowing
In the humble stable smiling
Jesu Christ in loving feeling.

Earth and heaven join in praising
Lord and Saviour Christ for saving
Humankind from winter chilling
For His Spirit-Sun warms willing.

See the birth of His Light shining
Mightily the Sun is beaming
That the earth a sun becoming
Human hearts are purifying.

Peace on earth to men is spoken
Of good will be our small token
That we join in His Creation
For the work of His Salvation.

December 25, 2003
Los Angeles

Chapter Seven. 2003 – 2004 The Magic of the Stars New Poems

Dream

Dream, thou vision, poetry
Dream of possibility
Dream of wondrous majesty
Dream of mystic mystery.

Dream, thou poet, of the morn
Dream of being newly born
Dream of Christmas' Holy Nights
Dream of little starry lights.

Dream, and be fulfilled therein
Dream, and fondly dream again
Dream until thy dreams awake
For the melodies they make.

Dream in poems, songs of love
Dream of songs from heaven above
Dream in melodies so pure
All thy silent dreams allure.

Dream in melodies beyond
Rivers, lakes and meadow ponds
Dream above the ancient Moon
Dream of magic, dream now soon.

Dream, and let thy dreams abound
Let them soar, let them resound
Let thy dreams take flight on wing
Let them fondly soar and sing.

Let them linger there with ease
Let them hover on a breeze
Let them promise fragrant flowers
Let them bloom in rose-red boughs.

Let thy dreams suspend all time
Let them now eternal rhyme

Chapter Seven. 2003 – 2004 The Magic of the Stars New Poems

On a breeze of thought to be
Music played eternally.

December 28, 2003

Christmas Glories

Tell me, Mother
Tell me, brother
Tell me early winter stories
Of the wonder
Over yonder
Of the heavenly Christmas glories.

Earth and heaven
Rise with leaven
Join in praising Christ the Saviour
He most holy
Melancholy
From on high God shows His favour.

Now His splendour
Our Defender
In the darkness of the winter
Shines His beaming
Rays redeeming
In the Sun's birth of midwinter.

Love is showing
Fires glowing
Come we for our hearts to warming
By the Child
Mercy mild
Shapes of winter now are forming.

December 29, 2003

Chapter Seven. 2003 – 2004 The Magic of the Stars New Poems

Pilgrim Song

Feelings are the warmth inside,
Christ, the love-God, is our Guide,
Teaches us within to dwell,
Inner languages to tell;

Songs of joy and suffering,
Songs the angels heavenly sing,
Songs of Mary and the Child,
Songs of gentle mercy mild,

Songs like pilgrimages made,
Undertaking journeys said
To be precious, dear and all
Pilgrims hear the beckon call,

Follow paths and footsteps there
To the Goal, Christ Jesus fair
In their hearts to celebrate
Brother, sister, Sacrament.

Then the footsteps to the place
Of most holy Christian grace
Shall us lead to drink and sup,
Take the Bread and take the Cup.

We shall feel the meaning of
Christ, the Saviour's inner love.

February 19, 2004
Culver City, California

Chapter Seven. 2003 – 2004 The Magic of the Stars New Poems

Syllables

Syllables read one by one
Radiant shines the winter sun
All the little flowers smile
Colors are a little while
A little while they smile here
A little while colors appear

Then night returns to starlight and
Spirit-Sun shines warm and grand
Winter syllables repeat
We do harvest what we eat
Little flowers colorful
Little flowers wonderful

In a garden salad choose
Shall nasturtiums gladly use?
Shall we dandelions muse?
In our salad we peruse
Flower books and syllables
Stories, legends, lore, fables

Winter night draws to a close
Who was yesterday he knows
And this night of wonder tells
Magical charm all the spells
Dwell this night in mystery
Syllables be company

To the winter sun of night
Darkness' mystery delight
Tells us how to read a book
Stories take a second look
Wonder how the words do read
Passages poetic heed

Syllables and afternoons
March and April, May or June

Chapter Seven. 2003 – 2004 The Magic of the Stars New Poems

Mark your place, this book employs
All our earthly, children's joys
Little girls and little boys
Play imagination's toys

Be so young and play with us
Syllables and syllabus
Read this poem differently
Sounding loud where silently
Pauses make our music news
Music's, Poesie's own Muse.

March 4, 2004

Creation – A Poem of Celebration

Rededicate all movements, views
To thoughts and feelings to pursue,
And answer only questions of
God's abiding spirit-love.

The source of all Creation stands:
God's love, our soil, our ground and land,
From whence there springs and sprouts in joy
The life and color we enjoy.

Then come the little birds and beasts,
They sing and sound this holy feast,
And human beings crown it all,
We think with reason, sure and tall.

We need for this our work desire
Prometheus' burning, flaming fire,
Just as the animals need air,
The plants fresh water in their care.

The stones repose in solid ways,
And summer sunshine basks with rays;
Let our tomorrows be a joy,

Chapter Seven. 2003 – 2004 The Magic of the Stars New Poems

Let us be children, girl and boy.

Announce this passage, careful read:
The day prepares us for to bed,
When we sleep our nights in Thee:
God, the Father, restfully.

Nights, where in the starry realm
Spirit-Sun shines at the helm,
There among the dead we feel
Spirit-souls as only real.

Music of the spheres resounds,
Melodies play music rounds,
We, forever young, do dance
In the nighttime star romance.

Venus is our Princess fair,
See her lover Earth compare,
All is dream and all is real,
Everything we ask and feel.

Seek our answers when we ask
To fulfill our earthly task,
We, as poets, priests and friends,
To our daily work we tend.

Fill our days with melodies,
Birds, the branches of the trees;
Human words well spoken form
Into sculptures air-shaped warm.

We pronounce our poems well,
Each his story seeks to tell,
Then, in books of Poesie,
We make spirit-company.

Company of girls and boys,
Company of little joys,

Chapter Seven. 2003 – 2004 The Magic of the Stars New Poems

Let us play and let us be
Filled with thoughts eternally:

Thoughts of love, of warmth and light,
Thoughts of joyful, pure delight,
Thoughts as precious as a jewel
On the crown quite kingly rule

Princes, kings, nobility,
Such are our good company,
When we think in light-filled ways,
Our own sunlight shines in rays

In the world without, within
In our souls does shine again,
We are children of the Light,
Christ, our Father, in His sight.

We awaken from our sleep,
From the darkness of the deep,
Into daytime light and fields,
Breathing heavenly meadows yield,

Breathing heaven here on earth,
Giving heaven living birth,
Make reality a sphere
Of the sun pervading here.

Make the sun reality,
Blessing our humanity,
Then, with Venus, we shall see
Pictures painted lovingly,

Pictures dreamt of fondly, too,
Pictures dreamt of, now in view,
See the world in fantasies
Of the lovers under trees.

Venus, come and be my wife,

Chapter Seven. 2003 – 2004 The Magic of the Stars New Poems

With thee gladly spend my life,
I, with thee, would dare elope
On an impulse up the slope.

Princesses and queens "adieu!"
I have filled my day, ensure,
With the best of both thy realms,
I am singing Christian psalms:

Psalms of winter wilderness,
Psalms of pilgrims' pure progress,
At the destiny I reach
For to taste one holy peach.

Then, in eating of this fruit,
I, in pleasure, place my boot
On the dance floor for to waltz,
Taste sweet princesses, and salts

Of the kings whose sure command
Proceeds in governing the lands,
Provinces born vast and wide;
Who will be my little bride?

Who will marry my poetry?
Nature, be my bride to be,
Nature, thou art now my wife
We, together, joined in life.

Our own children in this verse,
Poems of the universe,
We give birth to numerous,
Earnest, light and humorous.

Children are our verses here,
Let them people pages there,
Let them play a Maypole dance,
Let them romp and let them prance.

Chapter Seven. 2003 – 2004 The Magic of the Stars New Poems

Nature, thou art to me wed,
Nightly take I thee to bed,
Venus and her lover Earth,
Other children give they birth.

We, as parents, fondly feel,
Joy, each moment, every meal,
For our family is good,
In the meadow, in the wood.

Up above the starry sky
Dreams the everlasting high:
Mighty God, Creator All,
He, the Father, hear His Call.

March 5, 2004

Chapter Seven. 2003 – 2004 The Magic of the Stars New Poems

Riddles of the Rose

Develop threads of thoughts sublime
Running rhythmically through time
All the answers questions pose
Are the riddles of the rose.

He who seeks to know their ways
He must breathe their fragrant days
See their red and scented flowers
In the noontime summer hours.

Steeped in feeling he shall be
Answered by this unity:
Roses red of dignity
Live courageous openly,

Die the evenings there where love
Blossom thorny plants above
Suffer in the faith of days
Die the nights in holy ways.

Mid-March 2004

Chapter Seven. 2003 – 2004 The Magic of the Stars New Poems

Cupid's Bow

Whispers of the cloudlike dreams
Whispering what seeming seems
Up among the sun's warm beams
I shall manifest my dreams:

Dreams of holy mystery
Dreams of holy company
Dreams of magic twilight hours
Dreams of starry blue-pink flowers.

There I shall without a pause
Sing my melodies because
Night shall musically surround
All my being with her sound.

Music of the night shall be
All-encompassing we three
We, who in the Spirit-Land
Music of the Spheres do stand.

Standing there in music's place
Music poetry's own face
Faces smiling in the Night's
Blissful darling dear delights.

Freedom is the song we hear
Freedom in the atmosphere
Freedom moves within, you see
In this holy company.

Then, by day, with birds we shall
Sing our earthly wonderful
Wonderful poetic dreams
Make our pictures real seem;

Semblances of night by day
We shall find our holy way

Chapter Seven. 2003 – 2004 The Magic of the Stars New Poems

With the sun, our Christ to live
Dying into nights we give

Our dear passions with a kiss
Venus share our holy bliss
Venus, lover of the earth
Cupid watchful over birth

Birth of love's enchanted bow
See how lovers close do grow
Fetch an arrow Cupid sent
To the lovers' dreaming tent.

In the shade of cooling dreams
Shall make music daytime seems
Pleasure for an afternoon
Pleasantries and pleasant tunes.

Sun, Thou Christ, dost bide with us
Though we many, numerous
Each receives his portion be
For his own humanity.

March 19, 2004

Chapter Seven. 2003 – 2004 The Magic of the Stars New Poems

Mornings

Grow to pleasant pleasing views
Strive to understand the news
Mornings are the newborn day
Love expanding in her way.

Sun appearing, golden rays
Beaming radiant every day
Smile with warmth in measure of
Clear, redeeming, sentient love.

Every lucid ray of light
Is a message to our sight
Tells of wonder magically
Opens windows for to see,

From the night of darkness be
Love's abiding mystery
Springs each morning bright and clear
Light bestowing, time is here.

Daytime brings her open book
Revelation now to look
Spells of wonder, hope and light
In the day of candid sight.

May we now in springtime's love
Send our thanks and love above
To the sun of Christ Who dwells
Everywhere His Light us tells

Of the open Truth and gaze
Springtime living in our days
May we fruitful with our love
Find enchantment like a dove.

On a morning sparrows sing
Melodies in offering

Chapter Seven. 2003 – 2004 The Magic of the Stars New Poems

Hope, that virtue so sincere
Every morning of the year,

Speaks and sings to us this day
Lifting hearts and souls our way
To fulfillment shall we climb
Mountain vista views sublime.

Promise did our Saviour God
Humankind this Land so good
We each give our best thereto
Toward this everlasting view,

That one day in future shall
Cosmic love universal
Sing with resolution bright
Victorious the living Light.

March 23, 2004

Sing Birds Towards Easter

Wonders of the elegies
Time and life and death in threes
Written down one morning's breeze
Blowing through the shady trees.

Little birds announce the day
Singing heartfelt in their way
Human beings long for song
Hear it in the birds belong.

Their heartfelt and their plaintive tunes
Carried through the afternoons
Make for joyous interludes
Joy and love their throats exude.

Little birds of wonder small
Making music Nature's hall

Chapter Seven. 2003 – 2004 The Magic of the Stars New Poems

Hear their gladsome little call
Come and join the joyous all.

Come and be my poetry
Painting words of imagery
Floral scene arrangements and
Sunsets painted over land.

These and other sentient scenes
Felt by princesses and queens
Make life beautiful and fair
Whilst the birds sing in the air,

Sing their sweetest thrilling songs
Perched on twigs, balanced along
They have won my heart this day
Their true songs my heart do sway

Into raptures of delight
Alternate 'tween day and night
Birds and angels music fair
Play my rhapsodies repair.

Birds the emblems fresh divine
Angels bending earthwards sign
To the joy of Man and Child
Mother Mary mercy mild.

Soon will life experience
Become Easter penitence
Crucifixion, darkness, Death
Resurrection, earth's out-breath,

Springtime when the birds exult
Soon transport us, catapult
Us to sun and star and cloud
Cosmic Christ makes Nature proud,

Lift us into summer's dance

Chapter Seven. 2003 – 2004 The Magic of thé Stars New Poems

Music-poetry enhance
At a bonfire leap the flames
Christ within our human Names.

March 30, 2004

Chapter Seven. 2003 – 2004 The Magic of the Stars New Poems

Christ, the Gardener

Pronounce this poem properly
Place it prominent to see
Like a sculpture form it there
In the sun-warmed, sculpted air.

Sing this poem-song of love
Sing it cooing as a dove
Like a Mother to her Child
Sing this poem mercy mild.

See this poem painterly
See it colored gorgeously
See it pictured imagery
See appearing visibly.

See it as a Rose above
Thorny bush's death of love
Resurrected in the Night
Lovely lilac loving light.

Paint this poem as a Rose
Rose of red in fires glows
Rose, an offering of love
Courageous loving heaven above.

Find this rose of heaven's place
Dignify our human race
Bold and vigorous she smiles
Her lips are pure and undefiled.

Rosy lips and rosy cheeks
Through Christ's holy Passion week
Suffer every human trial
Tribulation for a while.

Red, immerse my faith in thee
Red, keep in thy company

Chapter Seven. 2003 – 2004 The Magic of the Stars New Poems

Red, emerge come shine or rain
Red, emerge 'midst fear and pain.

Red, thou Rose divine and man
Glorify the Garden and
See, the Gardener he tends
Flowers caring hands he lends.

See, the Gardener appear
Before the empty Tomb now near
He, our Lord and Saviour-God
Christ, the Rose, the living Blood.

See, to Mary Magdalene
He appears and speaks again
She, the first to see Him now
Bears the news that others know.

Christ, the Gardener, the Word
Surrounding Him the little birds
Christ is Risen Easter morn
Now in Spirit newly born.

See His blazing Spirit-Form
Feel His wounded Side so warm
Thomas doubted, skeptical
Christ before him actual.

Christ is Risen every day
Each new morning in its way
Christ, the Spirit of the earth
Resurrects in Nature's birth.

April 2, 2004

Chapter Seven. 2003 – 2004 The Magic of the Stars New Poems

Inner Landscapes

Write, ye poets, of the land
Feel the mountains, mountains grand
See the sun, her disc of love
Shining, beaming up above,

In the heavenly sky of blue
Orb of sun all golden, true
Glorious deeds as the first day
Doth she live her coursing way.

We, the poets, greet her there
In our inner landscapes where
Fragrance fills the atmosphere
In a garden roses fair

We are tending flowers and
Feel the soil with fingered hand
Love and life and light are here
God created all so clear.

April 27, 2004

Chapter Seven. 2003 – 2004 The Magic of the Stars New Poems

Venus Fair

One gloomy, rainy, ghastly day, I lay my bed about
The Sun in all her majesty sought clearly to come out.

The birds of air chirped in the dank and dismal weather there
For in their hearts the sun still shone and cheered them everywhere.

Then I began to see the Light resemble stars of night
And mysteries of lavender urged me on with their might.

And lo, my Venus fair appeared as lovely as a queen
And magically addressed us all there gathered 'bout the scene.

In purple all her faerie-maids were singing in a dance
They played on music instruments and swayed like trees of chance.

Then Venus spake in honest terms, she smiled through parted lips
And placed her hands so lightly then upon her shapely hips

She said to let her perfect doves fly up to part the clouds
And stage a play like Shakespeare did, to please the gathered crowd.

And when the doves had flown up high, the clouds dispersing fled
And lo, the sun appeared on high, majestic overhead.

And Venus smiled her faerie way, the play became her well
And everyone felt warmed and pleased, expressing thanks did tell.

Such mysteries do sparkle and such magic works in ways
That even gloomy, o'ercast rain becomes a sunny day,

And everyone good cheer does feel and all the folk rejoice
And lift up to the sun above in unifying voice:

"We praise Thee, Sun, Thou highest One, we sing Thy virtues sure
And celebrate good Venus, our beloved Princess pure."

Let it be known this special day, Christ works in mysteries

Chapter Seven. 2003 – 2004 The Magic of the Stars New Poems

His magic and His might are there, He beckons you and me,

He calls with trumpets angels play; He speaks His Word most clear
That human beings join the song whenever He is here,

He says to each and every one, like Venus feel pure
And like the sun cast shadows out, for Christ alone endures.

His message is to all who hear, His Play we all play out
And history becomes the day we busy are about.

So join His Song, redemption's love is meant to touch each one
And be ye good, child Mars and Moon with Venus and our Sun,

Be ye good, child Jupiter and Saturn, Mercury
Our lives unfold according to God's Son, a mystery.

No one can change His Plan as we move steady forward and
Receive the future toward us comes with open, welcome hands.

His Breath we breathe, His Life unfolds in our humanity
With Sun and Venus fair we join in glorious company.

June 19, 2004
Los Angeles

CHAPTER EIGHT

2003 – 2006

THE MAGIC OF THE STARS,

LOVE & LYRICISM,

SONGS & ELEGIES,

MYSTERIES AND OTHER THEMES

Chapter Eight. 2003 – 2006   Magic of the Stars, Love & Lyricism,

My Tree

A distance turned and then became
The close proximity of name
My colors true without no shame
I took the shoe; I took the blame.

And when I felt myself to me
As far as distant mountains see
I stood as tall and large as trees
On stony cliffs before the seas

One lonely ship traced out a path
Horizon's geometric math
Could not have chosen better winds
And as for me, I held my sins.

Kept looking at the distant ship
I stood my ground and bit my lip
Until the sea in fog and mist
Did swallow hull and sail and mast

And so I turned from west away
To find a better Easter day
I took my tree of self and walked
The way I spoke and gesture-talked

The blowing trade winds favored me
They urged me on where boundary
Meant nothing more than writer's block
I was too strong to be in shock.

And soon I found some pasture-land
And stretched my open, gentle hand
Out to the world, the way I felt
And all the frozen cold did melt.

Now listen for a different bird
The melody of whispered words

And you will hear my final cry
My final plea for asking why

The answer lies within, you see,
Within my inner mystery
Within the bark about my tree
There flows the sap of greenery.

February 13, 2003

Every Memory

Sorrow knocks upon my door
Weeping teardrops on the floor
All the memories galore
Seem in retrospect quite poor.

They were clapping gay with joy
Like as children, girl and boy
Without cares or worries old
Precious memories of gold

Now I sit and look thereon
Like an old centurion
Many years seem to have past
Over oceans deep and vast

In my heart there beats a tone
As some thudding, sounding stone
Falling, falling in the sea
To the bottom sands beneath

Gives an echo to be heard
Like a calling water bird
Cawing as a crow of black
Melancholy in its track

Shall the sorrow empty me?
Shall the oceans transform free

Chapter Eight. 2003 – 2006   Magic of the Stars, Love & Lyricism,

Into great and luscious trees
Flowering visited by bees?

Then do I know sun and love
Golden rays streaming above
Warming hearts in deeper good
Warm as kindling firewood

Every memory is kind
Is a blessing to the mind
Only we do live it there
In our hearts and everywhere.

Los Angeles
February 22, 2003

Two Poems of February 22, 2003

1. Thinking

Sit and stimulate the thoughts
Rich with wisdom kingly brought
All the elements are one
Each and every little one

Music seems to sing in words
Human beings, also birds
We, the thinkers gladly know
Joy our thinking to bestow.

What a wonder every morn
Like a special infant born
Out of darkness of the night
From the heart into the Light

Now the thinking's born anew
Resurrection is in view
Called redemption is but love
Loving light from God above.

2. Feeling

Stillness is the quiet place
Of the radiant human face
Of the heart and of the mind
Set into the rhythms kind.

All my feelings are so dear
Precious as they are so near
Like a blossom's fragrance fair
Hovering a breath of air

If you watch the sun by day
You will find your sacred way
To be human in the sense
In which meaning does condense.

Culver City, California
February 22, 2003

Red Rose and I

I am an inner I and I
Approach my essence asking why
With every question that I pose
The answer's red and fragrant rose

My words and thoughts do hover there
About the petalled blossom air
But always standing there with grace
My perfect rose's budding face.

Soul Yellow

My soul is morning, dawn, sunrise
Is yellow magic sunlight skies
I traverse daily heaven's road
Within this body's earth-abode

I suffer life my yellow true

Chapter Eight. 2003 – 2006   Magic of the Stars, Love & Lyricism,

Through every tragedy of blue
And with the courage of the flame
Pronounce my golden yellow name

To take within myself at night's
Transporting sunset dusk twilight
That on the morrow's morning new
Begin the day as fresh as dew.

Late February or early March 2003

Chris

She wrote a book, herself the name
In pages crisp, her words they came
She uttered speech revealing much
In tones of truth, the truth to watch

And truth appeared, nor could lies hide
What was inside came clear outside
Her gift to see, her gift to hear
Her gift to speak all clean and clear

Brought out the truth which once revealed
My future life foretold and sealed
Not prophecy in common use
But plain and fact, nor any spruce

Quite unadorned, quite simple, bare
All unafraid with courage there
Straightforward, bold, yet fresh as blue
Yes fresh as life, all fresh and true.

Los Angeles
February 27, 2003

On the morning of March 9, 2003, having slept the night at the family home in Culver City (Westside, Los Angeles Basin, California), I awoke with the poem "Rosebush Green and Red." Immediately, I wrote it down, then telephoned Virginia Sease in Dornach. After I had explained the circumstances in which it was composed, she stated: "That poem is Rosicrucian. That poem comes from the night." As I did not know what this meant, Dr. Sease enlightened me to the fact that there are four Rosicrucian colors, which are also found in my poem. These are red, green, black, and white. (The yellow and blue in my poem are incidental.) 'Rosicrucian' is derived from the name of the reincarnation of the only person initiated by Christ Himself (Lazareth), Christian Rosenkreutz. 'Rosenkreutz' means 'rosy cross'. The rosy cross is the symbol for Rosicrucianism. We imagine the picture of the rosy cross with the black cross of death with green, blossoming with seven red roses, above which is white spirit-life. Thus we have the two colors of Easter (red, the color of Sun-Christ and of heaven, and green, the color of life in death and of earth), and black (the color of spirit in death) and white (the color of spiritual life), the four Rosicrucian colors, all in my poem, "Rosebush Green and Red." It is indeed a most special poem, which also happens to be my longest (38 stanzas x 4 lines per stanza = 152 lines).

Rosebush Green and Red

There is a dichotomy in my soul
Of green, of green and red,
The green, the green of life,
The green of human dead

The red of sun and fire,
The red of sunset glow,
The heavenly red above,
The earthly green below

My soul is like a bush,
A rosebush green as morn,

Chapter Eight. 2003 – 2006   Magic of the Stars, Love & Lyricism,

As green as hope newborn,
As green as painful thorn

A rosebush crowned in red
By budding blossoms gold,
As red as Christ the Lord,
As red as courage bold

A rosebush resting green,
Contented, in this way,
In harmonies of love,
Christ's Kingdom come by day.

A rosebush touched by sun,
Divine the plant become,
As human as the Lord,
Immortal mortal One

A rosebush become red
In passion's grief and pain,
Pure gracious dignity
Surrounded by disdain

A rosebush known to man
In feeling tenderness,
In aromatic breath,
In blood's sure pulsing quest

Red rose's perfect grace
Unmoving in the air,
The subject of the sun,
Beauty beyond compare

A rosebush resting green,
All simple without need
For doing anything,
For work or will or deed

But pleasant in the breath,

Neither white's spirit-life,
Nor black's dark shadowed death,
But free from any strife.

Contentment is in green,
In rest is satisfied;
We may in green renew,
Restore our souls green wide.

In green we know repose,
The beauty of the same,
On which the dear, dear rose
Speaks master of the Name

In green and red my soul
Meet paradoxically;
I want to heal, be whole,
Rest lackadaisically.

Yet ever deeper still,
Within the calm of green,
My red emerges clear
To meet the pain of sin,

To cleanse my inmost heart
In fires of Christ's pure Blood,
That I be pardoned and
Forgiven by my God

My red calls me to work,
To strive perfection find
The goal of every day,
The Christ of humankind

I know He leaves me not,
My true Companion, Friend,
My Brother, Sister here;
My wounds he heals and tends.

Chapter Eight. 2003 – 2006   Magic of the Stars, Love & Lyricism,

For me to know His red,
Dear suffering, my own,
I feel within my heart
In love which He has sown

I'm centered in this red,
In my own heart and pain;
I care not then if cold
Comes down in pouring rain

For I am warm inside,
In feeling in my heart,
Where Christ is my own Guide,
Life's meaning me imparts.

My mystery I know,
In green and red I go,
To live my life with hope,
And love courageous show.

These two meet in my soul;
I carry them within;
Where one the other is,
Green and red again

A rosebush lives in me;
I sit and breathe perfume
In light-warmed air around;
The scent fills my whole room.

I see the color red,
The deep red of the rose;
I struggle to be good,
To feel my pain and woes

To let the green allow
My suffering a home,
For heaven has a place
Here in my earthly home.

So red I feel in me,
And green expands around;
In silences I speak
The resonating ground,

The sound of red and green,
The Easter deed each morn,
Through dying, death and pain
My soul in spirit born

I love the green of hope;
I hold the red of Christ;
God's green is born the East;
In Christ men die the West.

The moment I awake
Must dying agony
Begin, and every day
Find human company.

Father, Mother dear,
And brother, sister, friend
Are special in my heart,
In loving thoughts we send

Each other find, that we
In love and reverence
For human deeds of Christ;
Gold, myrrh and frankincense

We offer to the Child
In our own hearts with love,
That He in us may die,
A sacrificial dove

And in our suffering,
That we know pain and grief,
And in the death of sleep,
In heaven find relief.

Chapter Eight. 2003 – 2006   Magic of the Stars, Love & Lyricism,

This earthly is the scene
Of nature and of man,
The hills pastoral green,
The human chin and hand,

Where divine worlds do work
And light the fires aflame;
The red divine appears
Within our yellow Name

Above the peaceful blue,
Receding in the skies,
Encompasses the world
In which the bird sings, flies.

Yes, green and red do meet
In me, and on the earth;
The rosebush changeless grows
Through dying, death and birth.

Culver City, California
March 9, 2003

Morning Song

In the newness of the dawn,
Earth begins to stretch and yawn
From the drowsy sleep of night
In the dream of magic light

All the flowers begin to dance;
Birds upon the wing do prance;
Men and women slowly wake
For another day to make

Everything sounds fresh and new,
Songs the birds are singing true;
Color fragrances of flowers

Capture fleeting morning hours.

In the early song of day,
Birds do sing and fly away
From the land of nighttime gray
Into music light and say:

"Love is born again, light's child,
Sweet and beautiful and mild;
With all nature heaven and earth
Join together praising birth."

And the morning now begins
To awaken among men;
Day arrives into our world
Like a shining color pearl.

Los Angeles
March 12, 2003

Green

Green is pleasant, mild
Soothing to my mind
Morning's hopeful child
Nature's Motherkind.

Green is soft and good
Tender shoots of grass
Sprouting from the wood
Weeping willow's lass

Green is patient and
Resting in content
Grazing pasture land
Cows' warm breath and scent

Green is poetry's
Imagination fair

Chapter Eight. 2003 – 2006   Magic of the Stars, Love & Lyricism,

Plant's sap arteries
Breathing in the air

Green is simple, calm
In a dream of hope
A breathing, balanced balm
Helping us to cope

Green is inner life
Felt in fronds and ferns
Green is maid, housewife
Helping children learn.

Green is rhythm's hue
In the breath of love
Ever old and new
Below meets up above

Green is middle's friend
Companion to the brave
Green's a nurse to tend
The patient's life to save

Green is ever here
Unchanging as it grows
Green is a good peer
Simple friendship shows.

Yellow

Yellow is a song
Friendly as the day
Birds which dance along
Sunlit path-a-ways

Yellow is a joy
Telling all the world
Like a smiling boy
Proudly helping girls

Yellow is a lark
Flying free and high
Conquering the dark
Way up in the skies.

Yellow is the light
Shining warm and gay
Sunny, cheerful bright
Singing every day

Inspiration's source
Yellow talks out loud
Energy's good force
Vigorous and proud

Yellow is the Tone
Singing high and true
Shining on the stone
Sparkling in the dew

Yellow is a word
Promising the best
Trusting as a bird
Flying from her nest

Yellow is my Name
Genius' ecstasy
Golden prize my fame
Magic's fantasy.

Yellow reaches out
Ever finds its way
Into every heart
Love's own streaming rays.

Blue

Blue is deep, inside
Inner mystery

Chapter Eight. 2003 – 2006 Magic of the Stars, Love & Lyricism,

Complex, sorrow's bride
Mourning's history

Blue is inward, strong
Its own company
Sadly sings its song
Death's drumbeat timpani

Blue is prayer and thought
Contemplative in word
Devotion fondly brought
A melancholy bird

Blue is tragedy
Melancholic pain
Depression's melody
The endless falling rain

Blue is heavy heart
The stone of every night
Set from the day apart
To sleep ourselves invites.

Blue is dark and cold
As colorless as ash
In middle age quite old
Is knowledge hidden stash

Blue is inward wealth
The secrets of the night
Suffering in health
Hidden from the Light

Blue is solid form
Is rock and iron ore
Freezes from the warm
Cooling to the core

Blue is hard and firm

Rooted in the earth
Blue is math and term
The death before the birth

Blue is deeply felt
Like Advent, Mary pure
Prayerfully she knelt
Before the Lord demure

Blue is tender drops
Of dew upon the leaves
Blue is crystal shops
Beautiful she grieves.

Red

Red is focused fire
The furnace of the flame
Passion's funeral pyre
The Christ of every Name

Red is love and strength
Is courage bold and brave
Suffers pain at length
Fears neither death nor grave

Red is earnest heart
Is will and work and deed
Emerges from the start
At once both fruit and seed

Red is inner self
Is pulsing blood in heat
Is gold upon the shelf
Is succulence of meat.

Red is valor's voice
To save the world He came
Red is painful choice

Chapter Eight. 2003 – 2006   Magic of the Stars, Love & Lyricism,

The Truth of every Name

Red is sacrifice
Is action from the thought
Intuition's sense
Color red has brought.

Red is sure and lives
The present full in flower
A rose in grace she gives
And dies in evening hours

Red is dignity
Is feeling heart and faith
Red is sanity
The warmth of living breath

Red is inner time
Embedded in the Word
Immersed in rhythmic rhyme
The pulsing sun is heard.

Red is chivalry
Is honor bravely lived
Leads on the cavalry
Christ's banner boldly waved.

Red is Sacrament
Is Jesus' Sacred Heart
To heal men's ailment
His Flesh and Blood imparts.

Red is good and still
Unmoved by vortex and
Assurance all be well
The sun above the land.

Los Angeles/Culver City, California
March 15, 2003

Wirklichkeits Glück

Ich bin
Am Rande des Lebens,
Am Strande des Meers;
Ich will
Durch Hoffnung und Streben,
Trotz Bange und Leer,

Mein Ziel
Für Selbstheit und Ich-Sein
Die Zukunft finden,
Mein Herz
Durch Liebe und Du-Dein
Mit Freunden verbinden

Wir sind
Bedeutung des Herzens
Und Wirklichkeits Glück;
Wir sind
Mit Mut Angst und Schmerzen
Genügend und Stück;

Die Welt
Mag chaotisch, kalt werden,
In Dunkelheit sein;
Der Mensch
Bezaubert Gebärden
Und funkelt gar fein.

Der Mensch
Mit Glaube und Liebe,
Mit Hoffnung und Kraft;
Der Mensch
Kann Totes beleben,
Was trocken wird Saft;

Denn Geist
Ist mystisch und zaubert,

Chapter Eight. 2003 – 2006   Magic of the Stars, Love & Lyricism,

Liebt Freiheit und Licht;
Der Mensch
Was schmutzig schön saubert
Und hellt sein Gesicht.

22. März 2003

Lieben und Ruhen und Schlafen und Träumen

Der Liebende, Ruhende, Schlafende, Träumende
Der liebet and ruhet und schlafet und träumet
Er grüßet die Kinder, die lächeln und spielen
Er hilfet die Greisen, die wachen und hören

Der gütige, christliche Priester, der Dichter
Beweiset nach Christus, er zeiget und zeichnet
Mit Finger und Bleistift, mit Auge und Stimme
Sein Antlitz erstrahlet, erleuchtet und glänzet

Die Stimme des Priesters, des Dichters erklinget
Ertönet mit Schönheit und Klarheit und Wärme
Die Worte derselben, sie sprechen und reden
In Rhythmen und Tiefen des Fühlenden Herzens

Beschreiben Gelände, Gebirge, Natur
Vorstellen Geschichte, darstellen Szenen
Die Hände derselben erwärmen und tasten
Und zeigen die Wunden der Nageln des Kreuzes
Die Todestat Golgathas des Herrn Jesus Christus.

Geschwister, Gebrüder und Freunden und Väter
Und Mütter und Kinder zusammen gemeinsam
Unter den Sammelnden wandelt der Christus
Segnet ihr' Herzen, beruhigt ihr' Seelen

Dann schlafen die Menschen ermüdet, veraltet
Und unter den Engeln, den Toten mit Christus

Verjüngern, verstärken sich, wärmen und trösten
Sie lieben und ruhen und schlafen und träumen...

Los Angeles
10. April 2003

A Poet's Dream-Reality

I exited the partial room
Of pilfered pink partitioning
And found regrouping in my gloom
A pure and tranquil offering

The muses gathered in the air
My Venus listened to my song
As speech unspoken summer fair
All carried on the breeze along.

My Venus dreamt in me a dream
Of earth's great life and happenings
Of my own heart, she did redeem
The Christ of Sun in suffering

'Twas then in Nature, I of Mars
Transmuted iron's orange ores
Into the magic of the stars
In mysteries and metaphors

But did I know that I was touched
By Venus-Christ, her dream of love
Enchanted by the faeries such
That shone my Christ a violet dove?

O violet fair, a virgin pure
O Venus-violet fond and true
Thou loves the Earth, thy lover sure
And I enraptured am to view.

So smile thou faerie-princess dear

Chapter Eight. 2003 – 2006   Magic of the Stars, Love & Lyricism,

And hold me warm in thy embrace
And I shall muse all through the year
In poetry of thy sweet face

And in the end of cycles' time
All rhythms motioned in my verse
All speech delivered into rhyme
Shall love become our universe.

Thy dream, my Venus, of this day
Reality of love shall reign
Together with my Sun, her way
Eternity and life shall gain.

Now which is truer, should I ask?
Thou red Christ-Sun in feeling there
Thou violet Christ-Venus task
Love's mystery and magic fair?

Surely, thou Sun sense mystery
And magic play in all beauty,
And Venus, thou Queen of faerie
Dost feel in Christ reality

Now in the Center, Christ, Thou art
In feeling there, in fear and pain
In mystery of love's pure heart
In magic rainbow in the rain

Let this be known to one and all
May storm clouds gather, thunder peal
May lightning strike and raindrops fall
Our Sun-Christ, He all sickness heal.

But afterword shall be a day
Shall be the Garden's faerie-mound
And mystery shall have her say
The magic light shine from the ground

Songs & Elegies, Mysteries and Others   Chapter Eight. 2003 – 2006

> So gather all ye martyrs and saints
> Ye Sun-Kings gather to this place
> Ye Venus-Princesses and paint
> Christ Jesus for the human race.
>
> Culver City
> July 9, 2003

Fünf August Abendgedichte

1. Hans Peter van Manen

> Mein Sonnenfreund
> Viel verdanke ich Ihnen:
>
> Ihre Freundlichkeit
> Ihre Lebensfreude
> Ihre stete Interesse an dem
> Was am Leben interessant ist.
>
> Durch Sie atme ich einen Teil
> Ihres sonnendurchtränkten Atems
> Der aus weiterer Ferne
> Zu mir, zu meinem Herzen weht.

2. Gedanken

> Die Verbindung die uns über
> Zeitliche and räumliche Distanzen überbrückt
> Ist ein Faden
> Von feiner Gedankensubstanz
> Die klar leuchtet
> Und die kleine Wesen feierlich spinnen
>
> Lichtsubstanz
> Liebe genannt
> Denn solche Gedanken in Seelen aufleuchten
> Uns einander begrüßend
> Herzlich erwärmen
> Liebeslicht sei Gedanken.

3. Abend Andacht

Rosapurpur Farbendunst
Ein Abendhauch der Liebe
Rosa und Blau des Himmels
Herrlich und andachtsvoll

So beendet sich
Der Tag der Farben
Und die heimliche Nacht
Geister erwacht.

4. Sonnenuntergang

Am Ende des Tages
Müdigkeit die Menschen veraltet
Doch wenden sie sich
An der Sonne
Die sie durch den Tag
Begleitet hat

Und sie sehen
Schönheit
Glühendes Rot
Das sterben bedeutet
Und die Liebesnacht
Eröffnet.

5. Liebesgeburt

Rosa, Blau und Violet
Bezaubern Herzen
Zur Liebe.

Lieb bist Du Lila
Lieblich und innerlich
Herzlich und christlich
Geburt Jesu.

Zarte Maria und

Zartes Kind
Des Himmels.

Westchester
23. August 2003

Einsamkeit

Einsamkeit
Da ich bin ein Teilchen hier
Ein Mensch von andren Menschen umgeben
Körperlich getrennt und individualisiert
Doch unter den andren
Das ich weiß, Ihr und ich
Wir sind die Menschheit.

Einsamkeit
Das ich durste nach Christus
Mein Bewußtsein durstet nach Christus
Brauche ich Seiner
Ich nehme Sein Leib – das Brot
Ich trinke Sein Blut – der Wein
Und zelebriere das Sacrament des Bewußtseins

Einsamkeit
Wo ich auf Erden stehe und gehe
Wo ich sehe in den Himmeln die Sonne
Bin von ihrem Lichte erwärmt und erleuchtet
Bin vom Winde berührt
Bin von der Erde unterstützt

Unter Tieren und Vögeln
Pflanzen und Bäumen
Steinen und Felsen
Und ich atme die Lüften
Und fühle mich nicht mehr einsam
Denn ich bin nicht allein.

Du, Menschenbruder

Chapter Eight. 2003 – 2006 Magic of the Stars, Love & Lyricism,

Du, heilger Christus
Du, Freundin Natur
Bist bei mir
Und ich bin bei Dir
Und wir bauen zusammen Drei Welten:
Irdisch, Himmlisch, Menschlich.

Natur-, Geistes- und Menschenwelten
Erschaffne Wesen auf Erden
Engelwesen in den Himmeln
Menschenwesen Hand und Fuß
Auge und Ohr, Lippen und wir
Freuen uns innig und jubeln in Weltengesang –
Wir danken Euch, Welten Gottes
Wir danken Euch!

September 2003

Tendenzen

Tendenzen – das Wort im Munde
Das Wort der Aussprache
Das Wort der Dichtung.

Tendenzen – ein Moment nachdem
Nach dem anderen
Wo die Vögel fliegen
Und die Häuser sich bauen lassen
Tendenzen

Bejahung – die Hoffnung
Die Erfüllung des Wortes
Die Erfüllung der Sprache
Die Erfüllung der Dichtung.

Bejahung – wann alles sich ausgleichen läßt
Und kleine Schritte sich belauschen lassen
Und die Engel sich zur Sinfonie vorbereiten
Und die Engel die Sphärenmusik vor sich geben

Und die Engel singen
Bejahung

Inzwischen liegen Bausteine
Bausteine und Arbeiter
Arbeiter die tüchtig leben und schaffen
Häuser bauend

Inzwischen erhöhen sich Wolken
Herrliche weiße Wolken
Himmlisch und gewölbt
Unter Sonnenlicht und Vögel

Inzwischen schreiben Studenten
Aufsätze für Kursen
Klassenexamen
Schulenprüfungen
Die Ferien kommen schnell.

Die Ferien – ein Weihnachtsabend
Wo das Kind eintritt
Und die Welt ganz anders wird
Denn Jesu Christ wird aufs neu geboren
Und Herzen jubeln
Denn Er ist gekommen.

22. November 2003
Los Angeles

The Song of Winter

The song of winter sings today
In its own pure and simple way
We taste its flavors in the air
Of apples red and white and fair

We smell its fragrances come by
In breezes blown from gardens' sky
We feel its warmth in inner glow

Chapter Eight. 2003 – 2006   Magic of the Stars, Love & Lyricism,

The hearth our hearts do flame and show.

Arise from Mother Night of sleep
Awaken from the realm of deep
And kindle hearts for love today
To hear the gentle song hold sway

The song of winter's melody
The song of sad melancholy
The song, repeat, the Saviour born
Has come our hearts anew to warm.

He is the Lamb of Easter Death
Before the Resurrection breath
That in our breaths we die in Him
And resurrect the morns again

Come, winter song, come sing to me
Of Jesu Christ's melancholy
Come blow to me, now melody
Come blow, now fondly, gently see

I am a humble poet-man
Who poetry doth give with hand
These Holy Nights, remember Light
Is shining memorably tonight

The Light of Christ doth shine all free
An offering humanity
Doth need to live, eternity
Has come again to you and me.

Inglewood, California
January 3, 2004

The Mountains

Hills and mountains, this I know,

Seem to rise, to live, to grow;
Large as bed of earth they loom
Up above the empty tomb

Sacred are the mountain lands,
Greeting sunbeams with their hands,
On a sunny afternoon,
February, May or June

They are hallowed bodies of
Earth's great radiant, shining love,
And we filled with strength behold
Their old stories to us told.

History lives in their mounds;
Ancient are their sacred grounds,
And we rest in them assured,
Christ's own flesh, the mighty Word.

Palmdale, California
February 1, 2004
Revised Los Angeles
December 19, 2012

I Sing

I sing
Such a sparrow or lark
Upon the wing
I sing.
I soar
Say an eagle or seagull
In the sky
I soar.

I speak
Am a poet or a priest
A person poetic upon a point
I speak.

Chapter Eight. 2003 – 2006   Magic of the Stars, Love & Lyricism,

Together we sing and soar and speak
Together we make creative live
Our inmost image

Together we: imagine the life of words
Inspire the songs of birds
Intuit the colors of plants
Our creative spirits seek
Each day, each week

To manifest our art
Sacred sacredness our heart
To reveal our most holy "I"
To stand aligned between earth and sky.

O sun, o earth
And Man thou art
Soul and Man thou art
Spirit incarnate
Body delicate
Pronounce the day
God's way

Be so good
A tree in the wood
Let no one pass by
Before he senses why
I stand and write
These words invite
I stand the shore
Distances before
The sea in motion free
Surpassing time to be

Movement ebb and flow
The waves they come and go
The mountain peak
Stands to rise and speak
Tall, victorious

Humorous-serious

God is great
He knows the date
Beginning, end
We men

Above us angelic hosts ceaseless active
And our Christ is
He is the One
Father, Brother, Genius of all
Hear His Call

His beckon Call
To one and all
To stand tall.

February 29, 2004

When Soldiers Die

Address his will – upon the day
Acquire the skill – upon your way
Announce the past – as plain to say
The die is cast – 'tis time to pray

The other men – seaworthy all
Do come again – at beck and call
These seamen brave stand upright tall
Not lowly knaves – these never fall

Such stalwart there – such soldiers dream
Of families fair – of peace, they seem
To dream of days untroubled by
These fighting ways beneath the sky

They lend a hand, they promise words
They walk the land, they love the birds
And when they fall and die to earth
The angels call their heavenly birth

Chapter Eight. 2003 – 2006   Magic of the Stars, Love & Lyricism,

They are so young, unseasoned by
Death's hand, unsung, these heroes try
To right our wrongs, they only pray
Their voice in song, they die away

And when the mark is met they fall
This murderous lark the bullets call
They tear through wind, they pierce their skin
Nor can rescind when battles win

These youthful men spill blood as pure
As water when the rivers were
Rolling restless to the sea
Like birds quite nestless helplessly

They breathe their last, this breath of life
So brief their past, their marriage, wife
They leave this place, this world's hall
Without a trace, without a call

Their souls depart to Spirit-Land
Their bodies part, their lifeless hand
And on an air and on a breeze
Their soft brown hair blows there with ease.

Los Angeles
March 1, 2004

On Pilgrimages

Avenues quite dusty lay
Ahead in their solitary way
We trod them bravely
And we felt their firmness
Beneath our sandaled feet

We marched and went
On pilgrimages
Wandering roads over mountains
Through valleys and across deserts

To the holy place.

We discovered ourselves and
The meaning of the goal
The fruit of challenges
Of trials and probation

To the sun and the Light Divine
Christ, the healer of our illnesses.

May 12, 2004

Song of Mother's Child

From silences to song
We clarify the poem: You and I
Like Mother and Child:

You, Mother of my art: Poesie
Cradling me, the Poet-Child;

You, Breast
Giving me milk to nourish my poetry;

You, Earth
Whence sprouts, buds my poem-flowers;

You, Mother of
My longing to speak, to sing

I sing to You
Mother-Friend:

In whose womb I grew in silence,
From whose waters I broke crying,
On whose lap I laughed and played.

Now I stand, a poet, singing my song:

Chapter Eight. 2003 – 2006   Magic of the Stars, Love & Lyricism,

A song of spring,
A song of air and light,
colored petals,
sparrows sweet,

A poet's song to greet you
Mother-Friend.

May 12, 2004

The Perfect Whole

Never believe in halves
When the perfect whole like a peach
Awaits your plucking
With sweet juice for the morn

Never go half-willing
When the work demands a full day's going
When the road reaches its destination
That of a pilgrimage

Let us make our way
You in your time
I in mine
Whole and complete
And all the way there

Then, like teenagers,
We will learn the skills
To take with us into adulthood
To the communion of spirits

We shall join the living and the dead
We shall see and hear awake
We shall think and speak and sing quite openly
Of the Savior in our midst

We, the men and women

Bearing witness to the Christ
Shall remember the Lord
Rejuvenated like children for the new day.

Culver City, California
May 12, 2004
Revised Los Angeles
January 7, 2013

Love Remember

Love remember well a day
Love remember in her way
All the daffodils and smiles
Every moment spent in whiles.

Love remember well a night
Love remember sweet starlight
All the faeries' songs and dance
In the Wedding-Light Romance

Love remember well the morn
Love remember life reborn
All the sparrows, squirrels, larks
Talking cheerful, glad remarks

Love remember well sunsets
Stones and other silent pets
Love remember dying pain
Reddish-ruby clouds and rain

Love remember times and spells
Of eternal moment-wells
Love remember poetry
Songs and paintings, sculptures free

Love remember queens and kings
Princes, princesses with rings
Lords and ladies, squires and knights

Chapter Eight. 2003 – 2006 Magic of the Stars, Love & Lyricism,

Dukes and duchesses' delights

Love remember poet-bards
Soldiers fighting holy wars
Clericals and bishops, priests
Nuns and scholars, birds and beasts

Love remember castle-lands
Fortresses and coastal strands
Love remember forest-woods
Hunting, fishing for fresh foods

Love remember fields of grain
Love remember falling rain
Love remember golden sun
Shining clear for every one

Love remember dogs and cats
Frogs and toads and hairy bats
Love remember cows and sheep
Pigs and ducks and foxes leap.

Love remember lakes and ponds
Ferns and grasses and palm-fronds
Evergreens and mosses green
Pasturelands where grazing seen.

Love remember spring and fall
Summer, winter, seasons all
Love remember night and day
All the villagers do say.

Love remember mountains grand
Love remember desert sand
Love remember oceans vast
Swamps and meadows, east to west

Love remember peace and war
Gold and barter days before

Songs & Elegies, Mysteries and Others   Chapter Eight. 2003 – 2006

Money was as commonplace
As our modern human race

Love remember legends true
Fairytales, stories grew
Love remember humble homes
Earthen floors and spirit-gnomes

Love remember undines, too
Sylphs and salamanders knew
Love remember farms and times
In the days of ballad rhymes

Love remember young lads groomed
Handsomely young lasses found
In the golden, sunny fields
Courtship offered, bent and kneeled.

Love remember marriages
Horses, wagons, carriages
Churches, sacraments, and priests
And the nights of wedding feasts.

Love remember childhoods
When simplicity still stood
Without complications or
Fancy art-deco décor

Love remember olden times
Nature's wealth was then sublime
Let us find our love once more
In her universal lore.

July 25, 2004

Poetry Reality

A poem is – now deeply peer
Into my soul, entering here

Chapter Eight. 2003 – 2006   Magic of the Stars, Love & Lyricism,

Into my heart, into my song
Into my poem's rhythm strong –

A poem is – now feel the sense
A melody, mystic-immense
A simple verse, a song of love
A pure and pristine turtle dove.

A poem is reality
Reality of mystery
Reality of blood and breath
Reality of life and death

Reality of suffering
Reality of pain so dear
Reality of deep longing
For spirit-life all radiant clear

Yes poetry – a poem is
A thing of beauty – 'tis, it is!
A beautiful reality
All shining warm and radiantly!

August 23, 2004

Höret! Die Sonne – Für Gérard Klockenbring

Höret! Die Sonne
Singet im Chore
Singet ihr' Wonne
Mensch, Tier und Flore

Höret! Die Sonne
Singet durch Tage
Singet gar schöne
Lieder im Sage

Höret! Die Sonne
Singet die Nächte

Sage und Märchen
Wahrheiten dächten

Höret! Die Sonne
Singet gar edel
Königins Herrschaft
Königins Regel

Höret! Die Sonne
Singend und sprechend
Dichtungs Gesangbuch
Weihnachten jubelnd.

28. August 2004

Night is a candle's dream

Night is a candle's dream
Night is pure Venus' beams
Purple and fair
Her songs everywhere
Poems of mystery's dreams

Night is a song of love
Night is a word above
A word of untold
Mystery's fold
A word of Christ's beauty above

Night is a poem, a tune
Melody's timeless rune
An inner door key
To the heart's mystery
A beautiful timeless rune

Night is a song so dear
A song of mystery here
Each night we retire
Her song does inspire

Chapter Eight. 2003 – 2006   Magic of the Stars, Love & Lyricism,

Our souls with her beauty here.

August 29, 2004

The Magic Kingdom

A magic kingdom in the sky
A magic kingdom up on high
I saw it golden in the clouds
Shining in bright, radiant shrouds

A magic castle up above
A magic mountain of pure love
I saw it in the heavens grand
A heavenly, magic mountain-land

A magic castle smiling there
In the golden, glowing air
A magic mountain mystery
Up in the heavens for to see

A magic kingdom where dwell them
Little elfin faerie men
A magic kingdom there of light
In the heavenly landscape bright

A magic castle in the air
Built of clouds all faerie-fair
Made of airy, radiant light
On a magic mountain bright

A magic castle robed in sun
On a magic mountain won
By enchantment 'fore the night's
Starry merry mystic lights

Now the sun has set in love
Now the faeries dance above
Join the heavenly mystery

Dwell the night most magically.

But remember sunset's love
But recall the clouds above
The magic kingdom in the air
The magic kingdom radiant fair.

September 9-10, 2004

Seek To Know a Cloudless Day

Seek to know a cloudless day
Breezes blowing fondly say
Yesterday was colorful
Yesterday was wonderful.

Tomorrow shall be once again
Color-rich and entering
Into sunsets 'fore the night
Color sunsets of pure light.

But today is clear and warm
But today is breezes born
By a motion and a song
Promises in spaces long

Today is breezy holiday
Today is different to say
Poetry's an open thing
Creation out of air, nothing

Today is time to sit and write
Songs into the day invite
Create your own birdsong of love
Create your own magical dove.

Today is time for poem's worth
Summer still seeks to give birth
Summer still exhales the earth

Chapter Eight. 2003 – 2006   Magic of the Stars, Love & Lyricism,

Summer still exports her mirth.

Today is still the summertime
Today is this small measured rhyme
Today is but an open day
Ask for poetry to say:

Write a song and be the one
Who is warmed by shining sun
Who is drenched in sun's warm beams
Who is bathed in sunny dreams.

Write a song today and be
Living, breathing poetry
Be the poem, be the one
Who creates, a co-God sun.

Let the breezes flow around
Let the air be cloudless sound
Let your song sing musically
Be a bird most cheerfully.

Let your pain merge into sun
Let your song inspire each one
Pray and hope and feel your love
Keep the faith in God above.

Today is open, cloudless song
Today is breezy all along
Today is poetry of air
Cloudless colors poem-fair.

September 13, 2004

America – A Song for Thee

America – a song for thee!
O pardon me, o pardon me!
America – how I love thee,

Land of the brave and of the free

Take thy freedom, brave and bold,
In thy fresh youth, not very old;
Take thy stand, and be so good,
Like thy forests, meadows, woods,

Like thy plains and glacier snows,
Like thy swamps and deserts blow,
Like thy mountain ranges grand,
Like thy ocean coastal strands!

America – this song I sing!
To thee a halleluiah bring!
Bestow thy wealth upon the poor,
And bring an end to fighting war!

Now educate thy children, see,
How beautiful thy cultures be!
How rich in life, variety,
All races, folks, ethnicities!

All foods we eat are here prepared;
All landscapes spread their tableau shared;
The sun is arises every morn,
And ushers in the newly born!

And in the evening at sunset,
The colors glow in dying breath:
The Passion of our Saviour Christ,
The Crucifixion in the West

And in the glorious, heavenly nights,
Arise, America in Light!
Lift thy choir of voices strong;
America, thou dost belong!

September 15, 2004

Chapter Eight. 2003 – 2006   Magic of the Stars, Love & Lyricism,

The Last Day of Summer

One open summer, summer's day
The birds do come, the birds do play
The sun is warm this summer's day
The sun is warm, the sun is gay.

The final day of summer's here
And autumn tide is O so near
The equinox tomorrow brings
When day and night are equaling.

Today is summer, warm and clear
Today is summer, cloudless here
Today the mountains do appear
Today the birds and children near

Do play and frolic in the sun
Do dance and play and frolic fun
Today is summer's final day
I thank Thee God, I ask and pray

For one last day of summer glad
For one last day not very sad
And then the autumn brave and clear
And then the autumn shall appear.

Today is summer's final day
I dancing frolicking do play.

September 21, 2004

Feelings Are Special

Feelings are special and warm like the sun
Romantic and sensuous or pure lovely ones
Feelings are tender and sweeter than dew
Like honey are feelings, my feelings for you.

Feelings are pleasure and painful as well

They feel good like sexual orgasmic play tell.
They hurt like the suffering from rosebush's thorns
The thorns that did crown our dear Saviour in scorn

Feelings are special like lilies and fields
Like poppies and meadows and grasses that yield
To raindrops are feelings, are feelings like rain
To raindrops which falling do soothe our sore pain

Feelings are special like clouds in the air
Like raindrops and sunlight, like raindrops so fair.
Like sunlight are feelings, like sunlight and smoke
From chimneys in winter 'neath mountain snow-peaks

Feelings are lovely like lilac and silk
Like lavender magic, like cream or like milk
Like violet-purple, like dear mysteries
Feelings are wonderful musically.

Feelings are tonal like melodies flow
Like streams in the springtime when snows melt and go
Like birds singing sweetly are feelings by day
I ask that you feeling do listen and pray!

Feelings are holy like incense and air
Like candle flames burning on altars bare there
Like paintings of holy events from Christ's Life
Like sculptures in marble, like Pietä's wife

Like Mary and Jesus are feelings so fond
Like Mother and Child another respond.
Yes, feelings are special like sunsets the eves
To him who surrounded by true love believes.

September 25, 2004

Rejuvenating Light

Rejuvenating Light Thou refreshes my mind,
Thou makes me light and heals my blind;
Rejuvenating Light Thou comes to me,
Thou heals the sick and makes free.

Rejuvenating Light Thou art the Light
Of Christ, our God, for precious sight;
Rejuvenating Light Thou appears as day,
And makes me good upon my way

Rejuvenating Light Thou heals my ills
And grants me peace; I climb a hill;
I climb a hill, ascend to Thee,
In holy space and company

The birds do come, they gather near,
When I am in Thy radiance clear;
The clouds of white do billow bright,
In radiance of Thy heavenly Light

And there above, upon the hill,
I sup with Thee and feel Thy Will
Of quietness, of sacred peace,
Of inwardness and strength increase

From daily sweat and labors good,
Thy Light doth shine from firewood;
And when I come, return to life's
Arduous path, Thou my midwife

Hath granted me a haven safe,
Where I do go and seek my cave,
My cave where light doth shine in me
Am ever light eternally

Rejuvenating Light Thou blesses him
Who suffers the darkness grim,

And in the night's pure sanctity
I am again in unity.

September 25, 2004
Revised Los Angeles
December 15, 2012

An Angelean Autumnal Sun

An Angelean autumnal sun
With loving light for every one
She shines both warm and clear this day
This is what I mean to say
She is a beacon of God's love
Shining to earth from heaven above
Beauteous is her heavenly light
A great and glorious, heartfelt sight
O Sun! to thee we send our love
From earth below to heaven above!

October 14, 2004

Sincerity

Sincerity –
Sweeter art thou than honey
With thee, dear sincerity
I am like the faithful worker bee.

Sincerity –
Thou art the honey of my love
The golden honey spun above
Thou do I spit from out my soul
From nectar of the virgin-flower of my heart

Sincerity –
I am gladly drunk on thy sweet ambrosia
Thou art my Muse since my newborn day
Thou inspires in me what I here now say:

Chapter Eight. 2003 – 2006   Magic of the Stars, Love & Lyricism,

Sincerity –
I love the sound of thy drops so sweet
Falling, plopping upon love's cookie sheet
With thy golden honey I do brown my cakes
When I then in love's oven freshly bake

Sincerity –
I make another wish
Come and be my fruit salad dish
Make dripping in thy honey each chunk of fruit
Like as to a sticky, golden suit.

Sincerity –
Thou art my best nature
My honeyed-tongue of Goddess' fair stature
My golden voice all warm a-glow
Teach me ever anew sincere to grow.

Sincerity –
One last pronouncement would I have thee sing:
Keep me friendly as thy friend in love
All kind and warm as a Mother-dove

Then shall thou pour freely from my soul
Into the chalice of my friends' ear-heart-bowl
Whereby my love is shared like honey dew
Sweetening even bitter grapefruit too

Sincerity –
I thank God that he gave me thee
Making me into what I could be
In human company and poetry

For sincerity does make that genuine
Which fickle in me changes like the wind
Like gold-lined clouds which pure do blow
And billow in the heavens, this I know.

Sincerity –

Through all times thou hast protected my aims
And firmly but gently taught me to tame
My horses' wild galloping
Into a lovely cantering

Sincerity –
Now keep me protected by Christ's Blood
That all men my heart understood
For I am a man with feelings of
Divine and very human love.

Inglewood, California
November 7, 2004

Einsamkeit und Licht

Einsamkeit steht trüb, darf nicht
Froh erlauben helles Licht;
Licht durchleuchtet Einsamkeit,
Strahlet in die Dunkelheit,

Schaffet Liebespoesie,
Eine sanfte Melodie,
Tönend zart durch Gegenden,
Tröstet alle Elenden

Wie die Wehmut klingt das Lied
Überbrückt all' Unterschied
Sieh! das Licht umarmt die Welt
Sonne der Nachtssternenzelt.

25. November 2004

Die Liebe

Die Liebe ist der höchste Preis des Menschenlebens
Erreicht, erlebt durch Schönheits glühend, glitzernd Glanz
Wir widmen unsre Kräfte Liebesleben strebend
Und schmücken Tisch und Tür mit Liebes buntem Kranz.

Chapter Eight. 2003 – 2006 Magic of the Stars, Love & Lyricism,

Die Milde, die die Liebe in uns zart erwecket
Ist wunderschön und hold und lieb und immer treu
Wir tanzen gerne durch die Räume Liebe decket
Und wie die Mädchen schauen offen sowie scheu.

Wie süß bleibt ewig Herz der Liebe, Liebesdichtung
Wie innig und wie fromm wir fühlen da
Wo Liebe uns berührt führt in jene Richtung
Wo Bilder schön erscheinen Dichtungskunst ist hier.

Gemeinsam singen wir so dankbar und so froh
Die Sonne glänzt in lichter, himmlischen Harmonien
Wir werden fein wo früher Wilder waren roh
Und tönen Weltenhirten Frühlingsmelodien.

28. November 2004

The Landscape

Heavenly clouds low in the sky
In the eve when God is nigh
Grey and white and peach and pink
As the sun dips down to drink

Up above a pale blue
Distant mountains rich in hue
Nearer trees of shape are seen
Trees with branches, leaves of green

Buildings also stand close by
Ask me, ask me, ask me why
I will tell you landscape of
God's November evening love.

November 21, 2004

Knabe Jesu

Die Liebe zwingt mir auf zu Dir
Zu Jesus, Kind des Menschen

Kind Gottes, Jesus-Knabe lieb
Du reichst mir Deine Händchen
Und mir zulächelst, winkend zu
Dein' Augen klar und gut
Ich fühle mich von Dir umarmt
Bekräftigt warm mit Mut

Du schläfst bald in mein' Armen ein
Und träumst von Gott und Mutter
Und alles ist gar still und süß
Wie Honig, Brot und Butter
Ich bin Dir gleich ganz zugewandt
Mein Herz und Leib erwärmet
Denn Dein' Gestalt ist weich und warm
Und meiner Dich erbarmet

Du bist der Lieblichste der Welt
Der Schönste Menschenkinder
Und niemand in der ganzen Welt
Ist treuer, lieber, linder
Ich träume bald von Weihnachten
Von Hirten und Maria
Und Dir, Du kleiner, Jesus-Kind
Du kommst in aller Gloria

So arm und edel bist Du hier
So gut bei Dir zu sein
Du kleiner, Jesu, Du bist mein
Und ich, ja ich bin Dein.

Wenn jeder Mensch der Gegenwart
Von Dir berührt sich würde
So wäre diese große Welt
Erfüllt von Gotteswürde
Und Friede würde überall
Wie Melodien herrschen
Der gute Hirte auf dem Land'
Sein' Schafe wie in Märchen!

1./2. Dezember 2004

Chapter Eight. 2003 – 2006   Magic of the Stars, Love & Lyricism,

The Shadows and the Light

When in the shadows seek the Light
When darkness seen remember bright
Does shine the sun, whose glorious rays
Pronounce the golden sunny days.

When in the depths remember near
The Light you're seeking, it is clear
When reaching up to see the Light
Seek for its lucid beams so bright.

When turning inward toward the Light
Remember dawn is streaming bright
When seeking inward Christ, the Sun
Remember He's the Radiant One.

Then every chilling shadow dark
Can only serve the meadowlark
For like the grey before the morn
The night precedes the newly born
And like the early morning dawn
The sun is rising, the night is gone.

Remember shadows only serve
The Light which throws them in a curve
They dance all restless, this their hour
The Light is come in its full power.

The Light is mighty, warm and good
The Light is brightly understood
The Light is clearly up above
Our heavenly Father, Christ is love.

Inglewood, California
December 3, 2004

Poetry – A Poem

Poetry is, simply said
What painting words encompasséd

Songs & Elegies, Mysteries and Others   Chapter Eight. 2003 – 2006

A scene, a land, a dream of there
A world itself all noble, fair
And equally beyond compare
And special there, unique and rare

It may be great as sun above
Or God, our Christ and heavenly love
It may be small, an epitaph
A tiny, little paragraph

Or anything there in between
A place where I have lived and been
My love for such a place becomes
A poem painted – re-union.

For poetry enables me
To grasp in words ineffably
Indescribable in prose, a song
A mood, a feeling, rhythmic strong
To paint it there and let it live
And linger in the sounds we give.

Culver City, California
December 14, 2004

The Beach on December 26, 2004

The beach is here this holy day
Before my vision clear
The sands are reaching to the sea
Which stretches beyond there.

The waters are so still and fine
The waves do crash and ease
And up above the heavens speak
In faeries' colors peace.

Today is but a mystery
Beyond the realm of time
It's measured in the dream of yore

Chapter Eight. 2003 – 2006   Magic of the Stars, Love & Lyricism,

In undulation's rhyme

In come and go of timeless sea
It's measured in its way
In timelessness it's measured here
In timelessness today

Today the ocean is a dream
Of vast eternity
It's stretched out there beyond my view
Horizon beyond me,

The timelessness and chartless world
Of all the wondrous sea
Becomes the meaning of today's
White winter poetry.

Los Angeles & Inglewood, California
December 26, 2004
Revised Los Angeles
December 19, 2012

Tiefrote Rose, Gérard Klockenbring

Tiefrote Rose, Gérard Klockenbring
Duftest herrlich, Vogel – sing!
Himmelskind ganz neu und frisch
Blühend Weihnachten zu Tisch

Tiefrote Rose, lieber Mann
Tod hat schenkend seine Hand
Nun bist Du auf ewig jung
In den Chören Engel 'Sang.

Tiefrote Rose, Gérard Klockenbring
Warm und saftig, Mut Du bringst
Christusknabe lebest Du
Weihnachtsfreude jubelst Du

Songs & Elegies, Mysteries and Others   Chapter Eight. 2003 – 2006

Herrlich, andachtsvoll und klar
Golden scheint Dein Engelshaar
Golden leuchten Augen gut
Golden ist Dein Herz voll Mut.

Tiefrote Rose, Gérard Klockenbring
Stirbest Du des ird'schen Rings
Gebärest Du in Himmelsphär'
Ein neugesprossenes Rotneujahr.

Tiefrote Rose, lieber Mann
Gehörest Christi Friedenland
Leiden ist vergangnes Ding
Lieber Gérard Klockenbring.

1. January 2005

Why, Friend? – A Poem to Jeff Watson and to All Who Are of Too Light a Sensibility

Friend, – why do you not breathe the balsam-heavy air I send,
The scented, moistened breath of love, the fragrant rose aromas,
The honeyed dews which hang upon the morning grasses?

Friend, – why do you insist upon scattering yourself and the little love of this place to the wind, without a care or a thought for the heaven which dwells in this place in the heaviness of warm memories of those who've suffering gone before?

Take comfort in the little things, in the small drops of love's pure dew upon rose petals,
On spiders' webs and the leaves and grass blades

Take comfort in the warm breezes of memories you can feel wafting gently across your cheek when it is coldest, soothing your skin and giving you that old familiar feeling of home, if dim and barely lived.

Take comfort in the aromas of the rose-gardens of sequestered memories whose blossoms flower on the coldest winter nights, whose scents rise in the flames of holy love heavenwards like a prayer before inward sleep descending comes.

Chapter Eight. 2003 – 2006   Magic of the Stars, Love & Lyricism,

Take comfort, friend, and do not haste away your self in fretful fears,
For the dead are here, the dead who would console you even now with their songs by way of your remembering them

Someone died last night, my friend, someone special died to join with the others, with the poet-priests, in the choirs of angelic hosts who are sending all who remember their balsam-heavy Christ-breath of death to the living.

We may find Christmas, Easter there in re-membering them.

January 2, 2005

Dr. Martin Luther King, Jr. – A Tribute

Martin King, brave and good
Spoke true words where he stood
Walked the walk, lived his dreams
Changed the world with Christ-beams

Preached to all Jesus Christ's
Gospel of loving cost
Sacrificed his own life
Prophesied 'midst sore strife.

Sovereign King, fair and true
Justice lives in your views
In your words, in your acts
Martin King set forth facts

Positive, bold and good
Love of Christ where he stood
"I am Thou" was his way
Christian grace preached and prayed.

Changed the world, bore his cross
Crucified was the cost
Chaste and pure in his heart
Martin King lived his art

True, sincere, honest, good

Strong in Christ where he stood
Now he lives, works in ways
Spiritual are his days.

Inglewood, California
January 17, 2005
Revised Los Angeles
January 16, 2013

Dignify the Mountain-Land

Dignify the solid earth
Land of mountain, mountain-birth!

Dignify the mountain-land
Rocky cliffs and mountains grand!

Dignify the peaceful hills
Shepherds roam and farmers till!

Dignify the mountain-forms
Ancient ground long years was born!

Dignify the mountain range
Above changless earth the clouds do change!

Dignify the mountain lore
Scenery which we so adore!

Dignify the mountain-peaks
Rocks and snow through month and week!

Dignify the landscape of
Mountain scenery of love!

Sun Valley, California
February 2, 2005
Revised Los Angeles
January 16, 2013

Chapter Eight. 2003 – 2006   Magic of the Stars, Love & Lyricism,

Silence, or Time

Silence sleeps – a dim memory
Before when time was new
And youth was young.

Now middle age has crept in
Stealthily – like a cat
Whose jutting bones would be comical
Were he not hungry – a picture of age.

And age begins to grow old
The flesh droops and hangs like bags
From limbs of trees heavy in the late afternoon
Before the sun sets

Silence keeps me company
I listen to her daily
My companion and friend

But I am not lonely, for my Mother speaks
Her comforting voice reminding me
When I was a child
Before, when time was new
And youth was young.

February 17, 2005

The Mystery of Death and Love

Death –
You take away my friends
And bring them across to the other shore.

I feel them here
In my heart
But cannot fathom their mystery

Free –
They now roam with Christ –

The Sun of the Night
On starry roads
The wide heavens
And celebrate the Mass
In the great Church-Cathedral
Of the stars

They have become stars
My friends
To light my way
Through the dark, mysterious night
Through whose door
I too pass
In the mystery
Of death and love.

February 18, 2005

TOUCH

Touch
That sense of feeling
That warmth of hand, of heart
The fingering of the red soil
Of loam and clay
Of earth and sand

Touch
Teach me your realities
Tell me stories of stones and utensils
Of teeth and bones
Tease me with wet waters
Which run smoothly like soft silk
And dreamily caress the curves
Of maidens' breasts

Touch
Feel the forms so friendly
Fondle features fine

Chapter Eight. 2003 – 2006   Magic of the Stars, Love & Lyricism,

And trace silhouettes and shapes
Of rounded or angular edges
Of rotund or tiny places pleasing to pat.

Touch
Tempt me to embrace your torsos
Your bosoms bare
Your broad shoulders
Your muscular mounds

And, when I am still
Move me once more
To caress the warm cheeks
Of little children
Who chirp like larks in the springtime
Playing games with tiny hands
That touch today

Because touch
Is a sensitive sensation of

Very velvety
Smoothly silky
Softly sensuous
Durably hard
Sharply pointed
Watery wet
Slippery slimy
Dusty dry
And sandy grainy realities
Which we feel with our fingers.

February 18, 2005

Love and the Rain

Love listens to her own pain
Like falling rain
Whose drops caress the window panes

And dance like music in refrains
As clear and tapping as small elfin shoes
As lovely as the shades of many hues
As dreary as the melancholy, multi-colored blues
On Saturday afternoons
The rain pours.

Love gathers in her folds
Coins of precious gold
Wise with wisdom old
Warmth in midst of cold

Within her curtains of lavender silk
For her bedchambers of milk
Of white butterflies and chalk
Where circle-rings of faeries talk
Love gathers.

And the rains descending pour.

They pour down in broad sheets
In a ceaseless, never-ending repeat
Which lulls all and each to sleep
In the darkness of the deep

Distant memories of childhood keep
Infants and toddlers crying weep
Comforted by the raindrops stop
Forgetting their sorrows' melancholy shops
They smile at the rain.

The rain entreats us like choirs
Of descending angels which inspire
Gently soothing us with lyres
Washing away the funeral pyres
In a timpani of faerie lore
We simply cannot ignore
Anymore
Our hearts implore

Chapter Eight. 2003 – 2006   Magic of the Stars, Love & Lyricism,

The rains pour.

Love likes the rain
It soothes her pain
Heals the wounds of disdain
Every misunderstanding strain

Discord melts in its refrain
As the rain showers down the lane
Deep in dark forests, over plains
For the drinking of the golden grain
Love loves the rain.

Love and the rain
Remind me that I am sane
That I know from whence I came
When I was blind and deaf and lame

The rain creates pools of water for the lamb
To drink next to the ram
Becomes the green of sea-waves' foam
'Neath which the dolphins roam
Love and the rain

Love and the rain.

February 21, 2005

Evenings

Days we do, we active live
In will and work and deed
Then evenings we contemplate
We listen, write and read

For day is done, the sun has set
It's time for thoughtfulness
The deep unknown is our wellspring
Imagination's quest

Songs & Elegies, Mysteries and Others   Chapter Eight. 2003 – 2006

O days are filled with sun and song
With striving, struggle, strength
Then evenings we pause from this
We have achieved the length

It's time for pondering within
The depth of mystery
The Life of Christ does beckon us
The mystery we see.

O days we suffer with our faith
The pain and fear of men
Then evenings we turn our thoughts
To mystery again

The mystery of the unknown
Of death and love divine
The dove, the dolphin and the swan
Are Venus' loving sign

It's time once more to die in Christ
That in the nights we live
In holiness and sacrament
Of heaven we do give

Ourselves; our inward mystery
Is in the dark of night
The love of Jesus Christ, the Lord
Is living in His might

The Sun of Night does celebrate
The myriad stars around
For we have entered sacred space
We tread on holy ground.

O evenings are like a boat
That brings us 'cross the stream
Whose flowing banks and waters swirl
As in a limpid dream

Chapter Eight. 2003 – 2006   Magic of the Stars, Love & Lyricism,

We meet the ferryman who brings
We travelers beyond
The threshold of this world thereto
The starry spirit-pond

We stand as on the shores of here
We pause and see before
Us into mystery of night
That land of legend-lore

That fiery land of spirit-folk
The land of dead and Christ
Where angel hosts keep company
Beyond the sunset's West

And there a door is opened and
We enter through to night
The Spirit-Sun, our Saviour Lord
Christ Jesus greets us right.

We know He stands surrounded by
Angelic hosts and friends
He's waiting for us there to join
Him and His Hand He lends

To welcome us to mystery
To magic of the stars
The great unknown is our true home
Within our hearts not far

For the profound and secret dark
Of night does live therein
The mystery dwells in our hearts
Is fathomless again.

February 22/23, 2005

Taste, or Apprentice to Sais
(after Novalis' *"Die Lehrlinge zu Sais"*)

Taste the saltiness of blood, the Blood of Jesus Christ
The Blood He shed for us, His dying in the West
First eat His Flesh, the Bread of Life
Then take the Cup spilled for the Wife.

He is the Groom, His chosen the Bride
Beyond the Tomb, that's why He died
Salvation's Song does ring aloud
Here now the Tone! Remove the Shroud!

Reveal the face of Isis pure
If thou be he who shall endure
Apprentices come gather 'round
Novalis writes; Christ walks the ground

The world is changed; no one can hide
The Truth is out, is open wide
And each is free his lot to choose
Choose Jesus Christ, now feel His Bruise.

Take it to heart, His suffering
And therewith joy and offering
Offer the day a sacrifice
And live the nights, apprentice Sais.

February 27, 2005

When I Fold My Laundry

When I fold my laundry
The music changes
Perceptibly

The music creates small symphonies
Between my socks

And in the folded T-shirts

Chapter Eight. 2003 – 2006   Magic of the Stars, Love & Lyricism,

I hear minuets and bagatelles
In gentility
Like dancers at a costume party
Gliding across the floor
To the music of my laundry

And even my unmentionable underwear
They too sound there
In padded, muffled tones
The trumpets are sounding there
In my underwear

And my blue jeans sing sonorously
In the double bass's deep resonance
When I fold my laundry.

March 17/19, 2005

Passion Wednesday

We sink and mellow over time; we ask and say the words
Which for ten score and thousand years reminded men of birds.

They echo now in mystery before the sacred death
The Crucifixion, Christ's Descent, then Resurrection's Wreath.

We prayer for Easter hope and love, for sorrow's bridesmaid's friend
Who suffers now in eloquence; his time is at an end.

How shall he learn the mystery of death and love of night?
The Saviour comes to help him now from misery to might.

From inward penitence and grief, from darkness o'er the earth
From snows of Christ's dear Sacrifice in living, dying breath,

From out of tragedy the bridge 'cross death's sore heavy road
The faith of ages to be born anew, this is his ode.

We mourn for all who pray this day, preparing for the night

Songs & Elegies, Mysteries and Others   Chapter Eight. 2003 – 2006

For Easter morning follows death when darkness turns to light,

When painful questions seeking there unanswered by the world
Transform through pure experience into a precious pearl.

So hope with me the mystery of death and love this Week
And take the Sacramental Feast, Christ's Flesh and Blood now seek.

Partake of His good Elements that after death below
The morning new reborn above shall shine with inner glow.

This is the faith of simple men, the greatest share the same
The faith of ages we now need to pardon sins we name.

We are but human beings here, imperfect, incomplete
Come Saviour, Jesu Christ to me and teach me to be meek!

Come take my hand and lead me there where death is well the hour
That in th'event Good Friday speaks in silences may flower.

In silences of depths below, the Underworld of souls
Held captive by their sins' torment, by Christ's Deed are made whole.

And then the morning miracle, in faith we gesture now!
We seek for Easter in our grief, with love upon our brow.

With love for all, with love this day we ask forgiveness dear
We pray this day, prepare this day, we stand, our cross to bear.

For what is life but miracles, but faith and work and hope
But inmost feeling suffering with which we men must cope?

The miracles we know each morn, each inspiration gives
Renewal and the strength to go right forward as we live

So now, with courage on our breast, we ride to Cavalry
Before us rides our Saviour, see, His Banner waves now free!

He goes before us without fear, He rides now suffering

Chapter Eight. 2003 – 2006   Magic of the Stars, Love & Lyricism,

He is the bravest heart of all; He is our Company.

Yes Christ, the Sun, approaches night; the sunset has arrived
The Passion has begun and death bodes pressing us alive.

We fain would breathe all easily, but measured do we find
The Tempo of the Sacred One, the Tempo of mankind.

For Christ is our true rhythm and He steadies e'en the weak
He lends His Hand and helps the lost to find the mountain peak.

And now before the moment of the Truth of all our days
We may ascend to Golgotha; we find our inner way.

Ride on! Ride on! Now follow Him Who bravely knows the Way
He is the Way, the Truth, the Life; we follow Him this day.

And now, adieu, fair human friend, in future promise' hope
I shall with thee arise anew and climb without a rope.

I shall with thee ascend the hills and Golgotha shall be
The Sacred Hill of transformed earth, the Place that shines to see

The Sun of earth now points above to sun and stars of spring
Now pray, believe, it shall return, the song the sparrows sing!

Until that holy Easter morn we wear the cloak of death
And breathe now heaviness and loam the death of living breath.

And this is where we stand today, and this is but a prayer
And this is what I mean to say, and this is what I share.

Inglewood, California
March 23, 2005

Easter Morning, 2005

On Easter morning, bright and clear
The Risen One does fresh appear

Songs & Elegies, Mysteries and Others   Chapter Eight. 2003 – 2006

The Resurrection of the Year
Has come, re-born, is now and here!

O Christ, we feel Thy strength and might
In streams of radiant, warm sunlight
In lucid beams all clear and bright
A gladsome, cheerful springtime sight!

The birds with joy do praise this day
This Easter Sunday holy-day
As men and children go their way
The dawn is here, the Light is gay!

O Christ, Thy love returns all new
And with fresh hope our lives imbues
And in the morning, morning dew
The grain doth sprout, doth sprout anew.

And life returns, – but new, but new!
Is resurrected to our view
Is strong and brave through death, right through
The Other Side in lighter hues.

Raphael, Archangel of
Easter springtime sprouting love
Resurrection feelings of
Sentient hearts and flying doves

Clouds of white do billow bright
Emanating Christ's pure Light
Christ-clouds billow great and true
In the deep and heavenly blue

Sun is now our Cosmic Christ
Rising in the dawning East
Starry nights do fill the sky
In the everlasting high

Christ is Risen, yes, indeed!

Actual, His mighty deed
In all Nature do we read
Participate in this, His Creed:

"Join Me in My Presence there
In abundance everywhere
Where there's Life in all the air
There I live, there I appear."

March 27, 2005

The Mysterious Place

At this time some evenings
I enter into this place
The mysterious place,

Where love is good and kind
And relieves my tired mind
Freed from the daily grind
Where love I find.

I enter into there
This place of mystery
The mystery I see
And there I be
Holy mystery

Nor does anything outside
Can disturb
Or perturb
Because I am
Immersed and
Wholly there
In mystery.

April 12, 2005

The Winter Snows Have Fallen

The winter snows have fallen
In lovely lucid lallen
While whispers white and winsome
The snowflakes cover Vulcan.

The winter snows have gestured
In distinctive posture
In treasures' pleasures measured
At their azure leisure

The winter snows become us
In pleasantness around us
Quite arbitrary census
And scented burning incense

The incense curling, smoking
In heavy rising stroking
My selfishness revoking
All holiness invoking

The winter snows are outside
While flames are warming inside
In fires' figures dancing
The glowing coals are glancing.

Remember whether wonder
Is in the fields yonder
The bonds broken asunder
The storehouse is now plundered.

Remember in the fields
Snowflakes chilling yield
A breathless life and shield
To me always appealed.

The snows are falling faster
Than rhythms keeping muster

Chapter Eight. 2003 – 2006   Magic of the Stars, Love & Lyricism,

My uncle, brother, sister
Do circle in a twister.

The winter snows are falling
The voices are a-calling
The horses are now stalling
Though stable boys are pulling

The winter snows seem lighter
The sun's reflection brighter
The winter snows are melting
And spring is vaunted, vaulting.

The winter snows have left us
A memory of whiteness
The shoots of green about us
And roses red remind us

That Easter morning happens
The Resurrection beckons
We know rebirth within us
In Nature all around us.

Inglewood, California
April 12, 2005

TECHNIK

Technik – Du modernes Wesen!
Schreiben kannst du nicht, nicht lesen
Auch sprechen weder noch hören
Nur mannigfaltig stören!

Du kannst nicht denken, nicht singen
Dichten nicht, Schönheit bringen
Nicht sehen, nicht tasten
Nicht riechen, nur belasten!

Kalt bist du Technik, kalt und tot
Leblos bist du da, mehr Stein wie Brot

Keiner kann sich an dir ernähren
Du tötest das Leben, kannst nicht gebären!

Technik – Du kannst nur programmiert werden
Ausführen leblose Gebärden
Information ist dein Inhalt und Welt
Erkenntnisse Dir entschlüpft und immer fehlt

O Technik – künstlich bist Du und abstrahiert
Fotographisch, falsch manniert
Ohne Imagination oder Inspiration
Ohne Möglichkeiten oder Intuition!

Begrenzt bist du tote Technik
Begrenzt erscheinst du im Augenblick
Begrenzt heute wie morgen bleibst du
Begrenzt, was du nicht kannst ich tu'!

28. Mai 2005

Drei kleine Juni Naturgedichte

1. O kleine Honigbiene

O kleine Honigbiene!
Wie zärtlich du die Blüte küsst
Voll Glück den süßen Nektar trinkst

Trunken wirst du, kleine Biene
Und voll der Genüsse der Natur
Kehrst du nach Hause zurück
Den köstlichen Honig zu schaffen
Goldbraun und reich – die Liebe.

2. Gelbweiße Rose

Gelbweiße Rose
In den warmen Lüften zart duftend
Dem hellen Lichte eröffnend

Schön, milde und fein
Perfekt im Gleichgewicht
Harmonisch grüßend
Mir die Liebe hinreichend

Ich bitte dich -
Liebe mich
Gelbweiße Rose!

3. Die Ameisen

Ameisenleben
Ameisenarbeit
Ameisenweben
Ameisenstreben

Beschäftigung
Tagestun
Kleiner Ruhm
Ameisentum!

8./9. Juni 2005

Christ

Inward shines the inner Light
Christ redeems us in His sight
He is Sun and He is bright
Shining in the heavenly night

Christ is Saviour God is He
He is blossom on the Tree
Tree of Life is Christ is He
And His Branches shelter thee.

Christ is memory and all
Sacred sacramental call
He is present moment well
And the Future He foretell.

Christ redeems our thinking when
We do live in Him again
When our thoughts to Life become
Celestial starry shining suns

Christ does answer every deed
With His verses karma read
He is Poet of the World
He is Word of Life unfurled.

Christ is every little bird
Hear Him singing in the Word
Hear His Tone and see His Light
Think His Thought, now think it bright!

June 26, 2005
Revised January 16, 2013

In Merriment

In merriment to laugh about
Then quietly, nor stern nor stout
But eloquent, for such is love
And all the choirs sing above

Angelic voices sound around
The dear and sacred, blood-soaked ground
Remember life is mortal here
But spirit-life is full of cheer

So suffer brave all pain and fear
Eternity is O so near.

June 29, 2005

God Is Good

O Man remember
God is good
God alone is good.

Chapter Eight. 2003 – 2006   Magic of the Stars, Love & Lyricism,

We are but little
Little men, women and children
Who long for God

Seek after the Good
Seek to serve the Good
Seek to serve the Christ in one another.

There is God
There is the Good
There is our good God
There is our Christ.

Christ is love
Christ suffers there
In our human brother and sister.

"Truly, I say to you, as you did it to one of the least of these my brethren, you did it to me." (Matthew 31:40)

July 6, 2005

When I Write the World Happens

When I write the world happens
When I write the memories appear

When I write I learn what I have known and buried in my heart of gold
When I write my creativity flows in rich streams of love and thought-light.

When I write sceneries of my imagination are unveiled through parting mists
And the sun appears above, shining into my world of poetry

And the green hills bathe in the gold of the setting sun
And homes and castles dot these hills like secret gems

And the tall mountains reach up to the sky like heroes' hands
And travelers walk long and winding roads through lovely valleys

Songs & Elegies, Mysteries and Others   Chapter Eight. 2003 – 2006

And the mighty blue ocean's foamy waves crash upon the rocky grey cliffs
And the clouds blow billowing and white in the wondrous winds of time

And the little round birds chirp merrily among the trees' branches
And the flowers smile in colorful faerie dances

And the brown squirrels chatter and play chase tag with one another
And the dreaming human being walks deep in thought

Pondering life's inner meaning until he looks up at the sound of birdsong
And sees the love-disc of the sun in all her radiant splendor

When I write I pronounce my name and the world happens anew
And I am a man of heart and soul

A man of spiritual imaginations, a poet
When I write.

July 7, 2005

Nachtandacht

Abendstille deckt die Erde wie ein Kleid das sie umarmt
Die Sonne sinkt im Meere nach einem Tage ihrer großen Taten.

Die Nacht öffnet sich ihre Tür der Sterne, die funkeln und meinen
Der Tod sei Mysterium und Liebesboot zugleich

Der Mond scheint wie eine Schale, rund und weiß, hell und schön
Und die Menschen träumen Schönes, Kinder des Vaters im Himmel

O Nacht! Wie lieblich und zart bist Du!
Wie herrlich sind Deine Engelscharen, und die Sonne der Nacht
– Christus – auf immer und ewig.

Ewigkeit ist die Nacht, Ewigkeit und Treue
Und ich bin nur die Braut – der Dichter
Der Nachtgeschichten immer mit Bleistift im Buche des Lebens
dichtet

Chapter Eight. 2003 – 2006   Magic of the Stars, Love & Lyricism,

Schönheit bist Du, O Nacht meines Herzens, Schönheit und Liebe
Und der Traum des Vaters für Seine gläubigen Kinder in Seinem
Schoße.

17. Juli 2005

Henrietta – What You Mean To Me

Henrietta
What you mean to me.

Henrietta you are sweet as
Vanilla pudding
Chocolate chip cookies
Hot chocolate with marshmallows
Silky chocolate ice cream
M & M Peanut
Hershey with Almond

Henrietta you are salty as
Fritos corn chips
Capers
Kentucky Fried Chicken Original Recipe
Chicken broth
Extra salty H. R. Fish & Chips
Potato salad with lots of salt
Saltwater taffy

Henrietta you are spicy as
Flaming hot Cheetos
Tabasco sauce
Scrambled eggs with salt and extra pepper
Big Red cinnamon chewing gum
Spicy chicken wings
Beef tacos with extra spicy hot sauce
Steak with hot barbecue sauce

Henrietta you are pretty as
Pink ballet shoes
Pink lipstick

Songs & Elegies, Mysteries and Others   Chapter Eight. 2003 – 2006

Cashmere sweaters
A satin nightgown
Silk sheets
Rosewater
Fine lacework

Henrietta you are warm as
Toasted marshmallows
Mashed potatoes with melted butter and gravy
Fresh hot cinnamon rolls
Baked pink salmon
Broiled steak
A Jumbo Jack without cheese
A summer afternoon in L.A. in the shade

Henrietta you are feisty as
A small girl pronouncing the word "No!"
A horsewhip
A fire alarm
A steam engine going at full speed
A crow
A Mother bird defending her young
A rooster

Henrietta you are loving as
A Southern Californian sunset at the beach
The Pacific Ocean when it's serene
A big green lawn
A Turtle dove
Marian Anderson singing "Deep River"
The first light of day
A rainbow

Henrietta you are so much more to me
I don't know any more words.

You make me
smile
cry

Chapter Eight. 2003 – 2006 Magic of the Stars, Love & Lyricism,

mad
glad
sad
bold
sleepy
warm
happy

Henrietta
What you mean to me.

July 23, 2005

Colors

Emotions are the colors of my soul
They play therein their light and shadow roles
They shine all tenderly
In radiant harmony
I listen to them, seeking to be whole.

Colors are the feelings of my heart
They swim and dance and love do they impart
They mingle in the air
On summer mornings fair
I love with them each day to freshly start.

Moods are inner colors of my name
They smile or cry and ever changeless change
They happen everywhere
Returning to me there
Deeply cool or brightly as a flame

Colors are the scenery of love
I watch them in the heavens up above
They shine with radiance bright
They touch the earth with light
Bearing peace to me like turtledoves.

Feelings are the colors of a song
I sing them playfully and dance along

Songs & Elegies, Mysteries and Others   Chapter Eight. 2003 – 2006

They shimmer in the morn
And glisten newly born
In subtleties or movements sometimes strong

Colors are the wonders of my life
I see them as a husband does his wife
How fondly do I hold
The colors in my fold
Beholding them in shelter, keep them safe.

Music is the colors of a tune
Melodious on a springtime afternoon
The songs in nuance shades
In harmonies God made
Music plays in colors May or June.

Colors are a ship upon the sea
A-sailing o'er horizon beyond me
They dream of love this day
On tenderness' dear way
I see them floating gently by me free.

Love is but the colors of my soul
She dances to the tunes of pleasant roles
I join her with my heart
She sweetly nurtures art
And makes me sleep all quietly and whole

Colors are the lady of the world
They shine as one most precious oyster pearl
The lady smiles at me
She bids me her to see
How beautiful appearing as a girl.

Dreams are but the colors of the night
Between the deep blue darkness and the light
They speak in imagery
Profound in mystery
I know them by my vision, by my sight.

Chapter Eight. 2003 – 2006   Magic of the Stars, Love & Lyricism,

Colors are the waters of my eyes
They playful move transforming with delight
In fluid harmonies
A-swimming in the seas
Of color do I dip down from the skies.

Blossoms are the colors most divine
They flower with a flourish most refined
In bursts of beauty, see
How colors come to be
Belonging to my heart, becoming mine

Colors are the sweetest things I know
Giving birth and dying there I go
Each day with them begins
Then closing at the end
The colors do reveal themselves in show.

Colors are the moments special there
Their meaning indefinable as air
They merge in rhythm's time
Their substance most sublime
Resembling a goddess heavenly fair

Colors are the treasures of great wealth
They bear glad tidings of my inner health
I seek to die in them
To give birth once again
I share them then sequester them in stealth.

Colors are the windows of my art
I know their purposes in poems impart
They glimmer with a light
Between the day and night
The inner revelations of my heart.

August 10, 2005

The Beautiful Woman and the Christ*

She entered there – was beauty's shape
Her form was love – and love was draped
I saw her there as in a pose
Her fragrant lips smelled as a rose.

I kissed her there upon the lips
I touched her there, her shapely hips
I felt how in her company
And angel lived in mystery.

And yet she, woman, left me free
And I decided, let her be
For love was precious unto me
I dared not crush gentility.

She was a maiden of the earth
Yet thoughts of her gave spirit birth
And these appeared within my soul
Transforming in a spirit-role

And then I saw her once again
But then her way was not with men
But holy love she was to me
Appeared now clear and openly.

I greeted her; she greeted me
She was in heaven's company
Right here on earth in front of me
I saw my Christ most beautifully.

Transcending did mere bodily
Though beauty was, and strikingly
I saw her soul in clarity
'Twas love of one divinity.

And this her nature true to see
Appeared now open, candidly

Chapter Eight. 2003 – 2006   Magic of the Stars, Love & Lyricism,

I felt my soul in purity
Receive her gift in company.

As simple as a spoken word
I spoke to her, and she me heard
She turned to me; I heard her voice
She was redeemed; she did rejoice.

And so her beauty appeared unveiled
'Twas inner truth I saw and hailed
And love was shared 'tween her and me
And love is Christ our company.

And so you see earth was up raised
And heaven's Glory be now praised
The feminine as pure as snow
Awakened me to Christ to go

And this was moment's truth quite rare
Her beauty was beyond compare
And now I know the Temple of
Her soul is simply body-love.

August 14, 2005
Revised December 31, 2012

*Note: From an actual experience I had on Tuesday morning, August 9, 2005. The "kissing" and "touching" were with my eyes and in my thoughts only. The sharing of the Christ-love followed after I had the Sacrament in the form of cookies and soda I bought in the 49 cent store where she worked. It was when I returned to the store in order to greet her, as I had then a good, pure thought for her, and with the excuse that I wished to dispose of the empty soda can (which she helped me with), that I spoke to her the words: "Thank you. That was a good treat." She responded most openly and welcomingly, and with joy in her voice, and then we perceived the Christ in one another's eyes. She was the most strikingly beautiful woman, her face and perfectly-shaped figure both, I have ever seen in my life. She was not an American, with a somewhat brown complexion. She may have been from the Middle East or from the region of India, Pakistan and Bangladesh. Her eyes were brown and beautifully clear. Her soul was clear and light-filled. She was very trusting and appeared unconscious of her own great beauty.

Wisdom of the Stars

Wisdom, wisdom of the stars
I sense you sparkle not afar
But in the vastness of the night
Bring me inner, dear delight.

Starry heavens you appear
Nearer than the chair is near
There within my soul are you
Ponder spatially this view.

Now the little chair once more
Is my footstool to the door
To the blue celestial dome
Spiritual is our true home.

We do travel there each night
Deep within our hearts' delight
Only holy are the stars
Guide mankind the holy Czar.

Christ, the Prince, is Child once more
Christmas is the starry lore
Holy book astronomy
Teach me, teach geometry.

Then I may imagine space
Spiritual and Christly grace
Angels and archangels join
Spirits of the dead, star-coins

Chapter Eight. 2003 – 2006   Magic of the Stars, Love & Lyricism,

Shimmering as little suns
Let us join them, every one!

August 16, 2005
Revised December 31, 2012

A Song to Music

Music's melodies so clear
Sounding through the atmosphere
Radiant they now appear
Shining like the sun-sphere here.

Music awakens me by day
As I triumph on my way
To the golden Mystery
In the blue of heavens I see.

Music dreams the night in sound
Music of the spheres resounds
Music filled with life abounds
Music rumbles on the ground.

Music of the Passion of
Saviour Christ, His sacred love
Faith gives music holiness
Music suffers holy bliss.

Music resurrects each morn
As a sparrow newly born
In the modes the Greeks did play
Or the Middle Ages say.

Plainsong, chants and masses sung
Music sings for every one
Who does listen with an ear
For the Saviour drawing near

Music is an inner song

Songs & Elegies, Mysteries and Others   Chapter Eight. 2003 – 2006

    Played in heartbeats sure along
    To the rhythms of my blood
    Christ is pulsing, Christ my God.

    Music sparkles in the stars
    Planets sing through open doors
    Sun and Moon and Jupiter
    Sing for me and sing for her!

    Music listen, hear her voice
    Now we gladden, do rejoice
    Christ is but a Babe in arms
    Of His Mother Mary charms.

    Music, frolic with delight
    With the angels in the night
    With the spirits of the dead
    I take with me into bed.

    Music, fondly, see how I
    Reach for Glory in the sky
    To attain one perfect note
    Hear my Tone; now hear afloat!

    Music, come and dwell by me
    In the Garden's Mystery
    I am singing softly, see
    Playing on my flute for thee

    Music, thou art special for
    All mankind forevermore
    For thy place is ever free
    Music played eternally.

    August 17, 2005
    Revised January 16, 2013

Chapter Eight. 2003 – 2006   Magic of the Stars, Love & Lyricism,

Johnny George

Foggy day back in June
Played his drums out of tune
Was a lad, soldier too
Wore a shirt and one shoe

Johnny George was his name
Planted fields, hunted game
Sowed the wheat, fed the sows
Kneaded bread, milked the cows.

Johnny George help me be
Good as oats, barley tea
Mend the fence, clean the room
With a rag and a broom

Johnny George smile at me
I'm as weathered as can be
I've been lost out at sea
Now I'm tired, would be free.

Must go on, sailor's lot
Now in port, find my spot
Write my verse quietly
Peasantry poetry

Johnny George, where's your shoe?
Why are you, why are you
O so poor, work so hard
For a farthing and a yard?

Johnny George tell me now
Soiled shirt, sweaty brow
What's this life meant to be?
Plow the fields modestly.

Farmer's lot, swarthy boys
Country lasses, country joys

Summers hot, cool nights
Starry worlds bring delights.

Johnny George be so good
With the cows, in the wood
Help me see life once more
Poetry's earthly lore.

August 23, 2005

A Boy – A Poem Dedicated to Virginia Sease

A boy is a treasure; a boy is a joy
His world is playing; he plays with a toy
His toy is a question whose answer is love
That God keeps repeating to him from above.

A boy is a simple and trusting remark
He walks through the meadows; he walks through the park
He talks to the sparrows; he dances with joy
He splashes in waters for he is a boy.

A boy is a wonder and God loves him well
For he is a good boy who loves God to tell
His prayers and his troubles, his verses and plays
His stories, adventures each morning, each day

A boy is so little; he writes with his hands
In beautiful letters that all understand
His words are all simple yet meaningful, too
He's writing good letters; he's writing to you.

A boy is a picture that speaks and that sings
His picture is color and wonderful things
If you know the meaning the boy paints with love
Then you are most lucky the boy thinking of.

A boy is a world of trials and winds
Adventure's his weather; his friendship he lends

Chapter Eight. 2003 – 2006   Magic of the Stars, Love & Lyricism,

The people are stories; the mountains are books
Now read in the forests the faeries and cooks.

The boy plays with people, the faerie-folk who
Dance circles of magic and sparkle love, too
He wishes for glory a man to become
But he is a little boy—, and some then some!

A boy is a sparrow who flies in the trees
He eats from the flowers and prays on his knees
He knows in the evening to rest his small head
Each night he retires, retires to bed.

A boy chases rainbows; he loves the clear rain
That cools off his forehead and soothes all his pain
He loves the clear sunshine and then in the night
He joins with the Saviour in starry delight.

Remember this story of color and song
A boy in adventures who carries along
In his knapsack his playthings, in his heart all his joy
For he is a happy, a happy small boy.

August 21, 2005

Good Sevenfold Man!

Sevenfold Man, who art thou? we ask
What is thy nature and what is thy task?

Warmth is the body, the body of Man
In walking and willing he goes on the land.

Pure is the heart of the virgin, of she
Who chaste is untouched by the winds and the sea.

Beautiful is the true soul of she
Who shines with the Light of the Saviour, of He.

Stable the I of the hand who does lend
In helping his brother the love that he tends

Sound is the genius, the Name of the man
Who knowing himself knows to right understand.

Lovely the Kingdom of she who sustains
The love of the Lord of the fair, He remains.

Good is the Will of the man who extends
His hand in dear friendship, his service intends.

Sevenfold Man, thou art noble and good
Truly art fair, have we thee understood!

August 25, 2005

Where Are the Olden Days?

Where are the olden days when life was real
Life to imagine, the life you could feel?
When bread freshly baked greeted sunrise and air
And horses took women and men everywhere?

Where went the times when the family dwelled
In the love of fair harmony, in wisdom that held
Sagas and myths and the fairy tales rich
When the children still played while their grandmothers stitched?

Where are those centuries of long ago
When meaning still stood on the rocks down below?
When mountains were worshipped that led to the sky
Of evening sunsets when God was felt nigh?

Now life is all either plastic and clean
A metallic, computerized, urbanized scene
Or grimy and filthy, infested, diseased

Chapter Eight. 2003 – 2006   Magic of the Stars, Love & Lyricism,

A life that unworthy of men's human needs.

Where are those days that were homey and warm
That welcomed the children, the babes newly born?
That cared for the elderly, nurtured the youth
Sustaining adults with tradition and truth?

O where, my good friend, went the days, days of yore
When legends were lived, life was rich with folklore?
When pear-blossoms colored the gardens like dreams
And the searching of souls human beauty redeemed?

Yet every day the Sun reminds me
That God is the Father, Creator is He
Whenever the crow caws, honeybees I do see
The air of the dawn, something happens to me

And though life differs our post-modernity
I know Christ is with us; I know He's with me.

August 26, 2005
Edited December 31, 2012
January 16, 2013

Verses

A verse is living fables; a verse is living dreams
A verse basks in the sunshine of warm and radiant beams
A verse tells something stories in rhythmic, pulsing rhyme
Poetic songs are singing in sacredness of time.

A poem is the mystery of music and the night
A poem is the glory of resurrection's light
A poem is the darling of dainty, dear delights
A poem dwells in darkness emerging sunny bright.

September 13, 2005

Morning

See, emerging now a clear
Sunny morning, clouds appear
Dewdrops glisten, birds do sing
Daytime 'wakens happening.

All the mysteries of night
Disappear before our sight
The regality of light
Us refreshes with delights,

With delights of newborn mirth
Sun and heaven's radiant birth
If you answer what I know
Then my questions living flow

In the stream of limpid pools
Like some kingly after-jewel
On the crown of Lordship's Throne
He is heaven, He alone.

God is born each morning new
With His love ourselves imbue
Step in time, all things in view
This is music; this is true.

September 14, 2005

To Nature

Nature – I love thee dearly
Sweeter than the harmony
Of human voices in the throng
Of human struggles I belong.

Nature – I love thee, see
Thou are the sweet honey
Of drops of dew and flowers' blush
Your roses red do make me hush.

Chapter Eight. 2003 – 2006   Magic of the Stars, Love & Lyricism,

Nature – I love thee, how
My love for thee is on my brow
I swoon in all thy beauties rare
Thy beauty is beyond compare.

November 15, 2005

Morning Sun

Morning sun whose lucid light
Is salvation to our sight
Rays redemptive, rays aright
Bringing brilliance, blazing bright

Loving light doth stream from thee
Earthwards from the heavens be
Joy and love we send to thee
Heavenwards now thankfully.

September 17, 2005

Triumph

A triumph was a bird, you know
I flew the heavens, to and fro
And from above to down below
The love of life did feel and flow.

Yes, triumph is a gladsome thing
How glad triumphant songs do sing
And all the little birds on wing
Do frolic on the breeze they bring.

Now Nature, marry me today
As I go my merry way
And all the birds do sentient play
This fine September holiday.

September 17, 2005

Peace (2)

Peace is a thought and a white turtle dove
A snowflake in winter and white heavenly love
Peace is the stars and the moon up above
I'm dreaming of peace; I'm dreaming peace of.

Peace is a silhouette seen in the night
After the dusk and the shadows' twilight
Peace is the hallowed and magical light
Of Mary and Child, of Christmas' delight

Peace is the dream of the pools of deep
The semblance of day and reality's sleep
Peace is the breath of the chilly winds blow
They blow on my forehead in peace, this I know.

Peace is the quietude, prayer and a song
Peace is the tempo me carry along
Peace is the billowing clouds of Christ-white
Peace is my soul and my warm, sunny sight.

Peace is the morning before the new day
Before the new Light and the sunrise do say
Peace is the dawn's early song, this I pray
Peace is an eloquent, queen's holiday.

Peace is the mind on the Thought of the God
Who grants men the peace of His Son and the Word
Peace is the Life after death beyond earth
Peace is the Land of death's Spiritual birth.

September 18, 2005

Autumn

Birds on a morning at dawn in the air
Early is autumn and crisp everywhere
Cool our company, grey is our song
Stillness is reigning all peaceful along

Chapter Eight. 2003 – 2006   Magic of the Stars, Love & Lyricism,

Birds in the distance do sing to the Light
The sun is increasing; the day will be bright
And now all the birds, they are singing with joy
Their music is cheerful, as cheerful as boys

O when will the autumn become holy night?
And when will our Christmas sing songs of delight?
O walk to the Saviour, the Child and His Birth
Then we will celebrate Christmas with mirth

Until Christmas holy we walk bravely through
The autumn winds blowing, the rains falling too
The Light is now clearer and keener our thoughts
St. Michael He leads us with courage He's brought

Now follow Him going the Way of the Word
And listen to music, the music of birds
Then with the autumn shall we Christmas find
The Saviour of children, of all of mankind

Thoughts resurrected are beauty-light clear
Radiant and pulsing throughout the whole year
Warm are the thoughts of St. Michael so near
Heart-thoughts, the good thoughts; see, autumn is here!

September 23, 2005

Sun of Evening

Sun of evening, Sun of heart
Every morning fresh you start
Make your pulsing coursing way
Through each brilliant living day

Die the sunsets in pure love
Glowing colors heavens above
Enter secret into night
Everlasting dear delight

Sun I send my love to you
Radiant in the heavenly blue
Day is closing, thankful I
Do retire now from the sky

To asleep join worlds afar
Spirit-Worlds of sparkling stars
There with Sun of Night I find
The refreshment of mankind

On the morrow celebrate
Sun's rebirth of day-estate
Sun so precious art to me
Clear and warm in harmony
Counter-orb of love becomes
Disc of heavens, disc of Sun!

September 24, 2005

Peace is a Tree!

Peace is a tree, is a tree, is a tree!
I saw her in winter, in winter to me!
I saw her in springtime all sprouting in green
I saw her in summer, a heart-warming scene

I saw her in autumn, her colorful leaves
Kept dying and falling to earth in the eves
I saw my own peace, my dear tree far away
She drifted to sea as she went on her way

And now do I stand like a man on the land
Barren of tree with his peace in his hand
For his tree went away, went away to the sea
And left only pictures of seasonal trees

And left only pictures of trees in the sky
These pictures are clouds and they motion and sigh
These pictures of trees are fair clouds I release

Chapter Eight. 2003 – 2006   Magic of the Stars, Love & Lyricism,

The clouds of the heavens, the heavens of peace

I hold my dear clouds in my hands in the air
And picture my tree as a maiden so fair
She comes to me dreaming with long, golden hair
My tree is now dreaming my soul everywhere.

November 26, 2005

Prophecy

Somnambulant, o drowsy day!
O do not sleep your day away
And all the things that you might say
Do beckon backward holidays.

If any other omen old
My future life sealed and foretold
Then in the past could there be read
The moment when I would be dead

But death is such a mystery
And dying process prophecy
That only sudden certainly
Christ doth know as all things see.

We are but the men of earth
We witness here our human birth
While death invisibly transpires
Transporting souls above church spires.

So let the prophets spread their truths
They know not whence their words ensue
Yet truly speak they under oath
For Christ hath blessed them mystics both.

And what they speak does come to pass
Nor can else happen, requiem mass
Is only heard in churches held

The soul has fled its body-shell.

So pardon me if I've revealed
That hidden things to death must yield
Becoming spiritual anon
The physical is left and gone.

Until that pure and absolute
Day and time most resolute
We may our tasks well carry out
Our daily work make hay about.

Nor can our freedom otherwise
Alter our course for he who dies
But only daytime satisfies
Realities unseen belies.

September 29, 2005

The Rose – To Virginia Sease

An elegant rose
Verily goes
Rosy-red pose
Fragrance-pure nose

Noble and fair
Beauty repair
Fondness is there
Dear everywhere.

Virginia, thou rose
Transcending all foes
Transforming through grace
In dignity's face

Serving the Lord
The Christ, the pure Word
Virginia, the Rose

Chapter Eight. 2003 – 2006   Magic of the Stars, Love & Lyricism,

Christ, cheer my woes.

Virginia, my friend
The way to the end
Beginning soon comes
Until then the Sun

The Sun and the Rose
Virginia, she knows
Nobility, queen
The castle, the scene

The palace, the air
The sunlight so fair
The gardens of sight
The rose of delight

Virginia, the Rose
She goes and she knows
Deep insight her way
Each night and each day

The Rose and the Light
The Heart radiant bright
The Warmth and the Christ
The sunsets the West

Eternity's night
Replenish the Light
Virginia, thou rose
In stillness of pose.

Los Angeles
October 7, 2005

I Know in Me Myself Dwells Christ

Within my I indwelling might
There streams, unites in strength of light

Songs & Elegies, Mysteries and Others   Chapter Eight. 2003 – 2006

The heart takes in the feelings of
Courageous, bold and holding love

I know myself; I am the one
Who gathers forces, Christ the Sun
He gives to me the powers I
May focus there in pulling try

And do achieve myself I know
In friendship and Communion's flow
My brother-Christ and I do sup
We break the Bread and drink the Cup.

And then renewed do I then go
My thoughtful way I thereby know
There has transpired the sacred act
Consecration's human fact.

October 18, 2005

Michaélic Thoughts

Mighty Christ
Sun behold
Autumn leaf
Birds on wing
Blowing breeze

Rains do fall
Dying earth
Courageous heart
Walk to birth
Michaél.

October 18, 2005

Deeds of the Light

Light of my pain; light of my joy
I am your child; I am your boy
Child do I see worlds before

Chapter Eight. 2003 – 2006   Magic of the Stars, Love & Lyricism,

Worlds of light's glad company
Colors so rich, colors so dear
Colors I see throughout the whole year
Colors of light's deeds that I see
The meaning the darkness' encounter for me

The meaning of pain, the meaning of joy
I play in the colors of one little boy
I play in their dance as a boy with his toy
The colors I see and also enjoy

The colors I feel in my heart's inner song
Carry my pain clearly along
Clearly on deeds of the Light every day
Suffering now I go on my way.

October 22, 2005

Stimmen

Höret!
Die Stimmen der Kinder
Die Kinder die spielen
Die Kinder die lachen und meinen
Ihr Spiel sei Arbeit
Und Traum sei Wirklichkeit

Höret!
Die Stimmen der Dichter
Die Dichter die träumen
Die Dichter die dichten und meinen
Ihr Träumen ist wirklich
Denn sie singen ihr' Träume
In der Wirklichkeit

Höret!
Die Stimmen der Greisen
Die Greisen die sich besinnen
Die Greisen die fühlen und meinen
Ihr' Träume vergangen

Seien gegenwärtig
Denn die Zeit wird für sie ewig
Wird einfach Stimmung

Höret!
Die Stimmen der Kinder
Der Dichter, der Greisen
Klingen auf ewig
Werden Träume und Stimmung
In der Wirklichkeit.

3./4. Dezember 2005

Songs of Love and Romance –
Inspired from a Watercolor by Don Perryman

Immersion

Saturn, crown of memory
Passion born before the sea
Before the Sun, the Moon, the Earth
Saturn was the very birth.
Cosmic memory, now hide
Your secrets inwardly and guide
My body into mysteries
Of warmth indwelling rhythmically.

1. Trace

Moon become my mirror and be
The motion motionless white sea
The foam of life, the Soul of Moon
Now play, fair Moon, now play your tune.

And like a marble statuesque
Reminds me of a nymph burlesque
Whose sexuality is young
Like sepals sprouting tender sung.

Chapter Eight. 2003 – 2006   Magic of the Stars, Love & Lyricism,

2. Love

Venus, Goddess pure and dear
Your charm is grace of Mary near
The holy Night becomes your face
The Child, the Christ, of faerie race.

Yes, Jesu born to save mankind
In mysteries of heart and mind
Quite magical, the bosom of
Maria holds Him, dreaming of.

3. The Colors

Blue of Advent, deep, demure
Warmth of Saturn to endure
The final hours before the birth
The Child, the Saviour's holy mirth

White, the Color of the Moon
The Moon of silver-white in June
See her gaze attracts the beasts
Their sensuality released.

Purple Venus faerie-queen
Jesu-Infant, He has been
And is eternal song of love
The Child keeps dreaming, dreaming of.

4. The Night Sky

Now Saturn-blue, now Moon of white
Now Venus-purple Aphrodite
The moment of eternity
Has acquiesced above the sea

Look up and see both Saturn's glow
And Moon now full in brightness' show
But Venus twinkles shimmering

In magic mystical healing.

5. The Romance

These three planets paint the Night
The Moon shines through the dark in white
The background is deep Saturn's blue
But Venus is of purple hue.

And if you measure me a glance
Then shall you offer me this dance
Just take this momentary chance
For this shall be your last romance.

December 10, 2005

Women and Men

Women are a dream of love
Men are thinking, thinking of
Men are coats of black and white
Women colors of delight

Women seem to love and lure
All the men at sea for sure
Men remind me of the ships
Sailing to the maidens' hips

For to kiss them on the lips
As they toss and turn and dip
Men are sailors of the blue
Women are their mermaids true

Women are the gorgeous breasts
Men do come their heads to rest
Men are sinew, muscle, will
Women are the cups they fill

Women are the flavors of

Chapter Eight. 2003 – 2006 Magic of the Stars, Love & Lyricism,

Fragrances and scents of love
Men are travelers and hands
Working on the farming lands

Women are the torsos of
Soft and effervescent love
Men are tables, wooden chairs
Forests in the mountain air

Women are the moonlit seas
Men the triumphs of the trees
Women are the dreams of men
Men the handshake once again

Men are willing at their best
Women, women, feel the rest
Men are struggling, men are strong
Women are the pure birdsong

Women are the childbirth
Women are the holy mirth
Men are witnesses to life
Man take woman as your wife

Wed her, bed her, tend to her
Woman care this husband your
Be now lovers, couples and
Partners founded on the land.

December 11, 2005

The Holy Child

There will be a lovely morning
After night's deep mystery
There will be the dawn of Glory
And the Christ arise then free
In the air He shall ascending
Like a lark in gladsome song
He is music of the springtime;

He is Life of Nature strong.

But before the dawn of Glory
And before the Easter morn
Christ is Jesu, Infant lowly;
He is Christmas newly born
He is holy Child of wonder;
He is Son of God and Man
He is Christ Himself in Kingship;
He is Shepherd of the Land.

Now begins to shine within us
In our hearts the Mystery
Of the holy Nights of wonder
In our inner company
We do sense Him in the darkness;
His great Light begins to shine
Our dear Sun of winter beaming,
Our dear Saviour-God Divine.

Now do sleep, my Child, in peace and
Dream of things most sweet and fond
In the love of Mary gentle,
To her love do you respond
See, you smile in tender greeting,
Jesu Christ, the Child Who dreams
In the peace of heaven bringing us
Your warm and radiant beams.

December 23, 2005

Nachtgesang

Einst meinte ich das Leben wäre
Um so besser ohne Hindernisse
Dann aber aus meiner Arbeit gebäre
Der Dichter kleine Gedichtenüße

Einst wollte ich ja immer ernster
Damit ich die Tiefen erobere

Chapter Eight. 2003 – 2006   Magic of the Stars, Love & Lyricism,

Fand aber da nur Schattengespenster
Wollte schmecken süße Beeren

Einst tanzte ich mit Lust die Felder hindurch
Als die Sonne mir zulächelte ganz froh
Nun fang ich an in einem dunklen Loch
Hineinzufallen wie 'ne kranke Kuh

Die Tage werden alt und grau und düster
Die Nächte zeigen mir ihre Schätze reich
Ich verweile in ihren Sternenlichter
So daß die Gedanken werden mild und weich.

Morgens aber muß ich wieder Sachen
Handeln und schwere Prüfungen durchstehen
Gerne würde ich an alles fröhlich lachen
Muß aber mühsam immer weiter gehen

Hart wird das Leben mir wie Spitzennägel
Die in meinem Kopfe täglich gehammert werden
Ohne Sinn ich spüre sie wie Regeln
Unveränderliche Marmorsteingebärden.

Umsonst sind alle meine Bemühungen
Nach sonnigen Träumen oder Blumen
Weggegangen sind die goldne Schmetterlinge
Die Blütenkelchen und die junge Damen.

Die Welt wird arm und schattenhaft und lahm
Wie ein Bettler oder eine Greise ist mein Fuß
Der schmerzhaft jeden Schritt mir nahm
Und damit den warmen Bruderkuß.

Nur Eines ist mir noch geblieben
Damit ich weiter kann und will
Meine Freunde und die Mutter lieben
Mich und machen mich dann still.

Denn ohne Liebe kann man nichts und nimmer

Songs & Elegies, Mysteries and Others   Chapter Eight. 2003 – 2006

Geht das Leben ohne Liebe weiter
Ich dichte friedevoll in meinem Zimmer
Die Liebe macht mich inniglich und heiter.

Los Angeles
7./8. Januar 2006

The Newspaper and the Crown

Soaked and torn up – the newspaper
(whose pressed, black, inked letters
had already run unreadable in the cold, muddy rain)
Lay with a ticking, broken clock in the dumpster
Undisturbed by the rats who looked there for
food and shelter.

– What was that beneath the wet newspaper?
Dear, of gold
Sparkling with diamonds
A king's, a prince's, and magician's crown!
Inscribed in its radiant rim the letters:

LIFE OF CHRIST
IN GLORY HE RISES
INVINCIBLE SUN
DEATH CONQUERED FOREVERMORE
IT IS HERE WRITTEN
IN ETERNITY DIVINE

Now the dead, mechanical clock has stopped ticking
Now the HEART gives ITS RHYTHM
For LIFE has entered the picture
And LIFE ETERNAL CHANGES THE WORLD.

Like that rich crown He is lying in the Tomb (the dumpster).
The Grave is our cities (the broken clock).
The Grave is our sins (the newspaper).
The Grave is our hypocrisy (the letters).
The Grave is our lies (the running ink).
But CHRIST IS RISING (the crown).

Chapter Eight. 2003 – 2006   Magic of the Stars, Love & Lyricism,

The Future has begun.
He has appeared.
He does appear.
He shall continue to appear.
Some 5,000 years.

And CHRIST SHALL REIGN FOREVERMORE.

His Crown upraised.
His own taken up.
The Apocalypse has entered.

And CHRIST IS SORTING HIS PEOPLE FROM THE REST.
Some 5,000 years.

Let the newspapers be printed.
Let the rains fall.
Let the rats infest.

THE SUN IS RISING.
The Crown is untouched.
The Crown is eternal.
The Crown shall reign forevermore.
For CHRIST HAS CONQUERED THE WORLD.

February 15, 2006

Human Beings Change

Human beings experience things
Thinking, feeling, willing, loving, suffering,
Dying, death and resurrection experiences
Human beings change.

The external, emptying ones experience nothing, never change.
They have nothing to say, ever repeat the same misinformation
They are people machines, devoid of heart and soul.
Their cold, heartless, monotonous voices hypnotizing
They gaze out emptily in a blinding, black stare
Ever putting on an outer act, mocking, artless, nothing
For they are without value – devaluing

Lies, thieves, seducers, destroyers
The false ones are imitations, external, soulless.

Human beings are the artists of themselves
The master-builders, the re-creators, the co-Creators
The remembering, slow, cautious, aware, warmth-exuding, pictorial
The harmonious feeling, thought-ethical, disciplined knowers, aural
The mirroring, fun-loving, fine, fair lovers, poets, philosophers
The sweet, strong, struggling, incarnating, agitating, gestural
The discerning, present, inward, wise thinkers, romantics
The loving, virtuous, pure, blameless, imaginative, architectural
The healing & weaving, intuitive, ingenius, logical, tactile ones

Those who are living, suffering, dying and becoming
Ever change.
Human beings go through changes
In the process of becoming
Something they never were before.
Human beings are the special beings of the earth.

Pay attention to them.
Work with them.
Follow their progress with active interest.
Love them.
Help them
If they will progress;

Serve the human beings in which indwells the divine
For they are your brothers and sisters
They are human in a dehuman world
The children of Christ Jesus in heaven
Dear to Him and dear to us.

February 19, 2006

In the Woods

In the woods
Time stood still
Solemn, the trees
In the shadows' will

Chapter Eight. 2003 – 2006   Magic of the Stars, Love & Lyricism,

Under branches' hoods
Cold dark on knees.

But I stood up and
I walked in rhythm's step
A soldier marching to day
I knew the birds wept
Overshadowed in this land
Still I made my way.

But the woods remain
Yet unchanged
Nor time finds there a home
All is deranged
The trees stand, insane
While I write this poem.

Christ's Call

The stars came out
The night was bright
And Venus fair
She shimmered there
In her twinkling light

I dream tonight
Even now before I sleep
I wonder at the stars
At worlds afar
At the deep.

And when in tiredness
Asleep I fall
Into eternity
Divine reverie
I'll hear Christ's call.

February 20, 2006

Language

Language –
forms of paintings
carousels of horses prancing, galloping
trotting, walking, standing
color-horses kneeling in prayer to Mars
God of War and Sowing Seeds

Language –
the farmer's labor
the farmer's implement to hoe the gardens of love
the stall-boy's brush to comb the horses
who plough the fields of fate and fortune.

Language –
the harvest of golden wheat in the windy vowels
between the consonantal rocks against which the rains pelt
the whole grains of words ripening in the might of the sun
in the fields of lips and teeth and tongue.

Language –
the grain sown in the human heart
in the fields of earth in early spring
sprouting with word-power in the breath-warmed air
sculpting space like the hand with sledge hammer and chisel
carves the alabasters of summer into forms as varied as:

orphans and beggars
poets, lovers and lunatics
rustics and countrymen
peasants, farmers and foot-soldiers
marquises, counts and earls
lords, barons and dukes
martyrs and mystics
princesses.

maidens and trades people
doctors, damsels and knights
clergymen and clerics

Chapter Eight. 2003 – 2006   Magic of the Stars, Love & Lyricism,

friars and monks
educators, scholars and saints
kings.

Language –
when gesture-movements cease speaking
and the art of speech breaks through the mirrors of silence
shattering them into pieces
so that the common man sees the colors of Creation
afire.

Language –
the discovery of iron
the smelting of the metals
the blacksmith's anvil
the furnace' fire.

Language – speak against the winds
like bonfires burning black witches
casting out their spells into the ditches
freeing the people from their charms.

Language –
I know your lips
your bursting sun-power
parting the dark rain clouds
that men again see the sun-drenched day
of love, light and color.

Language – the palette of words
I paint reality with my lips
with the flame-brush of word-fire
the reality of the clays of earth
on which men walk and work each day.

Language –
through you the Souls of the Peoples
pronounce their inner selves to the World at Large.

Language –
the medium of poets and priests
peasants and philosophers
soldiers and statesmen
blacksmiths and brothers
Christians and crucibles
Popes and peoples everywhere.

Language – you are my word
Spoken with fanfare and fire
For the freedom of Man.

March 4-5, 2006

Inner Spaces Changing Blue

Inner spaces changing blue
In an inner spatial hue
Permeate me through and through
Melancholy does ensue

Now I breathe the breath of green
All the places I have been
Do remind me of serene
Inner grazing pastures scene

In a land whose wonders of
Holy, gentle beauty-love
Peace is like a turtledove
Soft descending from above

Now do acquiesce and be
In the silences of me
Like an inner melody
Singing sweetly inwardly.

March 7, 2006

Chapter Eight. 2003 – 2006   Magic of the Stars, Love & Lyricism,

Christ in Peach-Clouds

Peach-clouds of Christ at sunset
Glory and awe me fills
See in the heavens above hamlets
Wonders above the hills

See in the colors of sunset
The Passion and Death of He
Who is our Lord and Summit
Our karma and destiny

Christ in the clouds now pinkish
And in the blush of red
Beauteous His love for us
Sense Him in colors clad.

Sense we our Christ at sunset
There in the clouds of air
There in the colors' palette
He suffers with beauty rare.

March 12, 2006

Gründonnerstag

Christus – warum?
Warum, jedes Jahr
Musst Du leiden und sterben
In uns den Tod erleben?
In uns in der Unterwelt Menschenseelen –
Sünder helfen –

ICH WEIß ES SCHON
DU BIST ROT UND GRÜN
HIMMEL AUF ERDEN
GOTT WURDE MENSCH.

DU, O CHRISTUS
MUSSTEST DEN SCHWARZEN TOD KENNEN

DU, O CHRISTUS
STARBST, EIN MENSCH
UND DURCH DEINEN TOD
IST EIN GROßES WUNDER GESCHEHEN
DIE WIEDERGEBURT
DAS AUFERSTEHEN.

13. April 2006

Zwei April Nachostern Sonnenuntergang Gedichte

1. Die Möven

Sonnenuntergang
Stimmung Christi
Rötlich gefärbt
Mut und Liebe

Siehe:
Christus stirbt für dich
Für dich, du Mensch
Mit gutem Willen
Und die ewigen Möven
Fliegend, gehend und stehend
– Freiheit und Schicksal des Menschen
Sind die Möven
Beim Sonnenuntergang
Christi.

2. Ein Mövenlied

Möve – siehe, du fliegst
Die Freiheit kannst du 'langen
Möve – siehe, du stehst
Das Schicksal magst du tragen

Du bist nicht dieser Welt
Der Himmel dein zu Hause
Doch findest du dein Brot
Hier unten auf dem Strande

Chapter Eight. 2003 – 2006   Magic of the Stars, Love & Lyricism,

Wie schreist du so vor Hunger
Ernährst dich für die Reise
Dann schwingst dich plötzlich auf
Nach deiner nächtlich' Weise.

Der Mittwoch nach Ostersonntag
28. April 2006

The Daisies

In the histories of silences grow the daisies
The daisies we see in the heavens in the stars
The stars that sparkle in the night
Singing songs of light to the children
Who play among the silences of the daisies
In the summery sun

In the histories of antiquity
The Gracchi brothers' eloquent discourse argued
The plight of the slaves before Caesar
Caesar who turned a deaf ear and conquered distant lands
Distant lands where daisies grew in silences
For the Roman Empire in antiquity

In the histories of forests stand the oaks
The oaks that gathered mistletoe and wisdom
Wisdom for the druids who kept company
With the Moon and the stars of the night
Before the daisies appeared to the children
The children who play the future
In the silences of tomorrow

In the daisies dance the image of the face of God
The face of God Who smiles in the daisies
In the daisies that dot the meadows of love
The meadows of the love of the children
In the histories of song.

May 2/3, 2006

May Song

Do you remember once was yesterday?
O such was life the sweetest holiday
The years of childhood fled as in a dream
Like cooling, clear, refreshing water's stream.

Do you know today, or is it silk
Surrounding neck and shoulder, creamy milk?
Is it an uncle visiting the farm
A countrywoman, or a lady's charm?

Do you foresee tomorrow with an eye
In visionary truth, not blinding sky
Of deepest blue as dark as sullen seas?
The future bodes return of memories.

Do you not fathom mystery or white
The fate or fortune of forgotten sight?
Tomorrow's an unborn child whose Mother grieves
The present womb, and yesterday relieves.

Do you believe in destiny this day
Or does your freedom gaily hold its sway
In flight, a bird of light and feathered wing
The freedom every poet happ'ly sings?

Do you feel the weight of karma come
The burden that pronounces day is done?
Or do you know to find elixir of
Pure gold, whose destined freedom joins with love?

Do you sense the love of gentle night
Mysticism's darkness and delight?
O welcome in the summer Christmas deep
Remember in the heat the holy sleep.

Do you love the lilting dance of spring
Where children play at work of mothering

Chapter Eight. 2003 – 2006   Magic of the Stars, Love & Lyricism,

While parents borrow time from tasks each day
To celebrate the bountiful month May?

Thus ended this small verse or poem told
Before the truth of beauty agéd old
For youth is poetry and music's song
And every man to music does belong.

And every man reminds us was a child
His childhood lived in days of wonder mild
And fortunate, he roamed the meadows clear
A deer which wandered from the forest near

And childhood is a song sung by the birds
Before the human being spoke a word
For children love the animals of soul
The world for them remains one picture whole.

May 4, 2006

Love Was All He Vowed

Simply said – the breeze
In movements on my knees
My hair caught up among
The dances of a fawn
Within a forest of
Deep green and wildest love

Therein the faeries play
My thoughts in disarray
Belonging to the day
Of sudden silkworm say

Now utter nothing more
Than words begotten store
Then shall you poetry
Well borrow plaintively.

Because the poet strives
To measure number fives
His stars are mysteries
Above the stormy seas

And yesterday was told
Forgotten coins of old
The treasures spent on things
As silly playing rings

Today I asked him why
He did but once reply
"You've left behind the years
Of laughter and of tears"

Tomorrow is a glance
A festive hall perchance
Where maidens courtly dance
And suitors suit romance.

But I knew everything
The joys and suffering
My life was rich as gold
My story has been told.

Now bless this piece of bread
With smearing butter fed
To appetites as weighed
As heavy accolade

And time's a garland gay
And flowers a bouquet
And music is a song
But poetry is strong.

But poetry does sing
Her gifts in offering
Upon the altar of
Divinities of love

Chapter Eight. 2003 – 2006   Magic of the Stars, Love & Lyricism,

Yes poetry is lore
And legends mark for more
Each fairy tale is good
Would that each human could

Yes poetry is song
And effervescence long
But after time's affair
Will drift on sorrow's care

A grief unknown to them
Whose childhoods are a gem
They know not manhood's pay
Another future day

For the poet now
The future's anyhow
He toils and he turns
A final sunset earns.

He would announce this year
And make it very clear
But then a little leaf
Blows from the tree belief

And this he marks in words
Unknown to little birds
For poetry is man
And only poets can.

Remember he transpired
His sources he acquired
And then he spilled his wealth
In poems stolen stealth

He composed his songs
He noted what belongs
And left the rest to fate
Predestined for the date

But freedom is a thing
The man is sheltering
He shares it with a will
And pardons on the hill

He stands a troubadour
His songs entice, allure
Attentions of a queen
Her mercy he has seen.

She smiles most graciously
Upon the singer, see
Now surely you'll agree
He's in good company.

This is his final word
Now everyone has heard
Who listens to the bird
And wisdom has endured.

But all he will now say
Remains this holy day
"Love," he cries aloud
Love was all he vowed.

May 20, 2006

Transcendence—To Don Perryman

In the strength of harmonies
There laugh the faeries
There dance the little sprites
Suffer princesses delights.

In the powers of poetries
There muses she, Poesie's
Afternoon in solitudes
Transcendent in interludes

Chapter Eight. 2003 – 2006   Magic of the Stars, Love & Lyricism,

In the fires of languages
Mercy mine assuages
Every tree bears its fruit
Every kernel wears its suit.

In the tides of ocean songs
My mistress Nature belongs
We bear children there
Little poems without care

In the symphonies
Of joys and agonies
Collide enemies
Join hands autumn leaves.

There blow season winds
Mighty messages
Distances crossing sends
Courtiers passages.

If God heard the day
What would He then say?
"Come, child, into night
Join Me in the Light."

May 29, 2006

St. John's, Christmas

Every time the moment brings
Words a poet knows and sings
All the populace require
Music for their souls inspire

And the children differ not
For the songs the poet brought
Bring them joy and love this day
Answering the prayers they pray

So whenever you feel forlorn

Just remember Christ is born
Each and every night within
Sleeping, dreaming hearts again

And this mystery is fulfilled
Because of our God Who willed
That mankind new love might know
In the cool of nighttime so

Christmas happens every night
In the heat of summer's sight
Fall asleep once more in dreams
Of the sun in Christ's glad beams.

St. John's
June 24, 2006

Gardens

Easily the summer sings
Musically in offering
To the children of the sky
Always asking, asking why.

Then the spokesman for the faire
Complements the gardens there
With the hoe of love he shows
How the little flower grows.

For he works the earthen rows
And the plants he truly knows
They emerge, and blossoming
Dance like faeries in a ring.

If you would them represent
Tell the spokesman they you sent
You, the tidings of the flowers
Bring into the daytime hours.

St. John's
June 24, 2006

Chapter Eight. 2003 – 2006   Magic of the Stars, Love & Lyricism,

Kenelma

She walked. She smiled.
Her life was good, her measure mild.
Her smile was sweet, her heart as well.
Christ filled her soul, this I here tell.

Kenelma come, come speak to me.
I hear your voice. Your company
is gracious, kind, so thoughtful, warm,
as good as milk and love reborn.

Kenelma you are heart of gold;
your wisdom shines with light of old.
Your thoughts are clear, your tempo, feel,
is measured sure and all is real.

Reality stirs where you are.
In you Christ dwells and fear is far.
With you the sacred Heart of blood,
of Christ within is inmost Word.

I have no words, Kenelma good,
only my Christ you've understood.
For He is there where human souls
do feel and speak their inner goals.

My goal is not today or then.
Today is Christ, Kenelma tend.
Tend, yes you do, you're tending Christ,
in quiet ways, that troubles rest.

You're tending Christ, this do I feel.
And this is truth, and this is real.
The Christ is here; with you He comes.
He comes and sits for little ones.

I see Him in your heart and eyes.
Kenelma-Christ answer my why's.

Answer me you have done this day.
Christ has found me in your way.

Los Angeles
August 12, 2006

Suchet

Kinder spielen mit Augen
Lippen küssen und saugen
Tränen gießen und fallen
Lieder laufen und lallen

Wer das Leben verstehen
Der muß wandern und gehen
Heimat 'lassen und lernen
In den Weiten und Fernen.

Denn die Schule des Lebens
Bleibt zu Hause vergebens
Nur die Klassen der Jahre
Weisheit 'leihen, das Wahre

Suchet Menschen und Geister
Brüder, Lehrer und Meister
Findet Christus, der Wahre
Ziel, Bedeutung der Jahre.

14. August 2006

A Verse

Be good. Be still.
Be near God's Will.
Show quietly your scenic hill.
Your heart be warm,
good thoughts you fill
the fertile soil of love to till.

August 21, 2006

Chapter Eight. 2003 – 2006   Magic of the Stars, Love & Lyricism,

Imagination—For John

Clarity is light and beam
The way I see, imagine, dream
Is crystal clear, with thought as pure
As snow that melts into a stream

My thoughts then shine like memories
The skies are blue, the sunlight love
And children play as songs of birds
Who dance and sing on wings above

O when will life be holiness
A world transformed by princess' kiss?
O when will kings of saintly ways
Join martyrs of the faerie race

To finally establish here
Upon our earth so very dear
Jerusalem in new estate
And peace forever celebrate?

Yes clarity is love and light
The way I see is poetry
Is vision now of future come
Come quickly as the birds of song.

September 9/10, 2006

Love Is Like Water

Love is not solid like sinew or meat
Like wood or like stone, is not dense 'neath our feet
No, love is like water that moves as it goes
Love stirs in water which streams as it flows.

But love is still deep and profound like the sea
Like oceans is love, is Christ's love that it be
In currents of feeling, in depths felt within
The heart, there stirs love, understanding all men.

For love is like waters which deeply do run
Must penetrate into one's innermost sun
Love is there flowing as deep as the stars
In heavenly oceans 'tween Venus and Mars

Love understands to converse in the flow
Of human hearts she allows us to go
To the place of the radiance of Sun she would be
Yet generous and giving abundance is she

Like fathomless waters is love's Mystery
So love is not solid, but love is the sea.

October 18, 2006

The Roses—For Virginia Sease

The roses blooming in a mood
My inner fragrance understood
When by my rosy mystery
I sought their gardens by the sea.

They turned and offered me their face
As by the fortune of God's grace
But only children did remain
Beyond the answering refrain

To every flower a bird did sing
Requiting love in offering
A single kiss of sweetness' bliss
And that was love and that was this

The roses of my heart well know
Who is the Queen of men to show
The people who make greenery
Among the gardens by the sea

Now smell their fragrant scent again
And live their summers numbered ten

Chapter Eight. 2003 – 2006   Magic of the Stars, Love & Lyricism,

For this today is wealthy kings
Who roses give with golden rings

While troubadours sing songs of white
Beneath the silver of moonlight
And faeries all the magic make
That every one consumes as cake.

But roses red remind me of
The sentient dreams of sunset love
Before the night unveils her face
The Mystery of Christ, His grace

To each and every human child
Who sleeps on Mary's lap so mild
For she is Queen of faeries and
The Mother of all of mankind

Red roses blossom graciously
Unfolding riddles by the sea
For all the world abundantly
But only chosen men do see

Beneath the Moon by night they find
In essences of germ-seed bind
But only in the golden Sun
The roses red find union

For every garden is the home
(Though many flowers there do roam)
To a rosebush green and red
And red the Sun creates a bed

And red are roses by the sea
The foothills do accompany
And in the distance beyond me
There rise the mountains loftily

And up above the Sun so grand

Does shine on earth and all the land
She Who is the inner rose
Of golden red of sure repose

Yes roses red of inner grace
Smile in greeting from the face
Of queens and kings of dignity
And such is our good company

Queens and kings are roses in
The gardens sprouting green again
But these roses red do tend
That all may see Christ did them send

Into the gardens by the sea
They grace the gardens graciously
And such are our good company
The roses red most beautifully.

October 27, 2006

The Sea

Intent, he walked like burrowed breasts
Upon the shores his head now rests
Before the unity of sea
Engulfed him, water's effigy

Before the windy gales besought
His tethered sails now distraught
He saw another ship, of gold
Shining with sun's wisdom old

He tried to sail up to this ship
The waters cold, he bit his lip
But just before he reached the ark
The waves him swallowed, plank and bark.

And now he sleeps beneath the waves

Chapter Eight. 2003 – 2006   Magic of the Stars, Love & Lyricism,

Among the other sunken graves
Of sailing ships that failed to
Arrive at sunsets' colored hue

That failed to rise up to the skies
Of golden-orange, where he dies
Who resurrects beyond the nights
Of copper-silver love-delights

Instead his bed is ocean-floors
His treasures-chest behind locked doors
Of rusting orange iron ores
Among the soldier's metaphors

For stalwart bragging sailors or
Peasant-farmers ancient lore
Or rustic countrymen before
Modernity the past ignore.

So sleep in silences the sea
Keeps reminding me, o me
Whenever I accompany
The sailors dreaming wistfully.

October 29, 2006

Dream—For Linda

Where clouds do ponder sunsets sweet
There my heart and soul do meet
With Nature's loveliness and scene
I join the animals and dream.

I dream of evenings fond and rare
The moments hover in the air
The clouds are large as canopy
Of pink and peach I love to see.

And here on earth below I stand
Aligned am I 'tween sky and land

A single poet and a man
Who senses wonders unseen, and

Who dreams a poem with a heart
His pictures feelings do impart
Into a mood prepares for nights
Of everlasting star-delights

And now the day begins to rest
The sun has sunken in love's nest
Beyond the distant hills of lore
My poetry lives evermore.

October 30, 2006

The Little Sparrows—To Margaret

A songbird trembled in small joys
That only Maytime now enjoys
But autumn blows in windy songs
November tidings him belongs.

The little sparrows look for crumbs
They want not in the chill that numbs
The beggars, homeless, and the bums
Who wander streets and hold their thumbs.

The little sparrows are of God
They love the earth without a word
Then fly above in air's delights
Until their dreams encompass nights.

The little sparrows give to me
The tiniest of company
And yet they borrow my heart's love
I gladly share in dreaming of.

The little sparrows know the times
Of cold and winds and ancient rhymes

Chapter Eight. 2003 – 2006   Magic of the Stars, Love & Lyricism,

And yet they have all that they need
They need not books or glasses read,

But only crumbs and plants and earth
And after winters spring's rebirth
They know to cherish smallest things
Far distant from the place of kings

They visit ev'ry Christmas He
Who is the Prince of children be
The Child, the Christ, the sparrow knows
The little sparrow sings His woes.

And then the Child, the Christ is born
And brings the sparrow, once forlorn
Good cheer in humblest, mean estate
The sparrow freedom from His fate

The Child, the Christ loves sparrows small
Indeed each time the sparrows call
To us in songs of sweetness' cheer
We hear our Christ is with us here.

The little sparrows are my joy
With them within am I a boy
Not middle-aged, nor worn with cares
But child again, and all-awares,

For in the song the sparrow makes
The poet in me fresh awakes
And I grow still in inmost joy
A poet and a man and boy

The little sparrows sing for me
God is in their company
And this is sparrow poetry
I sing this song for you and me.

November 12, 2006

The Vineyards—For Isolde

Somehow within the colorscape
Of hills and mountains vineyards' grape
A dreaming sunset found in song
The distances I did belong

And hovering among the vines
Small birds did fly near flowing wines
And one lone figure walked along
The path that led to his own song

For this lone man a poet was
His tread conversed in scenes because
His poetry loved greenery
And green was his own company

And such a poem did he write
The sunset's fire did ignite
His mood into the chords of love
Courageous he was dreaming of

The grape the vineyards hanging held
Became the fruit the sun of gold
Did ripen into poems of
Colors' scenery of love

The poet laid his thoughtful head
Upon the vineyard garden bed
And soon he dreamt in song and star
Beyond the hills and mountains far

The colors of the distant realm
Of sunset feeling at the helm
Began to drift like waters of
The oceans women bathing love

Indeed did Luna, Goddess Moon
Play her cool, enchanting tune

Chapter Eight. 2003 – 2006   Magic of the Stars, Love & Lyricism,

Before she stepped into the sea
Beyond the sunset's scenery

And all was night of Venus and
Of Moon and starry, faerie land
Luna fair enjoined along
Aphrodite's lovers' song

And night became the poetry
Behind the Moon, behind the sea
Where Venus and the stars did shine
Christ, the poet's purple sign

And so, you see, his dream's my own
Nor any poet is alone
Though none his song can duplicate
And he alone does celebrate

His scenery imagined there
Above in magic's faerie-air
Becomes a poem rarest rare
Beautiful beyond compare.

November 15, 2006

The Prince—For Don Perryman

One noble, clear and star-filled night
I dreamt of many cherubs bright
They gathered close to me and played
The sweetest music heaven made

In circles formed they dances of
Waltzes, symphonies and love
Became the festive atmosphere
That holy night of Christmas cheer

And soon the Child, a babe serene
Asleep appeared as in a dream

Songs & Elegies, Mysteries and Others   Chapter Eight. 2003 – 2006

His Mother was the faerie-queen
Maria blue of heaven's stream

The Infant, Christ, was smiling there
Wrapped in stars of music fair
His face was peace, His heart pure love
The Christ-Child's birth of Christmas of

And this was midnight hour on earth
Deep midwinter was the birth
Where snows of white did blanket hills
Farms and cities, windowsills

Within a barn Maria held
The holy Saviour of the world
And all was still, save breath of beasts
And songs of sparrows' breadcrumb feasts

But then did heaven bow to earth
Maria heard the angels' mirth
Resounding from above in praise
They sang to God, their voices raised.

And so were earth and heaven once
Jubilating celebrants
The birth of Jesu Christ with joy
They joined around this little boy

And this is Christmas every year
Just a baby did appear
Maria, Mother of mankind
She holds Him, as we may Him find

Within our hearts these Holy Nights
When choirs of angels sing delights
The animals in dreams so fond
Do gather 'round the faerie mound

For Jesu is the Prince of peace

Chapter Eight. 2003 – 2006   The Magic of the Stars/Other Themes

The Prince of heaven without cease
And princesses and princes are
The faerie race of men and star

So come ye brothers to the stall
Ye sisters hear the angels call
For God does send to us His Son
His Name is Jesu Christ, the Sun.

November 16/17, 2006

The Birth

In the great darkness of midwinter
In the surrounding cold of the long nights
The Christ—the Light of the World—is born
He is born in our hearts
That we be radiant and warmed
He is born in the Earth
That She becomes a sun
For all the Angels to see.

December 19, 2006
Los Angeles

CHAPTER NINE

2007 – 2008

CHRIST, NATURE, POET AND POETRY

Chapter Nine. 2007 – 2008 Christ, Nature, Poet and Poetry

Beauty Is Clouds, Sometimes

Beauty is clouds, sometimes
I always thought within my rhymes
Like steps I climb into the skies
The clouds, they answer all my whys

Beauty is sleep, sometimes
I dream in stars and hold my signs
My signs are love and understand
The meaning held within my hand

Beauty is hope, sometimes
I wonder with sincere-felt minds
Minds of thoughts as ancient moons
As tremulous nights in Junes

Beauty is death, sometimes
I feel my loved ones in my times
My times of thoughts, when Christ I feel
The only One to me is real

Beauty is depth, sometimes
I whispered in the ears of lines
Lines that plumb the caves of souls
In inwardness my will in goals

Beauty is far, sometimes
Farther still than vistas climbs
Ascending high to mountaintops
Beauty far in snow-peaked shops

Beauty is quest, sometimes
Quest and question asked in mimes
In silences the questioner
Longs for answers that endure

Beauty is fruit, sometimes
Peaches, pears and plums defines

Chapter Nine. 2007 – 2008 Christ, Nature, Poet and Poetry

The shape and color of the tastes
That swell in sunshine, juices pressed

Beauty is age, sometimes
Translucent faces, wrinkled lines
Clear and shining, colored eyes
Brown- or blue- or green-lit skies

Beauty is thought, sometimes
Living lucidly aligns
With the Light of truthfulness
Rejoicing ever with gladness

Beauty is peace, sometimes
Lakes extending surfaces
Blue and glistening sunlight
Deeper than the old twilight

Beauty is gone, sometimes
Beyond the day she disappears
To merge into the night afar
To linger where the Venus star

Beauty returns, sometimes
More beautiful now she shines
The first bounty season's wealth
Beauty is the harvest's health

Beauty is clear, sometimes
Radiant beams of true sun shines
Into my world of poetry
Beauty now belongs to me.

January 1, 2007

Sailors

May I mention memories
Down by the docks of mysteries

Chapter Nine. 2007 – 2008 Christ, Nature, Poet and Poetry

Where ships set sail into the seas
Of yonder future gallantries?

The sailors do remind me now
Of stalwart schoolboys anyhow
Who bragging of their foolish pranks
Do play with toys on puddle banks.

But then these men of wave and storm
These sailors brave who know alarm
When ocean swells endangering them
Their ships do batter like a ram

Are far from boys who dwell in dreams
Whose fantasies are warm sunbeams
For sailors know the meaning of
Threats of shipwreck without love

And yet they also dream somehow
And know to shelter Christ the now
Within their hearts untouched by all
The dangers life of sea withal

For every sailor carries in
His heart a boy all young and grin
And such are they who work at sea
Who toss and turn the Mystery.

January 10, 2007

Today Was Yesterday

Now once the father's fame
Did gather 'round the game
Outplayed one gloomy day
Of history today

But this was yesterday
Another year or May

Chapter Nine. 2007 – 2008 Christ, Nature, Poet and Poetry

Today then gone away
Like boats that left the bay

Today I see them play
My boats of fame all gay
All this- and that-a-way
Like cows who munch the hay.

The tourists come like flocks
Of geese of Goldie locks
To photograph my nose
That great in length see grows.

They now astonished or
In disbelief ignore
The fact that I'm not more
Than poet was before,

That now an actor plays
Their stage my holidays
Their eyes and ears amaze
I do appear their gaze.

But we were speaking then
How in the future when
Today is history
My fame forgotten be,

Or notoriety
Just left behind the sea
Or deep below beneath
The waves' white foamy wreath

Upon the bottom floor
I exited the door
Of ocean's legend lore
When I was iron's ore

Today I think thereof

Chapter Nine. 2007 – 2008 Christ, Nature, Poet and Poetry

A poet dreaming of
Remarkable because
Today at that time was.

January 11, 2007

Christ

I found my sun of red
Before the night the dead
Did pass eternally
A hidden mystery

My sun of red became
My inner Christ, Whose Name
Was spirit, warmth and love
Courage sun above

My feeling heart entreat
In suffering replete
With fear and pain each day
I mitigate the way

To sorrowful extremes
Imbued with Christ's warm beams
For sun is warm indeed
All this you may now read

And fall asleep at peace
Of mind within release
The cares and strains of day
Christ accompany.

January 16, 2007

Memories

My mind measures meaning, math and myth
My heart its rhythms I'm breathing with
My hand partakes of labor and farm

Chapter Nine. 2007 – 2008 Christ, Nature, Poet and Poetry

Inside I am safe from chill and charm.

For I know to cherish in memory
Places beyond this time can see
Places and people who, dear to me
Remind me: look back faithfully.

And there in time's treasure do I see
And feel the light of warmth to be
For even when cold surrounded me
In my heart I keep Christ inwardly.

January 18, 2007
Edited January 19, 2013

To the Questioning Scientist

O World of many, so many
So many instances of objects I
see and hear
taste and touch
smell and feel
Where is Thy Spirit singular?

Where do I find Thee, noble Spirit of All
in this innumerable field
of forest and fountain
pebble and people
plant and pleasing perceptions?

In this manifold World of
whim and wind
white winter and waves
where art Thou
Who weaves in all things?

O how I long to know so much
in the minute boxes of my study
where I place each little fact that I find

Chapter Nine. 2007 – 2008 Christ, Nature, Poet and Poetry

like the smallest moments of my mind.

In Thy only Essence
May I find Thee
In every individual thing made by
Thy Hands: Thy Beauty
In Thy Eyes: Thy Goodness
In Thy Mind: Thy Truth
O One Unity: God.

February 5, 2007

Congenial to the Wind

Congenial to the wind
Leaving the surfaces of laughter
For the silences
Of the solid, still things
Ponderous and pondering
The inner weight of things
Of the solid still things
Congenial to the wind
Which way he may blow.

February 13, 2007

Time Passes Broad Things

Time passes broad things
When, by itself
The courses of rivers meandering
Stretch across many places
Distances, like time, transpiring
Distant spaces
Time passes broad things.

February 13, 2007

Chapter Nine. 2007 – 2008 Christ, Nature, Poet and Poetry

What Is?

What is an enemy
But the renown to disagree
But the opinionated King
Of my nose?

What is a friend
But the sympathies of forget-me-nots
But the antiquated, agreeing Voters
Of the popular Populace?

And what is tomorrow
But eternal Time that transcends
Enemies and friends
But the lessons of the past
Become presence forever?

What do I really know
Or what do I truly think
If thinking is but friendliness
Or disappointment?

Or is thinking, perhaps
Something else altogether
Something I, seeing
Perceive in all clarity
The thoughts in eternity?

Woe be to him who lives by whim
Of all passing sympathies and antipathies
Before the Dawn of Truth
Pierces his once-blind soul with the Light of Thinking
Forever.

Awaken!

February 13, 2007

Chapter Nine. 2007 – 2008 Christ, Nature, Poet and Poetry

Earth

Earth her love to us she gives
Like a mother by her lives
Every infant at her breast
Fed by love's milk that it rest

We of earth are men who brave
Weather strife of life and save
All our dreams at sea in storm
For the land where we were born

For the mountains of the earth
Mother lode who gave us birth
We now thank thee for thy love
Body of the Christ is of.

She is good and fortress true
Beneath a canopy of blue
Does her life of green so wide
Stretch o'er hill and dale with pride.

Earth to us replenishment
From our toils which life has sent
Do we lay our heads to rest
On her bed of pastures blessed.

Mother, Mother Earth, take me
Hold me in thy greenery
Thou of Nature's love beneath
Heaven do we find the heath.

Home our respite is before
Death does open heaven's door
To eternal life and home
Cosmic highways spirits roam.

But before Christ welcomes us
Across the threshold Inwardness

Chapter Nine. 2007 – 2008 Christ, Nature, Poet and Poetry

We find help our earth bestow
On all things temporal grow.

We, like elegies, compose
Our own lives around the Rose
Who, as heaven, on this earth
Does adorn the world with worth

Now we fall asleep once more
Like the little children poor
Smile, you baby daisy small
Christ does love you overall.

March 1, 2007

Elephants

Some elephants are things so fine
They grow their tusks around the vine
Then drink their food like holy wine
Or supping on potatoes dine

Some elephants do notice words
While others sing like little birds
But every one pronounces plain
The golden harvested wheat grain

Some elephants cause falling rain
Some right abolish green disdain
But every one a martyr is
To sacrifice on altars his

Some elephants are famous trees
Some elephants eat honeybees
But elephants on bended knees
Remind me of gigantic keys

All elephants are blue or red
And work and till the garden bed

Chapter Nine. 2007 – 2008 Christ, Nature, Poet and Poetry

They dream the nights when they are fed
By dreaming elephants, the dead

Dead elephants are souls of men
They shine like purple stars of ten
They dot the heavens once again
Dead elephants each night ascend

One elephant is more than nine
Continents or clouds entwine
Because the elephant is poor
We elephants cannot ignore

Because each elephant is large
We ride on them as on a barge
And travel distances of where
Our poetries relieve all care

Because the elephants cannot
Be borrowed, burrowed, blamed or bought
They are more precious than a lot
Of onions or what barons sought

These verses of the elephant
May well not be, or elegant
But then again, within a tent
With elephants would you repent?

For elephants do all things know
They play all roles and undergo
Most wonderful—remind me, oh!—
Transformations them bestow

My elephant may not be real
But if he were, I would then feel
Unaltered by these images
One elephant discourages

What's moribund, peculiar and

Chapter Nine. 2007 – 2008 Christ, Nature, Poet and Poetry

Unfamiliar, small or grand
So let these pictures elephants
Spontaneous appear nonsense.

March 18, 2007

My Love Is

Love is a mood in leather
With copper and silver stitch
Mine is a sentient flavor
Is diamonds found in black pitch
Mine is a sweet aroma
Like honey or dew on leaves
Mine is a true paloma
She gives me then receives

Love is a trace of silken
Platinum inlay ring
Mine is an iron token
Supporting a sacred thing
Mine is an Age of Fire
A worker of gold and ores
Mine is a blacksmith's choir
Whose hammer pounds molten Mars

Love is a dove or dolphin
A swan and poem serene
Mine is a peasant's proven
Method and fields of green
Mine is a farmhand's labor
A countryman and his wife
Mine is the sweet corn's flavor
The harvest I play on my fife

Love is a romance and children
A lover and smile and dance
Mine is a table olden
Of wood and square nails perchance

Chapter Nine. 2007 – 2008 Christ, Nature, Poet and Poetry

Mine is a supper of color
Of stew and bread and hot tea
Mine is a farmer's pallor
Ruddy reality

Love is a young man a-courting
A youth and a maiden perhaps
Mine is a man hardworking
Or taking in between naps
Mine is chores aplenty
Is sowing the seeds in hearts
Love-seeds for future bounty
Of feeling and greening arts

Love is a star, is Venus
Is princesses' laughter gay
Mine is a worker's bonus
A pilgrimage on my way
Mine is a hostel or outpost
A temporary abode
Mine is the mountains or seacoast
A traveler's winding road

Love is the faeries' Kingdom
Martyrdom's mystery
Mine is the song of freedom
A karma and history
Mine is a distant welcome
Approaching me every day
Mine is a meeting spoken
A silent embrace, we pray

Mine is a sacrament's moment
A tenderness fondly felt
Mine is a simple garment
A woolen scarf or a pelt
Mine is a radiant sunbeam
A sunset before the night
Mine is a poet's deep dream

Chapter Nine. 2007 – 2008 Christ, Nature, Poet and Poetry

The glorious golden Light

Mine is a toolbox laden
With everything that I need
To build me a home quite hidden
Where I can go and read
Mine is a book of poems
A shelf lined with answers and
A library filled with wagons
Traversing literature grand

Mine is a land of memories
Shining in hazy song
There would I dwell in glories
There my heart true belongs
There would I sleep in ages
Eternal in realms of peace
Finally step in stages
To my final release.

April 7, 2007

Serenity—A Poem of Easter Monday Evening

Serenity is not a word
Of solitude, a single bird
But glorious, Creation whole
That sings my heart, that sees my soul.

Serenity is not a verse
Of image short or picture terse
But beyond time and beyond thought
A sight that beauty gaining sought.

Serenity is not a poem
Of triumph far or quiet home
But in the distance beyond me
Does enter me entirely

Chapter Nine. 2007 – 2008 Christ, Nature, Poet and Poetry

But in the future beyond pain
The suffering I feel disdain
But somehow here today is of
Serenity is beauty-love.

April 9, 2007

Men of the Sun

The golden energies of light
Like angels of the sun or men
Who playing violins with might
Send dancers into flight again

Wherefrom the elders of the sun
Do gather 'round an oaken tree
As ancient as their wisdom won
By hearts and minds of warmth agree

They only when the Truth aligns
In gracious beams of sun's glory
Then do they set in motion signs
Of Christ in sacred mystery

They feel His Word incarnate once
In Jesu flesh became He man
Now working on in mankind hence
And in the earth of birth again

Each time the Holy Nights in hearts
His Light—the Child within is born
Each time His Passion deep as darts
Pierce feeling's Light to joy reborn

O Christ, Thou dwells in rhythm's Time
In human sentience those do go
Who emulate the Rose sublime
Are true alone the Truth to know

Chapter Nine. 2007 – 2008 Christ, Nature, Poet and Poetry

Like the sun remain they true
And faithful as the red of blood
Whose coursing regular imbue
The body of mankind with God.

May 13, 2007
Mother's Day

When Dreams Adorn the Heavens

Creative be the time of sleep
When dreams adorn the heavens
When daffodils upon the hills
Remind the soul of fragrance
When summer roses blooming waft
The scents of rising color
When red reminds the souls of young
Of children's fullness' flavor

When in the halls of dusk I dream
Of songs and smells of summers
When in the nights of holiness
My spirit sings and shimmers
Among the twinkling stars I go
And ask no more my question
When all is love and beautiful
Nor truth a small suggestion

When in the moment lingers speech
Eternity does answer
When timeless time upon the hill
Is all a bright enhancer
Is all a book of human Names
Bestowed by gracious God
Upon our heads before we knew
To read the sacred Word

To read the Book of Life before
The Tree of Knowledge happens

Chapter Nine. 2007 – 2008 Christ, Nature, Poet and Poetry

To skim the pages knowingly
The Book of Knowledge opens
Before we knew, but only dreamt
Imagination seeing
And all was Poetry and Song
And every man believing

And every man believing
A Poet dreams and seeing
A Poet sees believing
A Poet sings and being
And being sings composing
Composing poems seeing
Eternal is his sleeping
The Poet dreams in keeping
God and angels meaning
Christ and human being.

May 19, 2007

The Little Snapdragon

Somewhere sitting on the other side (the bright side)
The strangest little snapdragon saw me (reminding me)
That comely flowers blooming can see sometimes (see people sometimes)
How odd to be seen by a snapdragon (a little snapdragon)
But how many snapdragons have eyes? (hazel eyes?)
I guess it's not very many do (not many snapdragons do)
So I decided to look back ordinary (just ordinary)
To see what the little snapdragon would think (would think of me)
And do you know what he thought? (the snapdragon thought?)
The snapdragon thought I was unusual (unusual as in strange)
And he told me as much, yes he did (he did tell me as much)
He said I was unusual because I had eyes (blue eyes)
He said he had never seen a person looking at him before (that's right; he said that)
This made me feel funny, so I looked away (looked away from him)
Then that snapdragon adjusted his bowtie (his tuxedo bowtie)
And walked away to attend a funeral (that's what I said, a funeral)

Chapter Nine. 2007 – 2008 Christ, Nature, Poet and Poetry

I tell you, that was the oddest snapdragon (the oddest one I ever did see)
But don't quote me on this one (about the little snapdragon)
Because some people might think I'm strange (strange to have seen and heard such a thing)
But this snapdragon has ten brothers and sisters (that's right, ten)
And they're even stranger than he is (yes, even stranger)
They know how to do the foxtrot and sing "God Bless America" (just imagine that)
Well, don't be surprised, 'cause I told you ('cause I told you about this little snapdragon).

May (?), 2007

Diadem

Bequest he made, lest seasons turn
To ashes kept in earthen urn
But then the Saviour motions in
The rhythms annual again

And spring is Easter morning light
And summer beams St. John's with might
While autumn dies St. Michaél
Until midwinter Christmas tell

And Christ, He lives throughout the year
He makes eternal, time so clear
Transforming suffering to Light
Of beauty spiritual of night

From deeds of day when pain and fear
Cut and chill and enter here
The weary soul may know the deep
Of Christ in holy soul sleep

For Christ is deeper than men know
Who dwell unconscious to and fro
Or dream their days in fond attire
Like children's voices in sweet choir

Chapter Nine. 2007 – 2008 Christ, Nature, Poet and Poetry

And only those mature in Him
Immerse their hearts like diadem
Into the place, an altar of
Solemnity and feeling love

And there in quiet solitude
Make peace with self in inner mood
That all the storms of life surround
Tempestuous temporal found

While in their stillness hearts do know
Courageous dwelling as they go
Until they reach the altitude
Of mountaintop with sun imbued

Yes, Christ in them saves time from death
Eternity for every breath
But heaven touches earth with love
I smile in thinking Christ above.

June 15, 2007

Sweet Time

Time whispers
Grown thin from wide
A tall gentleman with cane
In place of rotund unable
To pass through sleep's keyhole

Time swells sweetly
Like fruits of summer juicy
Dripping with grace
From the faces of children
Who taste her bounty
Love

Time stops running
Like feeling warmed by suns

Chapter Nine. 2007 – 2008 Christ, Nature, Poet and Poetry

In clover fields
Meadowed valleys
My pastures
Time greens

Time, resound anew
In eternal chords' vibrations
Travel through spaces
Connecting thought-to-thought
Place-to-place
Person-to-person
Allow me, time
To hear

Time touches
Healing age and ache
Illness and hurt
Gentler than a breeze
Time's sweet touch
My friend

Time
Tend to the children of earth
Grant them peace and rest
Once more.

June 15, 2007

Honeybees

Sweet summer eves
Sweeter than the dew
When mankind believes
In the fewest of the few

I always write
For my love of you
Inspired by light
Shining ever new

Chapter Nine. 2007 – 2008 Christ, Nature, Poet and Poetry

Remember once
When children danced and played
Grace, elegance
My sorrows soon allayed

My sore distress
Dispelled by one red rose
Wore Nature's dress
In stillness and repose

"Come, come to me,"
The honeybees did buzz
Where blossoms see
The nectar ever was

So joined I in
The merry gathering
Flowed deep within
My soul the juices sting

But then the bees
Laughed scornfully at me
I did not tease
Or taunt so easily

Rather I marched
Away from company
My back all arched
I drummed my timpani

Still do I love
The sweet taste of honey
So think I of
The little bees so free

They play with zest
Among the flowers' glee
It is in jest
That they made fun of me.

July 9, 2007

Chapter Nine. 2007 – 2008 Christ, Nature, Poet and Poetry

Mystery

For love to die she must be born
From heaven of God she earth has worn
Then through a life of pain and scorn
She goes through death into Christ-morn

For birth is God to earth below
That all men see to us love show
But death is Christ, through Him does flow
Love, the bird, reborn I know

Death is truth, a sacred act
As birth an holy rite enact
But death does pass the soul most dear
Into the world of stars appear

When love once dies, she is so pure
That she must go, the dark endure
But on the Other Side welcome
The Christ, Who love is union

Love is mystery like death
The mystery unknown to us
The mystery of death and love
My spirit resurrect above

Each night a death in brief transpires
We sleep in holy spirit-fires
Each morn is birth, a life anew
The miracle of springtime dew

I only ask for nights of love
O welcome me o Christ above
Welcome me, I pray this eve
My soul, I feel, in Thee believe

Welcome me in sleep's domain
Where Father-One alone does reign
And day is but a mortal place

Chapter Nine. 2007 – 2008 Christ, Nature, Poet and Poetry

Left behind eternal grace

Death and love are mystery
Christ and dead alone can see
For we are human in the flesh
We ask Thy mercy, Christ, in death

We ask Thy grace each night in sleep
As little children in the deep
Christ does welcome little ones
Sleep, my child, where starry suns
Do twinkle in the skies of night
Lord of everlasting Light.

July 22, 2007

Genius

A genius is a thing or rite
That sings or plays or flames ignite
A man or woman filled with song
Or color, forms or tempests strong

A genius is a master's word
Composition's human bird
A poet's dream and thought and love
A sentient passion from above

A genius once descended lives
In all the genius does and gives
Become but beauty, truth or grace
Bestowed by God, dons heaven's face

Quite human from the spirit-realm
A genius flashes at the helm
And steers the captain's ship to lands
Of glory using all the hands

Yes, genius is a boatman's mind
The science of all humankind

Chapter Nine. 2007 – 2008 Christ, Nature, Poet and Poetry

The mathematician's reckoning
The physicist, who measuring
Penetrates to laws on earth
Where spirit enters depth and girth

Genius is the artist's place
Christ perceived and active trace
The one unique and special Name
Incarnate and mastered tame

Yes, genius is the quality
Of light or wisdom's royalty
Of kings and farmers, lovers, squires
Of doctors, clerics, monks in choirs

Of princes, barons, dukes adorned
Of poets, peasants, ladies gowned
Of duchesses and monarchs great
Of educators emulate

Of martyrs, mystics wandering
Of saints and scholars studying
Of bishops, minstrels, troubadours
Of rustics, soldiers, paramours

Geniuses are doctors, squires
Knaves and pages, vassals, girls
Lords and ladies, damsels, knights
And all the people, days and nights
Awaiting heaven's entrance here
On earth where Christ to all appear

For geniuses obtain and know
In consciousness they Christ do show
And well perceive in fellow men
The other's genius again

But if you genius would discern
Then listen, look and read and learn

Chapter Nine. 2007 – 2008 Christ, Nature, Poet and Poetry

To each belong his own and find
The geniuses of all mankind.

August 4, 2007

Trampolines

Trampolines are—everywhere
They grow like hair then disappear
But trampolines are not so bad
When all is told the truth be had

I once did see a trampoline
Amazing did it bounce and lean
Like boarders surf or buildings sway
My trampoline on this fine day.

August 9, 2007

Three Poems of Tuesday, late afternoon, September 18, 2007

I. Leaves

Thoughts—like leaves
Blow in the breeze
Deserting me for an eternity
Until—at Evensong
(or so I believe)
An image returns—in poetry
And with this image—this poetry
A thought returns—like a leaf
On a breeze (I believe)
Finding me
And I—receptive—find the leaf
Finding me
And I think of the leaf
Finding me
And thoughts—like leaves

Chapter Nine. 2007 – 2008 Christ, Nature, Poet and Poetry

Blow in the breeze
Finding me for an eternity
And I sleep—in safety
In the leaves of thought
And imagery.

II. Memory

Memories—of time
Returning like waves
Washing on the shores
Of my soul, tonight

And I keep repeating
In fondest greeting
That memory is most kind

For memories—of time
Wash my feet like waves
In healing on the shores
Of my soul, tonight

And I keep repeating
In gratitude greeting
That memory is most kind.

III. The Thoughts of Light

A poem without flaw is beautiful
Like a flower blossoming colorful

But I love the time
Of a delicate rhyme
When the air and the light are wonderful

Because such a time
Meets my thoughts sublime
And then do I see Christ bountiful

Because Christ to me

Chapter Nine. 2007 – 2008 Christ, Nature, Poet and Poetry

Is the thoughts I see
The thoughts of light most meaningful.

September 18, 2007

Die Lieder

Menschen sterben
Menschen erben
Erzählungen, Geschichte
Gedächtnis und Gedichte

Die Menschen lieben
Die leiden, geblieben
Wie Steine oder Lichter
Liebende und Dichter

Aber im Momente
Erdenelemente
Räume und Zeiten
Menschen begleiten

Bis nach deren Tode
Wie ein schön' Kleinode
Der Christ und Ewigkeit
Wilkommen Seeligkeit

Seelen und Geister
Werden Sterne und Meister
Mit dem Vater im Himmel
Verlassen Getümmel

Ruhe und Friede
Werden die Lieder.

19. September 2007

Love

Love is like a flower
Blossoming an hour

Chapter Nine. 2007 – 2008 Christ, Nature, Poet and Poetry

Fragrances as lovely
As her color comely

Love is sweet as nectar
Round as dew of moisture
Pure as hearts of faerie
Of Jesu and of Mary

Love is something tender
Softer, milder, gentler
Than the moss of forest
As the Infant dearest

Love reminds me alway
Of the twilit skies, pray
Ask me why I evenings
Sensing love's sweet meanings

I will answer, maybe
Love returns, a baby
In the nights like winter
Christ, the Child, does enter

Human hearts are stirring
Love amongst us caring
We are human being
Christ is human meaning.

September 24, 2007

I Always Noticed

I always noticed changed things
Like diamonds crushed into sparkling dust
Or silk unraveled into strands of threads.

I always noticed changes in things
Like leaves to soil decomposed

Chapter Nine. 2007 – 2008 Christ, Nature, Poet and Poetry

Or wilted petals of rose
Or talkative lips gone still and silent

I always noticed transitions fleeting
Like twilight and avenues
Across which shadows lengthen
Or the bodies of adolescents newly pubescent
Filling with bosoms and bottoms, and sprouting with hair
And scents and fantasies of love
And awakened thoughts, newly won independence, freedom and responsibility

I always noticed separations
Like departing from home into strange places
Or leaving school behind for destinations traveled
Inner or outer, or both

I always noticed times of retiring
From long days of work
Into dusky evenings of thoughts
Penned on paper like leaves of ash
Into nights oblivious to thought and unrest

I always noticed transitions
Like shifts in time into timelessness
Where space moves inward
And the pulse becomes free inwardly
Like a prayer in me
Deeper than time or the sea

I believe
Always transitions in me
I see
And I pause
Because transitions cease to be
When, finally
Quiet descends and lends
Incorporeality to eternity
Momentarily

Chapter Nine. 2007 – 2008 Christ, Nature, Poet and Poetry

I always notice things three
Like Christ, you and me
Brotherly
Safely
Within me
Or fork, plate and food
Or table, chair and family
We are always three

Three hands
Three words
Three eyes
Three times three
Times three
Equals three.

September 29, 2007

The Chair, the Table and the Tableware

The chair sits patiently.
The table stands faithfully.
The tableware is placed at hand.

The chair sits before the table.
The tableware is placed at hand upon the table.
The chair, the table and the tableware respect the silence of the room.

The room houses the chair, the table and the tableware.
The room is gracious to the chair, the table and the tableware.
The room entertains the chair, the table and the tableware.

The chair, the table and the tableware experience the room.
The chair, the table and the tableware notice the sunlight shining through the window into the room by day, and the moonlight by night.
The chair, the table and the tableware whisper about the sunlight and the moonlight.

Chapter Nine. 2007 – 2008 Christ, Nature, Poet and Poetry

The window hears the chair, the table and the tableware whispering to one another.
The window clearly thinks the chair, the table and the tableware are gossips.
The window does not hide its thoughts regarding the gossiping of the chair, the table and the tableware.

The chair, the table and the tableware cannot keep from whispering.
The room tells the chair, the table and the tableware to be quiet as the guest is expected.
The chair, the table and the tableware still their lips because they do not question the authority of the room.

The guest enters the room without the slightest knowledge of what has transpired between the chair, the table and the tableware, and the window and the room, because all is quiet when he enters and during his meal in the room.

After the guest retires for the evening, the chair, the table and the tableware gossip about the guest amongst themselves.
The window sheds light on their gossiping.

The room is gracious and allows the chair, the table and the tableware to whisper.

October 2, 2007

Times To

Times to consist in afterludes
When voices quiet in quietudes
When all the people acquiesce
And nights ascend after sunsets.

Times to recede in inwardness
When calm endures till quietness
When my own soul ent'ring returns
And thoughtfulness again discerns.

Times to listen to inward songs
Gone are the voices of the throngs

Chapter Nine. 2007 – 2008 Christ, Nature, Poet and Poetry

My attitudes the past belongs
And mystery absorbs my wrongs.

Times to weigh a weightless thought
On scales of feathers God has brought
When all else fails, and time transpires
Timeless in eternal fires

Times to pray on bended knees
Like futile efforts, backward trees
Devoted with humility
In gratitudes beyond now me

Times to fill my heart with breath
With meaning felt, and close to death
When spirits roamed depart from day
The night has come without delay.

Times to listen to silences
When truth begins in entrances
To sound aloud in cadences
Between the words it balances.

Times to pardon, first my own
Then the beings I disown
Then the troubles of the times
Then the verses of my rhymes

Times to whisper and to stay
When my voice alights my way
And history becomes a road
I have traveled in this ode.

Times to sit or stir or write
Poetry and songs ignite
When the land of symmetry
Transforms into elegy

Times to meditate or ask

Chapter Nine. 2007 – 2008 Christ, Nature, Poet and Poetry

When my story is my task
When my verses antiquate
Out of style and out of date.

Times to breathe of perfumes sweet
When the fragrances of wheat
Fill my soul in ethers mild
And I return and be my child
And I return to poetry
And I return the truth to see
And I return to poverty
And I return the Mystery.

October 17, 2007

CHAPTER TEN

2008 – 2009

THE HOLY TRINITY AND GOD

Chapter Ten. 2008 – 2009 The Holy Trinity and God

God

Gifted with God I dwell and go
In personalities human, I know
Perceive I they in hair and breath
The living God in breath of death

God is good; I thank Him for
His goodness on the rich and poor
His Hand in blessing that men sleep
On His Lap within the deep

God is love; His Work is done
Creation is His Deed; His Son
Is Christ, the Word, Which had begun
From the very start and Sun

His Spirit is the Truth, the Light
And God is spirit, day and night
That men nightly hear His Voice
In Him alone may we rejoice.

God I thank Thee for this day
Now I pray I go Thy Way
To rest in sleep, Thy little child
Merciful Thou art and mild.

October 22, 2007

Kim

Stillness is a gift sometimes
Where Christ becomes my hand sublime
And I repeat in simple rhymes
My hand of Christ uplifted mime

When, though the world in tumult sways
And human children feel dismay
And one lost child in sickness stays
My hand of Christ remains today

Chapter Ten. 2008 – 2009 The Holy Trinity and God

When illness fills the child possessed
With thoughts, like chaos, say "distress"
When all is troubled in unrest
"Forgiveness" I did speak and blessed

But this lost child a feeling knew
Beyond her words "revenge" ensue
A feeling of the heart of few
Christ was present she felt, too

Hard to bear whose life is storm
Whose childhood scars and tears are worn
Whose body agonizes form
Whose mind is filled, whose soul forlorn

One child to witness jealousy
One child molested sought mercy
Cannot forget, like leprosy
Does plague and haunt and blindness see

For there in horrors Christ she knows
Her karma stands her life bestows
She senses, fights Him with her blows
That is, her voice and mindless goes

He does not leave her, night or day
He would her deepest fears allay
But first forgiveness ask repay
For karma is her truth today

She holds her Bible like a child
But her soul is often wild
And then, exhausted, see how mild
Her Jesu sleeps quite undefiled

She loves her Jesu pure and love
She loves His love, a gentle dove
She dreams of heaven up above
She longs for peace in dreaming of

Chapter Ten. 2008 – 2009 The Holy Trinity and God

For finally, when quiet stills
Her ocean-mountain calmly wills
There Christ abiding on the hill
Of Golgotha on cross is ill

He suffers with her day by day
He is her karma she must pay
And so to Jesu does she pray
She cannot have another way.

November 22, 2007

The Garden

My only arm is tortoise shell
Or—shall I say?—an open drawer
Where ministers small sermons tell
And congregations dance the floor
My followers like flower-petals fell.

My only harmony is holy poems
Like little ladies listening alone
They seem to sit on silent silver stones
And singing songs on undulating tone
Remind green gardeners of hallowed homes.

I am the garden. All my fragrant flowers
Are simply poems blossoming because
Their time has come in gentle morning hours
Their colors shimmer love and without flaws
Between the rains in alternating showers

I was the child before I knew Christ shine
I was the youth; I quested far and wide
But then the Light did stream so fine
Soul's shadows mine no longer hide
And now, illumined, I began to sign.

My Name, like Glory, is a song of love

Chapter Ten. 2008 – 2009 The Holy Trinity and God

Bears Trinity and also Michaelmas
Belongs each child to God above
But Christ I knew before the Mass
Before in poetry I dreaming of.

Then spoke my soul too much, I knew but ill
Did suffer karma and adulthood, fell
Nor child nor gardener to till
But yet the garden I did tell
My verses covered over every hill.

I always shared my love of greenery
For what is garden but the plants of earth
A leaf, a stone, a shrubbery
Awaiting Easter growth's rebirth?
My verses scent was seasoned harmony.

The loneliest, I learned the very start
Never was alone, could not be once
For every brother with a heart needs heart
Humanity is but the human sense
The Uniting when felt first apart.

My flowers blossom in a poetry
Of flowing wines in vineyards' canopy
Beneath a sun of Christian artery
I drank His Blood, the Cup of Christ to me
Became my blood in grapes of gallery

And what are grapes but words' own windy vowels?
And what is wheat but consonantal power?
We form the rhythms' vigorous rolls
Of light alliteration's tower
Interspersed with rhyming world souls

My door I opened wide to show mankind
My inner light all radiant to smile
My wisdom suffered with a mind
That only hearts can bear awhile

Chapter Ten. 2008 – 2009 The Holy Trinity and God

Who brotherhood and love can ever find

My beds of earth like humus rich
Soil of succulence, sense and sound
Such am I, a garden which
Both greenery, the growth and ground
My Christ, the Sun, shown dreams upon my ditch

The gardener does daily dig
In rows of poppy, purple and
Blossoming, a cherry twig
Petals pink fall on the land
The girls all grown, my garden wore a wig

I penned there poems faithfully
Through every season all to see
My beds, like satin, beautifully
Announced the blossom and the bee
Pronounced the people pleased and plentifully.

For what is harvest but autumnal sun?
And what is summer, every little one?
And what is Glory, when in spring my Christ
In me does resurrect in morning's East
An Easter deed, time changed, when time I asked?

But the Child keeps dreaming deep
In the winter's holy sleep
I join small Jesu, bosom of
Pure Mary, Queen of faerie-love
A God, our Christ descended from above.

In silences I sit and write
My songs of sentience in the night
Do dream and dance in dear delight
Awaken in the morning light
To sun of pulsing gold of splendid sight

My poetry is but the times

Chapter Ten. 2008 – 2009 The Holy Trinity and God

I dedicate to sacred sounds
Of words of spoken souls and rhymes
And energies of granite grounds
Or gestures mimicking a million mimes

I am the garden still, my hill
Of flora keeps surrounding mounds
Of flying forests, firs that fill
The vast voracious garden grounds
One maiden sits forlorn by window sill.

If anyone should ask why leaves
Keep falling from my trees the eves
Say garden I my maiden grieves
My soul my maiden is, believes
She is the gardener my paths relieves.

I am the garden of my life and when
My soul, the gardener, a maiden lives
She goes among the flowers, my verses then
In them breathes life, her soul to them she gives
Until they blossoming die once again.

Now, you may ask, who is the earth?
I am the garden, love sun's light
The earth is death, Christ's
Heart and Birth
The sun is sentience, soul and sight
The rain is tears and blessings, mostly mirth.

The air I breathe is wind and song
Repeats repeating birds along
Who borrowing eat the fruits belong
To history, the future strong
Myth-amethysts keep healing all my wrong.

The seasons are all rhythms of
My flowers and cycles life and death
The stars, the angels, dead above
Eternity; my fragrance breath
And time—sweet time—is living, lasting love.

Chapter Ten. 2008 – 2009 The Holy Trinity and God

So now you know the world where I
Surround myself, a poet or
A garden beneath a gracious sky
A poetry, my special lore
My task my answer to my karma's why

Keeps blessing me with suffering
For what is fair but rose' disdain
Does crown the thorn in offering
After the never ending rain
Beauty's love redeeming radiance bring?

December 1, 2007

Holy Dreams

Sit and dream like evening
When silence stirs in everything
And longing likes to linger on
Like ever after age along

Remember gold or silver dreams
Of heaven's sunny and moonbeams
Before the questioning returns
I meditate on meaning's urns

Like ashes from an ancient war
When bodies were cremated for
The rising spirits ageless or
The stars and planets long before

But here on earth the homeless go
They wander in the coldness so
That inner light within their souls
Remind their hearts of childhood goals

Each Christmastime where Advent leads
Us to the manger's quiet deeds
Among the animals who breathe
The Child of Mary we receive

For every womb belongs a heart

Chapter Ten. 2008 – 2009 The Holy Trinity and God

Our souls like Mary stand apart
We wander like the homeless do
And seek a shelter, give birth to

The Child, our Christ, He would in us
Be born anew in agelessness
For Christmastime eternal is
Our lives are guided stars us gives

The sign beneath which, in a stall
The shepherds find the Christ so small
Who lies asleep in dreams thereof
The holy wonder Christmas love

So dream with me these Holy Nights
Beneath the heavenly starry lights
And gently rock the cradle where
Christ Jesu sleeps in God's good care

If only we like Mary pure
Prepare a place which can endure
Throughout the year, a sepulcher
The human heart shine love-demure

Then shall we offer our gifts, too
Humility shall then ensue
Glad cheer we warm our hands within
The inner stall, our souls again

But be prepared, for soon He comes
He would be born as many suns
In human hearts for human thumbs
And little sparrows who seek crumbs

The sparrows small sing songs for Him
The Prince of Peace may enter in
Yes they rejoice when we within
Our hearts make merry joy Christian.

December 12, 2007

Chapter Ten. 2008 – 2009 The Holy Trinity and God

Grace

Immerse, imbue in inner man
The heart, the hearth, on sunny land
In feeling warmth in evening
When night begins the darkness bring

And with the darkness cold attains
Its properties like snows and rains
In mid-December grows one rose
Of red in stillness' fragrant pose

This rose of beauty-graciousness
Reminds me of redemption's kiss
Of soon the Child of Mary dear
Of Jesu Christ and the New Year

But first in snows or rains of cold
Of midwinter very old
We bring the Child our offering
Of love and cheer; our warmth we bring

For Jesu Christ, He sleeps in dreams
Of love and feeling's fondest beams
Beneath the heavenly stars above
The world surrounded is by love

Now take this small remembrance mine
With it yours alike entwine
'Tis but the grace of God, Who good
Laid Jesu Christ in manger-wood

Within the stall we find Him there
Our fondest dreams us reappear
And magic of the night of air
Stirs in us and everywhere.

Los Angeles
December 15, 2007

Chapter Ten. 2008 – 2009 The Holy Trinity and God

Ist die Kunst

Stil ist der Kunst Oberfläche, Schönheit ihr Leben und Liebe.

Meinung bedeutet ja nichts, denn die Kunst ist Gottesangesicht.

Farbe ist Fülle und Feuer, Schwarze ein Ungeheuer.

Schlaf ist mein Bruder und Freund, die Kunst gibt uns Ursprung kund.

Die Welt ist der Kunst immer rund, die Worte der Dichtung ihr Mund.

Licht ist die Liebe des Tags, Sonne der König und Pracht,

Schönheit der Stoff Wirklichkeit innerhalb Kunst und bereit

zu schaffen und tun eines Dings künstlerisch abends umrings.

Ruhe ist Friede gar still wenn man nach Gott neigt und will.

Mehr "Ist"

Kraft ist ein williger Macht, Denken 'ne Fähigkeit sacht'.

Das Denken ist philosophisch, Erkenntnis anthroposophisch.

Glaube nach Nächte wohl führt; Hoffnung des Morgens gehört.

Liebe ist Kinder der Nacht, die spielen und träumen erwacht.

Sterne sind Engel und auch Toten mit Atemweihrauch.

Gott ist der Weltall und ganz Liebe und ewiglich Glanz,

denn Er will leuchten in Dir, in Christus Er kommet, ist hier.

Christus ist einzig und gut, für uns Er gosset Sein Blut.

Sterben ist Pfad nach dem Gott des Ewigkeitsfriede gar hold.

Chapter Ten. 2008 – 2009 The Holy Trinity and God

Süß ist der Schmerz Christi lieb, teuer Er bleibt wie Er blieb.

Engel singen Flügel und Geist, der Mensch stirbt, nach ihnen er reist.

1. Februar 2008,
21. Januar 2013

Good Friday

Sentience seems a somber thing
This Good Friday happening
Christ is crucified and died
Mercy, we have killed the Bride

Jesu Lord did suffering
Lamb of God, His offering
Now we bear the weight of death
In the moisture of our breath

Shall the morrow mourn for Him
In the Land of Dead again
That on Day the Third He rise
Christ of nature, sun, stars, skies

But we first must feel this grief
From which we find no relief

Sorry is the world today
Follow we the Son, His Way
Make it through another day
This is all we ask and pray.

March 21, 2008
Good Friday

I Saw a Song

I saw a song.

I saw my song I was singing because

Chapter Ten. 2008 – 2009 The Holy Trinity and God

My dreaming was awake and,
Piercing my silences,
Spoke words to all:

The beloved dead who are not dead
The beloved living who are dreaming or awake
The beloved creatures I know with my senses
My God of heaven and of earth
Who makes certain my path for His Good.

I saw a song
This, my song.

August 20, 2008

Beyond An Age

Once, beyond an Age
Time had changed.

All was lawful
In the Age
Beyond the metals

Neither stone nor wood
The Ages long gone by
Neither gold nor silver
Neither bronze nor iron

Only spirit in the New Age
Time had changed.

August 20, 2008

Friendship

Only friends can deepen thought
Into feeling meaning brought
For to another dear are they
In their hearts concern holds sway.

Chapter Ten. 2008 – 2009 The Holy Trinity and God

Sincerity is true, you know
If you lack it, lies do show
If you care, then show your hand
Help and share and understand.

Friends, I say, are true and good
They suffer in the ways of God
They learn by their mistakes then heal
Their wounds, though dearly do they feel.

Who, today, does care I ask?
Friends do care; this is their task
None can change this, 'tis good will
I place my foot upon the hill.

Keep your feelings dear, right close
Allow not others comatose
Remember friendship is a word
Nothing else allow be heard.

Take the time for thoughts of heart
Begin the day these thoughts do start
Then follow through all travellings
End the day in evenings

Of thoughts of heart into the deep
Of inward-going holy sleep
There you and I another greet
For by the day we Christ did meet.

Friendship is a soothing balm
Find times and places for its psalm
Moments when to share it there
With the others who do care.

August 21, 2008

Chapter Ten. 2008 – 2009 The Holy Trinity and God

Evergreen

Remind the thinker still to be
To enter Christ, the Mystery
Beloved by the inner sea
Of feeling and of love in me

Let all the troubles wash away
Like long forgotten yesterday
Where only peace remains to stay
And holiness abides alway

When you go to bed this eve
All that's left is to believe
Into the warmth of night and sun
The deep of sleep is God and Son

There in heaven holy find
The spirit-essence of mankind
The Holy Spirit is a song
I greeted and I did belong

Then on the morning mankind rise
Find sun of day up in the skies
The earth becomes our work to till
The meaning of the solid hill

And all the children of Divine
Are innocence and younger sign
The Father of us all, He holds
Each one of us safe from the cold

His Hand is strong and sure, right well
The human story we do tell
We read the Book of Life to learn
The whereabouts we make and earn

Remember, then, tomorrow brings
The hope sincerity in rings

Chapter Ten. 2008 – 2009 The Holy Trinity and God

That the world becomes the scene
Of life and death and evergreen.

August 24, 2008

Chorus

Heaven is a mist I saw
When trees are blooming in the ground
Before the night began to show
Her stars in heaven's darkness round

The little birds, their chirping glad
And air as cool as freshly some
And breezy blew the face of lad
The world-all was new, handsome

And then I felt the day was good
And only small in passing touch
The fires like passion burning wood
The park did mean to me so much

And then I saw a family
The parents with their girl and boy
Hand-in-hand they joyfully
A-walking 'round, yes with dear joy

So summer was a holiday
And pleased the people said and smiled
Like, though 'twas August, month of May
My heart a treasure, loving mild

I feel still the evening breeze
The sunset is in color Christ
A wonder and a flame of light
The day in dying toward the West

Such beauty Glory ne'er surpass
Only the God of mercy make

Chapter Ten. 2008 – 2009 The Holy Trinity and God

Before the dusk this sight compass
And Christ devotion ask awake

I dreamed before now am awake
The light and air do make it so
The vision of the sunset take
As end as quickly brought I know

The deeds of sun are good and whole
God has performed mankind to bless
All Nature joined for sentience' role
Now sense with me this holiness

To close a peace of night shall dream
And earth to bed in sleep all still
The sun of night become the beam
Of warmth and love, divine God's Will

And stars of Angels and the dead
Sing in chorus glorious sound
And play on instruments of gold
And all is love and one and round.

August 29, 2008

The Math

Eloquence is since surpassed
Just take the time and do the math
For if you figure everything
Words become but borrowing

And fond expressions lack amount
The calculated sums that count
And poetry is but a word
Without a quantity is heard

But mathematics plagiarize
They cannot versify the whys

Chapter Ten. 2008 – 2009 The Holy Trinity and God

Nor understand true poetries
Imaginations, sans degrees

Yes only poets can do sing
Their suns in love's imagining
They conjure forth ephemeral
Imagery original

For poets dream their dreams in soul
Their poetry unusual
Quite unquantifiable
All un-mathematical.

August 21/22, 2008
February 23, 2009
January 6, 2013

The Suicide

Dedicated To
David Foster Wallace
(1962-2008)

Suicide*
You know the dizzying inner pain.

Can you, elegizing, meditate on the suicide?

Would that you knew
this your pain
will only compound
        multiply
                intensify
for the dead know this
and more.

Can you elegize the suicide?

Suicide—in a hall
        extrapolate
your dark thoughts

Chapter Ten. 2008 – 2009 The Holy Trinity and God

       embattled in
              a mental tin
of pain.

Can you elegize the suicide?

O, the man
the woman
        turning inwards on oneself
           knows a hatred
              and a grief
as a shadow sensed unseen.

Self-demonize
        the suicide
I elegize.

Suicide,
       have you chosen
           to succumb
               to a notion
of impossible escape?

No one can escape
       the pain
for pain belongs
       to songs
           of life—
death cannot obliterate
       the insane pain.

Endure
       a soul Christwards

Find in life
       your cure.

October 20, 2008
Revised September (?), 2012

Chapter Ten. 2008 – 2009 The Holy Trinity and God

[NOTE: David Wallace was an award-winning American novelist, short story writer, essayist and Pomona College creative writing and English professor who committed suicide. This came as a shock to many who knew him and to all who had been his students. He suffered for years prior to taking his own life. Suicide is a choice. (See, below*)]

*For those suffering intense pain, suicide may appear as an option to escape the pain. This poem will show suicide only compounds this pain in a terrible fashion. The soul longs for experiences denied it by premature severance from the body. This denied longing is experienced as indescribable pain. We know this, but in far more detail and with much greater exactitude, from Rudolf Steiner's spiritual-scientific research. This great Austrian seer and thinker Rudolf Steiner (1861-1925) researched higher dimensions (the Spiritual Homeland) using the scientific approach but with higher organs of perception and thinking—in full consciousness. What makes Rudolf Steiner's work particularly significant for us is that although many today are awakening in soul to spiritual reality in full consciousness, he was a 'spiritual scientist' and thus brought detailed results of his research into the hierarchies few today can perceive in the form of thought. Thus anyone who is unbiased may think Rudolf Steiner's thoughts and decide for himself if they are reasonable. Rudolf Steiner is the greatest thinker of all time; he is also the greatest 20th century teacher and leader of humankind.

Inside the Library

The mesmerizing attitudes of wandering people filled the room, while the spirit of the evening lifted everyone's hearts, creating motions and movements of love in the limbs, in the hands and arms and legs of the people. Every one was talking, talking and walking about, and for an eternity that was a reverie, the library ceased to be a library but a place of verse and rapture, a place poetic and uplifting. All was love inside, while outside the dark night listened, listened to the wind and the stars, and to the cars and the streets the cars rushed by on.

But here inside the library, the spirit of an autumn evening reigned in everyone's hearts, moving silently amongst us, though few were aware of the wonderful community of which they were a part. Only the children played in this spirit. The children always understood, while

Chapter Ten. 2008 – 2009 The Holy Trinity and God

their parents impatiently watched over them, worn by the cares and strains of the day. But here in the library, the adults forgot the day's distractions and joined in with the children, for the books and the lights and the very carpet breathed with life and love and happiness. The walls seemed to disappear, and it was a glorious evening inside the library, gracious and protected by love and by light, while outside the earth slept in her dream of stars, blanketed in the darkness and the air of the night.

This was unrepeatable, a once-in-forever proposition, but the children grew up in such moments, for they lived in such invisible joys, in the spirit of such a library, only quieting down when their parents or teachers read them stories or tucked them into bed with a kiss on the forehead, for the children loved the magic, and they were like little dancers who ran lightly through the halls of day, chattering and laughing, giggling and huddling with excitement and in their secret understanding, long forgotten by the adults called grown-ups who, for a moment, paused on this wonderful evening in the library to consort a special book and inwardly rejoice like a small reverent child with a wish or a prayer or a tender smile for a beloved playmate or a toy handmade of wood, or for a rag doll of linen and buttons that it kept long after the realistic toys had lost their interest.

Only the occasional Mother or kindly father still bent down to greet the little child, to caress its small face, to murmur encouragement or listen to its earnest questions or sincere looks of trust with a smile, for those of us who still know our children still know to guide and love them while they play at their important games of work performed each and every day. And inside the library on this wondrous evening, the spirit of autumn roamed freely, alighting on my shoulder, too. That's why I thought I'd write it all down and share it with you here.

Los Angeles Public Library, Robertson Branch
November 17, 2008, evening
Los Angeles

Chapter Ten. 2008 – 2009 The Holy Trinity and God

From a card from Virginia Sease, Ph.D., written in Dornach, Switzerland, April 13, 2009:

….
> Your essays and poems continue your manifestations of creativity and indeed in many subject spheres. I experience your Christ-related poems as your deepest source.

Cosmic Christ—
To Evelyn Francis Capel

O great Being, Sun of radiant light!
Ascension Christ this morning is so bright!
From this earthly realm of man below
To the spheres of heaven above You go

Men see only before the dawn the day
Christ anoints for us the holy way
Angel beings greet the rising Sun
Christ for them is also shining One

We on Earth do witness life and death
Christ has lived and here breathed His last breath
On Easter morn He for us arose
From the empty Tomb in Spirit goes

Company of heaven not comprehend
Life and death on Earth for Christ and men
Are mystery; Ascension brought them light
Of Sun, resurrection's power bright

See the Cosmos bright indeed become
Expands the Light while rise the arisen Sun
Now we men can only look with awe
The ascending Christ in heavenly law

We would feign with Him ascend to star
Here remain on Earth, the heavens far

Chapter Ten. 2008 – 2009 The Holy Trinity and God

That the Angels, too, may join in song
Praise the Saviour's deeds of Life so strong

Easter is a seed of morning new
Up above in heavens opens the blue
Christ becomes the Cosmos wide and true
Dove is resurrected high in view

We rejoice each morning with the Sun
Born again from darkness to light won
See the Mystery of Life begun
Christ in Victory for every one.

Culver City, California
December 31, 2008

Peach

Some consider wantonness
I allow them, nor distress
But before the Mind of God
Thoughts awaken of my Lord

He is clear and bright as day
In my heart has come to stay
All the other people teem
In a restless illness dream

Poetry is other word
An incumbent healthy bird
Flown into my mind in thought
Merry answers questions brought

See the thoughts of poetry
Shine in words creatively
My own star of night appear
As a sun of soul so clear

Nothing else can trouble me

Chapter Ten. 2008 – 2009 The Holy Trinity and God

Nor the deepest stormy sea
For the air in victory
Fills with streaming light, you see

Any child of God will know
Heart does care and make it so
That the feelings of the eve
Deepen in the word believe

This is Christ in inner realm
Of the heart of sorrow's psalm
Sung in Masses of the choir
Suffered by the saints inspire

Every human being know
Who the Christ received Him so
This own feeling warm with grief
Only in within relief

For within experience
Suffering its story hence
Like a pilgrim on the road
To the cross his timeless ode

Every pilgrim walks alone
By him Christ companion
Then alone with Christ he goes
On his journey with his woes

Pilgrimage is mystery
Deeper than the eye can see
Deep within the warmth in me
Is the Christly Mystery

Now involve the Thought alone
In which history was sown
In the Heart of Jesu, Lord
This is God, the Christ and Word

Chapter Ten. 2008 – 2009 The Holy Trinity and God

For this Thought originate
In the Mind of God, Son's fate
Nothing else does this pre-date
Only this I now relate

Christianity is Rose
Red above the Thorn see grows
Heaven's Glory rises o'er
Suffering is more and more

Suffering becomes most dear
Only I immerse me there
In, within my heart is here
Christ is pilgrimage in prayer

What is poetry but prayer?
But the road the pilgrim fare?
On an old and timeworn earth
There within my ancient worth

Poetry sings past in myth
Poetry is hieroglyph
Poetry of future gift
Would my heavy heart uplift

But I now immerse with care
Me in poetry in prayer
Find in suffering my source
Christ of feeling my remorse

Christ of feeling deepening
In the truth within breathe in
Then breathe out and feel within
Pulse of blood repeat again

Destiny is future reach
Destiny is plucked, a peach
Holy is the distance I
Almost taste my peach of sky

Chapter Ten. 2008 – 2009 The Holy Trinity and God

This my peach divine I see
Peach of heaven's company
Peach of holy Trinity
Peach above the Mystery.

February 14, 2009

Everywhere

A poem is a song, a music fair
Until the song is sung, the music air
Then poetry is done, and all is where
The dreaming fills the all and everywhere.

March 15, 2009

From a card from Virginia Sease, Ph.D., written in Dornach, Switzerland, May 22, 2009:

> Again, my gratitude continues for your thoughtfulness in sending me your letters, essays, poetry and books. Keep up the creativity—it is also beneficial for the angels!

Sophia

Christ flows in the stream, I know
The stream of life in living flow
The stream of light inwards bestow
The light of love on earth below

I love to dream of Christ each eve
When by the sunset I believe
In His Passion One sad day
No one follow Him His way

Each one who loves Him does today
Find love in crucifixion gray

Chapter Ten. 2008 – 2009 The Holy Trinity and God

Above the cross was night, though day
A black before in grave He lay

Then Easter was a deed on earth
First Christ helps souls who lost their worth
Then on the day the Third rebirth
Arise, Christ joy in joyous mirth!

My attitude must inwards turn
To find the meaning of an urn
For what is left behind on earth
But only ashes without birth

Yet this tells not of life unseen
The spirit lives not here is seen
The Mystery unknown to us
A thought unthinkable it was

The thought is spiritual as deep
As when each night we fall asleep
The body to the day belong
The soul to spirit dreams in song

That is what this poem is
A song I heard, angelic 'tis
For the Angels sing in choir
My poetry in love inspire

Sophia, She of feminine
Is purity and Spirit-tin
The Godhead, She is wisdom or
The figure holiness adore

Sophia, bless my poetry
I ask Thee now in prayerfully
Thou art Song eternally
My heart uplift that Thee I see

Sophia, Thou in heights above
The Queen Who holds the Infant love

Chapter Ten. 2008 – 2009 The Holy Trinity and God

The Child, the Babe is Christ Jesu
Caress His little face of dew

He is fresh, pristine and new
Like Thee art Maria blue
Heaven, Thou Sophia true
Enrobed in Sun of golden hue

Thy feet repose on Moon of white
Like slippers shining in the night
Thy head a crown of stars adorn
The holy Virgin Christ is born

Sophia, I Thee eloquence
All my verses heaven sent
Aspire to Thy holiness
Thou the night doth each night bless

Now join me, reader, in my Song
Of wonderful we all belong
To the beautiful and true
Sophia all the heavens, too

She is higher than the high
And wise and mighty Seraphi
She of Trinity remain
Purifying as the rain

O, drench our Earth, Sophia, Thou
Of Song the Angels do endow
Like forests rich in green of bough
The Christmas tree this night and now

Sophia, Thou of Christmastime
Bestow upon my little rhyme
A smile that Jesu Christ in dream
Of love the world anew redeem

Gentle art Thou Lady high
See protect the Lord is nigh

Chapter Ten. 2008 – 2009 The Holy Trinity and God

Thy embrace to shelter love
This the meaning poem of

One last word I sing to Thee
For the human family
Thou art friend and kind to me
Sophia of the Trinity.

May 8, 2009

Pictures of Places and Faces

Pictures—of places
Of unseen faces
Of traces of places
I see these places

I see these faces
They are pictures
They are real places
They are real faces

Pictures—of faces
Faces of Christ
Faces of Sainthood
Faces of Martyrdom

Faces
Christ-faces
Pictures real are faces
Christ-faces
I see faces

Pictures—of places
Where men have walked
Where men have spoken
Where men have thought

And pictured faces
Have seen Christ-faces

Chapter Ten. 2008 – 2009 The Holy Trinity and God

Men with Christ-faces
In places
Real places
I see pictures of places

Pictures arise
I see pictures before me
Pictures are faces
Christ-faces of Saints and Martyrs

Christ-eyes
Christ-noses
Christ-lips
Christ-ears
Christ-cheeks
Christ-chins
Of Christ-faces
I see Christ-faces

Pictures—of places
Places green in sprouting springs
Places green in greening summers
Places of colors of flower-blossoms
Of leaf-autumns
Places barren of life
Of death's winters

When Christ, the Babe is born
When Christ, the Light is born
When Christ, the Light is born in the surrounding darkness
When Christ, the Light of warmth is born in the surrounding cold

Brightening in the darkness
Warming in the coldness
Christ in barren winters
Life in sullen death
Birth in quiet places
Christ Jesu, the Child of midwinter

Chapter Ten. 2008 – 2009 The Holy Trinity and God

Pictures—of places
Places of spring joys
Rebirth of New Life
Rebirth after death's shadow
Covers the Earth

Of crucifixion on Golgotha
The place of the Skull
Of darkest death where Christ died
Many places of death
Where shadows bend to Earth
Golgothas everywhere
Human crucifixions
Places

Pictures—of places
Many rebirths
An Easter Resurrection
Where Christ rises
Rising from the Dead
Places on Earth
Places of rebirth

Pictures—of places
Real pictures
Real rebirths
Real risings

Places here on Earth
The dead have risen
The dead are rising
The dead shall rise

Until the World shall be the place
Of the many risen ones
And the Earth shall rise from death
And rebirth shall be real in all places

See the pictures of faces, of places

Chapter Ten. 2008 – 2009 The Holy Trinity and God

See the pictures
Now the future has begun
The pictures are the signs of the future

Of many faces and places
Of the Face of the Earth
The great Picture is the Sign of the future

See the pictures
See the signs of the future
See the great Picture
See the Sign of the future
In pictures
In the great Picture of the future
Today.

May 20, 2009

Accompany

The Son of Man, the son of Mars
The Night of Christ, the Night of stars
The afterglow, the sons of light
The geniuses of God tonight

The avenue of promenade
Of poplar, birch, of tree and God
The quiet place of domicile
The reverence, the holy mile

The aftermath, the funeral
The sorrowful ephemeral
The spirits of the newly dead
The Bride, Bridegroom, soul to Christ wed

The similar compare today
Dissimilar another way
The inward pull, the Christ within
The presence of the Christ 'mongst men

Chapter Ten. 2008 – 2009 The Holy Trinity and God

The Christ doth move amongst the crowd
Unrecognized beneath the shroud
Of spirit-heart protected thrice
From outward life, from purchase' price

From chaos' sounds, the tumult or
The restlessness Christ doth ignore
He brings in me His stillness' peace
The others fill the room release

The spirits stir like whirling breeze
Whilst Christ untouched in me makes ease
The Son of God, the Son is love
The son of Mars, the Venus dove

The Sun of all our brotherhood
The Sun resounds; the Sun is good
The Sun is warm; the Sun is light
The Sun is day, the Sun of night

The Sun is Christ of human heart
The Sun each day doth newly start
The Sun in me my inwardness
The Sun in me my verses bless

The Sun become the World-Light
For all men see before the night
The Sun reveals the Christ by day
The Sun will heal the sick God's Way

The Sun is Christ; He paints the Earth
With colors of the dawning birth
Christ paints the Dome of sky of blue
Christ paints the clouds of white of hue

Christ paints at close of day in chords
Of colors dear the sunset towards
Eternal night and Son Divine
Sophia is the heavenly sign

Chapter Ten. 2008 – 2009 The Holy Trinity and God

Now one last word is erudite
To learn the day, take into night
The learnéd sage the teachers are
They guide mankind both near and far

They write the books of spiritual
We read their hands Divine of Will
For what is pen's philosophy
But God's clear Christianity?

For what are letters and the arts
But bonafide and thinking hearts?
For what is thought but Christ today?
Christ is the sunlight's golden ray

Christ is rabbi; teach me well
Thy lessons of the water well
Feed the hungry; give to drink
Care the sick; on naught else think

Visit lonely; tend the child
Love the loveless, mercy mild
Help the hurting family
Of the one humanity

This is Christ in you and me
This is Christ before the Sea
This is Christ accompany
Us on our way to God, to He.

May 25, 2009

Vision Kindness

Thine eyes see kindness
A vision sweet and fond
See love and beauty's peace
A Mother to her child respond

Chapter Ten. 2008 – 2009 The Holy Trinity and God

Thine eyes see wonder loveliness
See purity and grace
See joy and holiness
A vision of the human race

For in the quiet
Of the early morn
When all is still
And day is newly born

When at the dawn
The sun soon rise in east
Begins the journeying
Ending the holy feast

I blessed the Christ in Thee
He showed Himself to me
And this is love
The human family

And this is love
And this is miracle
Which Christ bestows
On poets lyrical

For what is song?
Poetry musical
And what art Thou?
My friendly whimsical

Yea, in the eyes of God
Who grants men each new day
Beautiful love
Onwards ever and alway

The music of the day
Brings joy, sings verses wonderful
And that is love
Imagination triumphal

Chapter Ten. 2008 – 2009 The Holy Trinity and God

And that is love
And that is poetry
My song for life
The human family
My song for life
I sing for Thee and me.

July 17, 2009

Monk Poetry

Devout, my inner monk sustained
A prayerful sentiment remained
And all the poverty I blamed
On penitence I now arranged

Like nails of biting eloquence
In wood of bleeding penitence
My mind a place where sentiments
Seemed out-of-place as common sense

My actuary lost his job
My dignitary I let sob
My old remorse began to turn
Into refrains I daily earn

And now I listen patiently
The silence breathes all heavily
And I am caught immobiley
In grief and metaphorically

I sing the psalms of tragedy
No one else to blame but me
All I own quite mentally
Is sorrow's load and time for me

Is fitting for a monk to be
In robes of sackcloth ashenly
My face except for sun that tans

Chapter Ten. 2008 – 2009 The Holy Trinity and God

Would pale as Moon all color sans

The corridors of mind and song
Do echo wilderness belong
This monk in circles walks around
Unceasingly the holy ground

Where Christ, my brother, sister near
Keeps company all everywhere
Never lonely, I remain
Most thankful, even I insane

I am the monk of future wrote
A book without my fate of note
But only work and quietude
The nights my days each time ensued

My only customary way
Is rise the morn, great the new day
And sleep—yes, sleep—is all I say
My mortuary mind repay

A single curse, the dead in me
Keeps living quite alive, if free
To read and write abundantly
This is my oath to Church to be

The Church is rooms where all is words
I read and write devoid of birds
So silence keeps me company
This monk endures, if heavily

My step I sit the hours in prayer
To mourn in place of my despair
I thought I heard a voice repair
Then fade to distance disappear

I love the silence, tolerate
The want of joyous elevate

Chapter Ten. 2008 – 2009 The Holy Trinity and God

For quiet is the time I own
Where sleep is deep and thoughts disown

The places I within do roam
Are mind and word and breathing home
I am without the other kind
Of freedom found in all mankind

And now I close my book of prayer
Be disillusion in the air
The sacristan and chalice of
Communion sacrifices love

Until all people whispering
O friends! I cannot offering
The Church would brighten with my song
When all I feel forgive my wrong
One day I end my journey long
To find another place along

Until that day I read and write
In monasteries of the night
I read the books by candlelight
Illumine softly is the light

I love the colors of the eve
The sunset of my Christ believe
My monk becomes the poet I
Keep writing this my lullaby

For colors are my poetry
Surely all is imagery
My readers can most easily
In reading find within and see

The monk within my mystery
Is love and feeling poetry
Is faith and patience every day
My voice unspoken must delay

Chapter Ten. 2008 – 2009 The Holy Trinity and God

The hour when fate my fortune is
The future beckons me because
No other way does God me find
My purposes lie for mankind

Such is the hand my destiny
Keeps writing living poetry
Such is this monk my imagery
Is filled beyond the Church in me.

July 23, 2009
Final three stanzas
July 26, 2009
Los Angeles

CHAPTER ELEVEN

2009 – 2013

ALL PREVIOUSLY

UNPUBLISHED POEMS

Chapter Eleven. 2009 – 2013 All Previously Unpublished Poems

Children

Christmas lovely winter mild
After sunset comes the Child
Holy prince, now bringing peace
Angels singing without cease

Earth and heaven gather 'round
Mary and our Christ renowned
Blesses all the Father good
We, His children, understood

Sleep, ye faithful; come to rest
Life has been to suffer test
Now the night begins to sing
Join we favored by our King

Lord and Saviour of the World
Christmas wonder holy Child
In the dream of prayer we see
Christ is Jesu tenderly

Ox and ass keep with their breath
Warm the Prince of Life from death
Born to save the world from cold
Sun the Light the prophets 'told

Children, sing ye carols sweet
To the Infant at His feet
Offer shepherds gifts thereof
Wool and flask of milk and love

And a lamb this Lamb of God
Even as a babe the Word
Destined for the Cross to die
Human death the reason why

That the death-experience
Good is from that moment hence

Chapter Eleven. 2009 – 2013 All Previously Unpublished Poems

We begin as little ones
As Christ Jesu we are sons

Go the road of life, we pray
Christmas is a holy day
To the Holy Week of trial
Suffer for a little while

This the Passion of our Lord
Crucifixion of the Word
On the day the Third He rose
From the Land of Dead foretold

Resurrection Nature is
Scene of Sun and stars He lives
See, resplendent in the joy
God of suffering and boy

Christmas is an holy time
Sing we in this little rhyme
In the night we sleep in Thee
God the Father restfully

There with Christ the Son, our Lord
And Sophia, Spirit-God
Trinity the meaning of
Peace and light and holy love.

Culver City, California
First fifteen lines
December 23, 2009
(rest of poem lost)
Last thirty-seven lines
February 23, 2010

A Christmas Night

I climbed a mount on high to cloud
Until the night fell o'er the sky

Chapter Eleven. 2009 – 2013 All Previously Unpublished Poems

And cloaked the earth
My hand reached up unto the stars
Below the mount in stillness kept
A Christmas night

My song at peace like lullaby
I gazed with wonder heavenly light
'Twas beauty-love
Returning down the mount to morn
A Christmas fresh as newly born

I love the earth; my friend is she
Encompass all the land and tree
My gaze is bright with light where sun
Does reign o'er all in dominion

A day is motioned deeply life
I feel in sound all men can hear
Beneath the quiet stones do sleep
Above a star is beauty keep
And love is night I wonder-dream

And angels in a chorus sing
And animals awake on earth
Do feel the stillness of the stars
Where my soul with Christ appear
Every night is Christmas clear

But now this moment of the year
The spirits of the dead are here
The spirits of the dead are near
I love the song of chanticleer
Like calls of animals I hear
The night to me is peace appear.

January 19, 2010

Chapter Eleven. 2009 – 2013 All Previously Unpublished Poems

From a letter from Virginia Sease, Ph.D., written in Dornach, Switzerland, August 22, 2010:

…..I very much appreciate everything which you send me even though time constraints prevent me from mentioning most poems and essays. I am especially moved by your poem "America! Soul of my Heart" which you wrote on your birthday. It is my wish that many people born in America such as we are and those who still find asylum in America may experience the qualities which lie behind and within your poem. ….

America! Soul of My Heart

America! Soul of my heart
I join with thee in every start
Thou dost renew in me my song
The strength in me again grows strong
That every day I take the deep
From within me into night's sleep

And with the dead, in Christ I dream
The Sun of night my sacred tomb
Is shining bright with sun-drenched beam
I feel in me the Godhead-womb

My light – Thou Christ – my dearest Sun
Warms Thou my heart, and every one
That on the morn I am reborn
A victory, my pledge I sing
Is every day and every morn
The Sun of day my heart warmth brings

America! Song of my heart
I love thy Word; my poetry
Is springtime's life and promise' start
Is vision of the Sun to me

Chapter Eleven. 2009 – 2013 All Previously Unpublished Poems

Thy Name is soul and strength to be
The land of will and bravery
The land of lore and of the free
The land of life and greenery

America! I sing to thee
The world sings thy song for me
The world climbs thy mountains; see
The world walks from sea to sea
The world gestures 'cross thy plains
O'er desert, forest, fields of grain

Down canyons, rivers, over lakes
O'er hilly land. The world makes
A place where all the peoples of
The earth do work and live and love

In childhood and youth do give
Adulthood, middle age, do live
Then dying into old age, go
In death, all ages, men must know

All peoples of the world announce
America! I love thee. I
Am young with thee, all doubt renounce
And reach up to the bluest sky

Rejoice, for life is beautiful
I shake my brothers', sisters' hand
Thy fruits of life are bountiful
I work the soil, the richest land

The landscapes various, and songs
Of languages of every folk
Are heard like music's dance along
The halls of heaven, gods invoke

Enthusiastic is my voice
I join thy story and rejoice

Chapter Eleven. 2009 – 2013 All Previously Unpublished Poems

For history and future. Come!
I celebrate the seasons' sun

America! Thou art my word
My element, my friend and bird
My birthday, Wedding, funeral
My death's rebirth, my spiritual
Life and blood, my native breath
And when I die an ancient death

My ashes join the fields of wheat
Into a spring eternal greet
My praises raise; I lift on high
My voice to thee, a lullaby
Of love and gratitude to thee
Land of the Good, God's friend and me.

August 5, 2010
my 48th birthday morning

Rose of Heaven

The essential man – in spirit-soul
Untouched by earthly illness-role
Yet deeply felt in union
A karmic Christ-communion

Warmly feel I in my heart
Permeates my being art
Each night my body do depart
Each morn anew I waking start

My faith is brotherly, my friend
My warmth of feeling loving tend
I mingle in the atmosphere
Of Christ-kindred in the air

Then, by God, His blessing gives
Under God my karma lives

Chapter Eleven. 2009 – 2013 All Previously Unpublished Poems

Is my soul for art described
Pictured in my words like scribes

Scribes of Christian properties
Scribes of words and prophecies
Scribes of vision poetries
Scribes of wisdom-love that sees

I be scribe; my poetry
Is my vision tenderly
Christ within my heart to me
Felt in warmth of breath I be

Christian stirs in inwardly
Pulling feeling into me
There I find the altar of
Future worlds of stars and love

Sun, my heart, I enter thee
Deepening right into me
In my dreaming visionary
Is my song sight luminary

Animals delight each morn
In the day is newly born
But the birds of song proclaim
Hear Christ quickening call out His Name:

"Come!" writes John, "Come, quickly!" speaks
We do follow, we who seek
In our hearts a fire shows
Ignited for the heavenly rose

Rose of heaven red appear
On the rosebush earth, right here
In the sunlight shining clear
Christ is streaming through the air

Christ is coming; He is near

Chapter Eleven. 2009 – 2013 All Previously Unpublished Poems

Christ appearing everywhere
Christ is calling every one:
"Children, join Me in the Sun!"

August 16, 2010
Revised January 9, 2013

I Am the Passage

I am the passage
The only passage
To where I am ever
Coming and going

I am the passage
I swim and I wander
I eloquent somber
Come and go yonder

I am the passage
I stand up and motion
I walk in commotion
I feel with emotion

I am the passage
My heart is a message
The message of passage
Through which I travel

I am the passage
Within my heart I
Know worlds of dreaming
Dreaming ascension

I am the passage
In dreaming ascend I
To heaven with father
With Arne and Mother

Chapter Eleven. 2009 – 2013 All Previously Unpublished Poems

Mother, dear Margaret
Father and Mother
Friendship Virginia
John and the others

I am the passage
My heart is a message
Through feeling I travel
Through feeling I'm moving

I am the passage
Moving and motion
Stirring and sounding
Die and devotion

Birth and communion
Speech elocution
Magical potion
Drink with devotion
Make evolution….

August 26, 2010

Pearl

The waters are not shallow
The thoughts of life run deep
In feeling stirs around me
My heart in dreams of sleep

I wonder at the heavens
The starry worlds of night
The Mystery abounding
In the stillness of the light

The oceans are but sorrows
Which wash on shores of time
The mountains the foundation
Eternal and sublime

Chapter Eleven. 2009 – 2013 All Previously Unpublished Poems

The clouds sign Christ's returning
The Sun in glory shines
In radiance of morning
I journey and I climb

The distances so lovely
The distances of days
My quest is seeking always
The golden sunny rays

Then at the sunset evening
Descending into night
The Sun is sacrificing
A death before my sight

She glows her passion's colors
In oranges and gold
And somewhere red is telling
Of warmth offsets all cold

And when the night appearing
In stars of myriad lights
I wonder and I wander
Forever in delights

For nighttime is eternal
Forever young and fair
Is spirit with the moonlight
Refreshing in the air

Is spirit in the starlight
My fiery friends aware
Of Christ in all His Glory
Beyond all human care

The One and only lasting
The Lord salvation brings
Celestial in answer
To princes and to kings

Chapter Eleven. 2009 – 2013 All Previously Unpublished Poems

Heaven is His palace
The Shepherd in His fields
Keeps watching o'er His children
All souls of the world

The Shepherd's flock keeps tending
His mercy do I yield
The Shepherd peace is bringing
Contentment, joy His pearl.

August 30, 2010

Where Wisdom is a Verse for the Dead

In Thy presence Christ,
Thou heaven's priest,
All human death is passage.

Souls depart
From bodily abode
Where illness, pain and dying
Do cripple men and women
On death's bed,

Age and sorrow bring
The soul, long suffering,
Disappears from outwards life
In mystery appear:

Heaven's bodiless
Weave and heal, unseen,
Unheard, but dearly felt,
I know. The dead

Are young and warm
In infancy; heaven is birth
And festive life
Of newly-entered souls;

Chapter Eleven. 2009 – 2013 All Previously Unpublished Poems

We sing the chorus' Mystery;
In tombs we go
Down halls of ages,
Crypts and vaults;

Remains, like relics
Of the saints,
Remind me of my song
I sing is sacred

In the atmosphere
Surrounding me,
Within me,
The heavenly bodies,
Warm in death's birth,
Move about;

The Mystery-Reality
Is felt in me;
All around me
The dead live and go;

They come to comfort
And console
The living left
On earth behind

The earth is house,
The dead the company
We keep;

Surrounding me,
Reality,
Unseen, unheard,
But palpable as breath
As movements of the hands;

The dead with angels
In our midst. They come

Chapter Eleven. 2009 – 2013 All Previously Unpublished Poems

Are here, as near
As we to them
In heavy hearts
In mourning;

They warmly love us,
Angel-children
Smiling, standing,
Seeing, touching

The dead
Are keeping company;
Heaven is here
Where hearts feel,
Where eyes see,

Where wisdom is
A verse for the dead
Who listen to
Our inwards prayer

Of warmth of hearts
We say inside,
The room we keep
For them to visit us;

They come,
Will always come,
When they in our hearts
Feel, through our eyes
See, with our hands
Touch.

The dead are presences
In us on earth.

September 3, 2010

Chapter Eleven. 2009 – 2013 All Previously Unpublished Poems

Sounds of Evening

Sleep softly, serenity
Sleep sweetly, soliloquy
Sleep lightly, listening
To the sounds of evening
Sounds of animals preparing
For the nights of offering

Sounds of households quieting
Families their children bring
Sounds of sunsets coloring
Clouds with light of sun setting

Sounds of heavens darkening
To the sound of wandering
Moon so bright and beckoning
Poets in their fond dreaming

Sounds of oceans distancing
Waves of waters crash crashing
Sounds of motions motioning
Days into nights transforming
Sounds of angel choirs sing
Glories of the heavens bring.

December 13, 2010
Revised January 9, 2013

Internalize These Thoughts

Internalize the thoughts I heard
Felt, then thought, a little bird
Before the night of cloud and star
I dreamt of fields and forests far
Acquainted with the happenings
Of scholars, visions, sainted kings

The Sun was deep and deepening
Into the silence evening

Chapter Eleven. 2009 – 2013 All Previously Unpublished Poems

A sunset colors offering
All mystery and pardoning

Then did announce in Christ the Sun
A man incarnate, only one
Once for all of time, He knew
Suffered, God died in Jesu

Sacrifice most precious, dear
Mystery of pain appear
Cross of darkness, green of death
Dove of Light above His breath
Final Deed, then life of red
Suffering turned joy instead

Easter is the Mystery
Death no mortal man may see
Spirit-birth invisible
Son of heaven favored well
All men might know possible
Saviour's resurrection tell

"Come," the Shepherd Good hear call,
"Come unto me children all
"I am Life, now safety feel
"With the Father I do heal
"Future is my promise' day
"Sure abide in me alway."

God in heaven, He abides
All His universe resides
This is morning hope renew
This is Easter Sunday view.

Christ is deeper than the scope
Of a constable or Pope
He is deeper than the noise
Than the fanfare chaos' boys

Chapter Eleven. 2009 – 2013 All Previously Unpublished Poems

They are but a tempest storm
Christ the waters calms to form
Restlessness stops movement of
Stillness brings to us the Dove.

Peace brings God ordained above
On the earth Sun thinking of
On the earth of death and form
Resurrect to spirit born

On the earth the fruit does fall
There within the seed is all
Future mountain-forests grow
Sun the earth becomes we know
And these mountain-forests are
Dignity upheld and law

In the Sun abide they still
Weights of Intellect and Will
"Join us," call the Sun-folk, hear,
"New Jerusalem is near."

This my poem enter in
Hearts and hearth and home within
Internalize these thoughts of light
In the Mystery of night
On the morrow new begin
Praises to the Sun again.

December 31, 2010
January 3, 2011

Johnny

A bluebonnet became a little boy
He sat on a stool and played with toy
He sat and sang and played with joy
He supped with a frog, much did enjoy.

What was his name, this bluebonnet boy?

Chapter Eleven. 2009 – 2013 All Previously Unpublished Poems

What was the stool he sat on with toy?
He name was Johnny; I know he's good
His seat was a toadstool made not of wood.

Johnny was a bonny bluebonnet boy
Johnny led a lovely lively life with joy
Johnny played games and with many a toy
With a frog he supped, his days did enjoy.

Johnny became my friend; we made
The funniest faces while games we played
Johnny and I not once dismayed
Johnny and I drank lemonade.

June 13, 2011
Los Angeles

Menschenbruder

Ich finde mich
Im Äther
In meinem Innern
Im innren Herzen
In meinem Fühlen
In meinem Atem

Ich ruhe mich
Im fühlenden Denken
Das warm strahlet
Im Äther schwebend
Wie ein Hauch atmet
Mein Ich

Das Ich meines Herzens
Das warm rühret
In meinem Fühlen
Dich zart grüßend
Menschenbruder
Du, den ich liebe

Chapter Eleven. 2009 – 2013 All Previously Unpublished Poems

Christus.

29. Juni 2011

Human Brother

I find my Self
In the ether
In my within
In my inner heart
In my feeling
In my breath

I rest
In feeling thought
That streams warmly
Hovering in the ether
My I
Breathes like a breath

The I of my heart
That warmly touches
In my feeling
Greeting Thee gently
Human Brother
Thou whom I love
Christ.

June 29, 2011

Love and The Meal

My human brother, sister,
Father, Mother, friend
I loved you in my childhood,
A youth my love did send

A young man born in freedom,
My love became my heart
I suffered in my feeling

Chapter Eleven. 2009 – 2013 All Previously Unpublished Poems

With love the dearest hurt

And by my inmost suffering
Within my heart I found
In soul most tender feeling
My love for you the grounds

Of human language forming
My poetry and mood,
In imagery and thinking
My feeling for the Word

This my song here singing
A bird of love awake,
A boy again and Poet
A smile I feeling make

A smile the lad he kindly,
Again a youth and child,
With human love surrounding
His person, good and mild

Who is this lad and Poet,
This bird and man and boy?
He's Alan Lindgren deepening
In feeling love and joy

Now when not sorrow tender
In sadness' sympathy
He joyous reaches cheerful
Your friend always will be

His face and eyes see brighten
From out his shining soul
His inner light in greeting
The Christ in you; he's whole

Communes with you in sacred
Moments meaning much

Chapter Eleven. 2009 – 2013 All Previously Unpublished Poems

'Tis love these moments tending
When Alan found your touch

Your touch become Christ's blessing
As warm as sun above
The Hand of Christ was touching
As sunlight streaming love

On earth Christ finds me daily;
I open and we sup
My heart is table laden
With broken Bread and Cup

Together we this Meal
Partake for sustenance
Then into life are strengthened
Christ's flesh our nourishment.

June 30, 2011

The Little Shoe

Feelings figments of an arc
Rigid rainbows print a park
Curves called crescents of the Moon
Ask me why I sing this tune

I will tell you honestly
Words are sounds and voice to me
Consonants keep counting more
Military men ignore

Who will pass the time in peace?
Words are answering release
Bulging bigger boulders blue
Of an able avenue

One last moment in this verse
Free from dormant universe

Chapter Eleven. 2009 – 2013 All Previously Unpublished Poems

Like a wave of swelling hope
I write poetry to cope

Life is riddled ruggedly
Climbers clamor cleverly
I am slow and ponder blue
Is the color of this shoe

Little shoe an elf once dropped
No one bothered when he stopped
To return it quietly
Now I write this homily

If you see an elf alone
Ask him if he wears a gown
Pearls and a little shoe
Tell him I have one, it's blue.

August 15, 2011

Birth

Summer was an ideal I knew
In the heavens I laughed in blue
But my eyes returned to earth
Green kept giving summer birth

Age is autumn, winter's death
Summer is the living breath
Spring is rebirth or the smile
Raphael is painting while

Roses blossom on the cross
Crucified above the moss
Is the Christ in sacrifice
Life of heaven, death the price

Winter is the inner birth
Children understand the earth

Chapter Eleven. 2009 – 2013 All Previously Unpublished Poems

Memories of Christmas are
Simple as a shining star

Bethlehem, now come to me
Bring me one small Christmas tree
I will decorate the green
With the light my eyes have seen

Poverty is like a child
Who needs wealth when mercy mild
Is the love of Mary for
Jesu ope the heav'nly door

Now we enter mysteries
In the night where elegies
Cease, and magic ever new
Births eternally our view.

August 15, 2011

Painted Patterns

Painted patterns behind leaves
Touch anointed altar eves
On a sunset each believes
Of our God Who all achieves

By His hand with colors weave
Countless distant clouds receive
Until paintings eyes relieve
Many hearts of sorrow grieve

I remember sunsets deep
I remember before sleep
How I pardoned all the day
In the passion's color-way

Passion, crucifixion seen
In the dying colors been

Chapter Eleven. 2009 – 2013 All Previously Unpublished Poems

I was echoing the scene
Sadly I beseeched the green

Sacred, sacred breath to me
Is my personality
God has touched my mind with thought
Of the Christ of Christian sought

By the seekers over time
Up the hills of green they climb
Painted patterns of the vine
Tell of resurrection's wine

Painted patterns all connect
Every one mankind collect
No one need left out neglect
Choice is I have you respect

When the evening his tired head
Rests upon the earthen bed
Sun descends; it's twilight hour
Stars begin above to flower

Painted patterns disappear
In the night of chanticleer
Where a myriad stars appear
My, the heavens, Christ is clear

All may see His crown and day
In the Mystery hold sway
Day is now the night alway
Everlasting time God's way.

August 26, 2011
Santa Monica, California

Light

Blue heavens with clouds
Vast and white and grey

Chapter Eleven. 2009 – 2013 All Previously Unpublished Poems

Stretched out beyond
The mainly month of May

I thought I saw
Maria pray
Blue of powder
On this day

I look up
And see the grand
Upside-down
God's greatness Hand

I wonder and
I awe the blue
The brilliant white
Of white of hue

The deep blue sea
Of sky overhead
I dreamed above
I dunked my head

And love was sky
And day was all
As large as heaven
I was small

My eyes; they opened
Received the call
Of heaven's heights
Of heavens tall

Blue skies with white
With clouds of light
Bursting brilliant
With sun bright

I knew I saw

Chapter Eleven. 2009 – 2013 All Previously Unpublished Poems

In clouds above
My Christ in awe
Clouds white of love.

Santa Monica, California
September 4, 2011
Revised Los Angeles
January 9, 2012

Know God

Semblances of shoulders say
Breast is breath of life alway
Silhouettes of shadows nigh
Tell of sunlight in the sky

If you contact mysteries
Maybe come in homilies
Stirring life and death in threes
Shall you linger elegies
Find the Moon divinities
Christ is God though enemies

May construct another text
Christ can never be duplexed
God the Father gives context
In His universe complex

Who is Christ? The ignorant
Ask when Christ is true Advent
Ask when birth's eternal lent
Ask; His love is spirit-sent

Who is God? They do not know
As they come and as they go
"Hear," commands the preacher, lo
"Hear, Know God," he beckons so
Knowledge is of God, you know

Chapter Eleven. 2009 – 2013 All Previously Unpublished Poems

Heaven above and earth below.

Santa Monica, California
September 7, 2011

Truth

Truth is science on the earth
Truth in heaven's spirit-birth
Truth of life is pain and mirth
Truth of men is human worth.

Who is the Truth of science? Say
Who is the Truth of death today?
Who is the Truth of pain, who may?
Who is the Truth of men repay?
The Truth of each is Christ alway.

Santa Monica, California
September 7, 2011
Los Angeles
January 22, 2013

Dreaming

Never let the universe
Extend beyond the poet's verse
Though he rhymes in rhythms terse
Beauty's heaven is a nurse

Caring for her patients, stars
In a hospice bed like Mars
Sheets and pillow white as Moon
Heaven sings a plaintive tune

Wears a uniform of love
Shapely princess Venus-dove
Her hair is golden as the Sun
Garlanded in silken spun

Chapter Eleven. 2009 – 2013 All Previously Unpublished Poems

By the angels playing song
Harps with strings of prayer are strung
Sweet their voices' melodies
Music making harmonies

See the celestial starry night
God ordains eternal light
Christ is babe, whose beauty-love
Heaven dreaming nurses of

Christmas is the midnight hour
Sun in light begins to flower
Holy is the night; the Son
Dwells with God in union.

Santa Monica, California
September 8, 2011

The Park

A great old tree stood solid in its branching way, planted rooted deep in the brown grounds of earth, assorted small leaves decorating its forked branches greening a high crown, while sunlight only flitted through the shaded space called Nature's house and home to birds. I sit beneath, reflecting in the cool outdoor room, spacious as the park entire, and place to many tree and happy bird.

Outside is human habitation, populated by the citizenry folk, whose lives in timeless time I see transpire, lives in my fifty years, now early twenty-first century after Christ, but echoed down millennial halls of ancestry-progeny, generations' lineage of man, common to our humanity, a multi-chambered mirror in which are seen the changes of the ages. From primitive ritual to fields of harvest; from simple humility of the holy family to glory-art; from science to machinated technology, so strange to Nature and our human being, and pervasive of our time. We march ahead to the destination of mankind. New Jerusalem beckons; we tarry not.

The red Sun remains creative of each day, the dogs or cats beloved pets as pigs or chickens before them. The solitary human being walking as

Chapter Eleven. 2009 – 2013 All Previously Unpublished Poems

alway, though dressed in casual in the comfort fashioned to today. The air invisible we still breathe, the Sun's light's ever clear and warm. The clouds the gorgeous minions or of storm of dreary rain shops or of silent white-pure snow-blankets, the green text of broad Creation still read in verdant luxurious life and growth, the Earth-foundation of the kingdoms four (stone, plant, animal and man, as we well know), the Sea eternal as before in hearing of the death-white Moon.

I wonder now that heaven sings. Changeless is God's place, the homeland of all worlds as everlasting stars of night. On earth we men and women, as once the Child, are born to live and die (and we be born anew) for learning and for work. So is our evolution: time and space, eternity, then time and space again.

Life is an ancient poem, written in languages both dead and changed and heard today. We eulogize our song; in warm and resonant baritone a monastic Mass is heard in requiem chanted to damp dusk at twilight's gathering mist in the graveyard of our lives, where angels touch the tombstones with their feathers fine. In Christ the dead depart; it's returning hour. On earth God's morning is reborn. This park is radiant with the golden Sun on green's beauty-lawn.

Culver City, California
September 9, 2011
Revised Santa Monica, California
September 10/October 5, 2011

Fonder

Inquire in incandescent mind
My heart of feeling inward find
But first remember humankind
Mother precious, Mother kind

In readiness now write; inquire
The truth of feeling first require
Like posts of virtue do inspire
In songs called verses, voices choir

Chapter Eleven. 2009 – 2013 All Previously Unpublished Poems

Recall with me the ancient rite
Of sacrificial sun ignite
Where burns eternal fire in light
With leaping flames bright in the night

I often sought in afternoon
A pleasant solitary rune
To sing a softly gentle tune
And acquiesce beneath the Moon

Now listen with me, gracious heart
I stand before you quite apart
The music soon begins to start
And every actor plays his part

If you feel secluded far
These verses by excluded are
Only think on yonder star
Then you'll join me fonder are.

September 17, 2011

Measure

Measure is a rhythm or
A solar pulsing regular
An olden man of wisdom near
He knows the tempo with his ear

Who is the measure rhythm so?
The solar pulse is regular
The olden man of wise and near
The tempo is the Christ appear.

Santa Monica, California
September 17, 2011

Chapter Eleven. 2009 – 2013 All Previously Unpublished Poems

Herbstanbeginn nach Weihnachten schauend

I. Sensibelsein

Sensibelsein wird empfinden
Empfinden wird Fühlen
Fühlen im Herzen
In Herzensgründen

Herzen, die fühlen
Herzen, die träumen
Herzen, die schauen
Geburt Liebe Christi

Geburt Liebe Christi
Geburt Leben Christi
Geburt Lichte Christi
Geburt Sonne Christi.

II. Sonne

Sonne meines Herzens
Scheine in Finsternisse
Lichthell und strahlend
Kraftvoll mit Wärme
Warm in die Kälte

Sonne Christi
In mir aufleuchte
Meine Seele
Erleuchtend
Mein Herz
Erwärmend.

Santa Monica, Kalifornien
23. September 2011
Culver City, Kalifornien
22. Januar 2013

Chapter Eleven. 2009 – 2013 All Previously Unpublished Poems

Radiance

On an ancient holy altar
Flames in incense rose reminding
Me of sacrifices Psalter
Monks in monasteries finding

Harmonies in churches holy
Voices richly sing resounding
Men of God devoted only
To a life austere and grounding

Then a bird of small, a sparrow
Heard, I heard in quaint song loving
Telling not the Saviour's sorrow
But of joy, Prince of peace proving

So I opened wide my window
Welcomed this small sparrow tender
In my arms I gently fondle
Gave him crumbs and quiet shelter

Do you know, this bird of joyous
Entered softly singing cheerful
Joined the monks, the holy chorus
Praising God in Christ, an earful?

Christmas is for sparrows' gladness
Christ is come; rejoice ye faeries
All rejoice, the Child now born is
Ye good children, holly berries

Decorate the homes of poorness
Christ was born and laid in manger
In a stall, no room in richness
Angels sang, good news harbinger

Jesu is a boy; He love is
Little boy, yet God in Him lives

Chapter Eleven. 2009 – 2013 All Previously Unpublished Poems

See His eyes of earnest gazing
All the angels God are praising

He was born huge sacrifices
Suffer pain and death so dearly
Christ redeemer, us suffices
Deeds renew, Sun's rhythm yearly

Who knows death besides we human
Beings? Who has suffered darkness?
Christ has death known; became human
Suffered life and died He for us

Through death's portal went, the Mystery
With His Light the dark dispelling
Radiance, His Sun appearing
Warming hearts, His Spirit willing

Now not darkness fear, nor death we
Christ our beacon shining ever
See, the Sun of life and light He
True abiding, leaves us never.

Santa Monica, California
October 10, 2011
Revised Los Angeles
January 9, 2013

Destiny

A sorry lot who sadly mourns
It seems no one exempt forlorn
Like troubles crowned by thorny thorns
Each child must suffer who is born

In Christ shall know the shadow's tree
Like Hades' Underworld on knee
Within the inner mystery
In which men in the darkness see

Chapter Eleven. 2009 – 2013 All Previously Unpublished Poems

Grants every soul another light
Of magic who in Christ unite
Imagination frees their sight
To dreams called pictures all invite

Like Christmas does, come children, come
By the hearth shall warm the sun
Who born within the temple's heart
Grants all God's children a fresh start

And that is light the darkness banned
Thus freeing my soul upon the land
And that is warmth the cold did melt
I know it, I have by it felt

The meaning of the sun in me
Within my heart is hallowed be
The love of Christ in feeling lives
Transforming me as beauty gives

Another sentience dear to me
Deeper than the eye can see
Untroubled by old chaos, we
Join hearts and hands in destiny.

October 31, 2011

The Eternal Present

The present is eternal
Eternity in time
I always sing the present
Moment within rhyme

The present moment singing
Becomes the Moon of night
Until the Sun of morning
Returns me to the light

Chapter Eleven. 2009 – 2013 All Previously Unpublished Poems

The light eternal greeting
The day of radiant sound
The day of radiant color
The day's immortal ground

Keeps walking in the silence
Of the stones, while Man
Is speaking, He the Poet
Of Sun and of Earth's land.

November 19, 2011

The Banyan Tree – To Richard Levin

I knew a man as small
As the sky was tall
Yet his mind was large
As a lunar barge

He floated on the sea
Of turbulence and me
He sailed and thought of life
And death by human strife

He dreamed while half awake
A lover pulled to take
In love and beauty he
Sought peace and harmony

Was sensitive and frail
Like plants who grow and ail
His illness was the world
He suffered like a pearl

In an oyster shell
Of copper like a well
Kept dunking in the night
Beneath the nude moonlight

Chapter Eleven. 2009 – 2013 All Previously Unpublished Poems

In answer to his thoughts
Revealed himself not
But the other while
His secret did not tell

Although he was quite small
His soul of large did call
Across the waters deep
Whose surface rippled sleep

Like a plant he lived
Quiet, sensitive
As a Christian
He loved all things within

That he them understand
Their mystery and sand
Of timeless time before
Eternity was born

His name like Eden, see
Was future, prophecy
Flowers purple light
In gardens of delight

Was lover, Richard, friend
Without beginning, end
An endless poetry
Beneath the Banyan tree.

November 20
December 27, 2011

Children (2)

Children offer wonder true
Like an answer ageing blue
Keeps out-raying yellow warm
Before red became my form

Chapter Eleven. 2009 – 2013 All Previously Unpublished Poems

After season middle age
Blue recedes, an inwards stage
Green becomes the welcome scene
Dying rest where I have been

All of good of God above
Born from Him, His heavenly love
Every child who ponders Him
Reverent sleeps in God again.

November 27, 2011

Advent, or Chanticleer

Advent more then hope of birth
Prepares for me my heart like Earth
Receive the Child of Spirit as
The Christ in Bethlehem born was

With Angelus Silesius
We know if many, numerous
Births of Christ in Bethlehem
Not in our hearts it were in vain

In my heart will Christ Christmas
Be born anew the radiant Light
A miracle again shall pass
And Christ shine warmly in my sight

For what is sight but Sun in us
But in our hearts the radiance
Of Sun, the inner birth of Christ?
And this is Holy Nights of bliss

A joy like reverence and all
The angels join in songs of praise
We hear their voices earthwards call
The animals in dreams like rays

Chapter Eleven. 2009 – 2013 All Previously Unpublished Poems

Of Sun in inner hearts of men
Like shepherds we find Christ again
From fields of love of Bethlehem
We gather 'round the Child when

The news to us is brought by God
Our flocks in stillness rest in sleep
We heed the call the newborn Word
Arise from dreams of heavens deep

We go to Him, we feel but cheer
Immerse our souls with smiles here
We find the little baby there
Within our hearts of chanticleer.

Santa Monica, California
December 12, 2011

Christmas Eve and the Meaning of All Humankind

Do you know on Christmas Eve
When with the Earth our hearts believe
The Child, the Light, the Christ so soon
Be born again beneath the Moon?

The Sun of hearts shall shine within
Shedding light the world of men
As we await with animals
The Saviour's birth this festival

On Christmas night at midnight hour
The inner light begins to flower
In souls of men bright joy appears
This light in radiance so clear

Like children we are small this night
Expecting we this babe of light
Whose birth surrounds us with delight
Like smiling faces radiant bright

Chapter Eleven. 2009 – 2013 All Previously Unpublished Poems

Into the darkness brighter grows
The Light the world renews and knows
For at this time the Mystery
Of birth appears for us to see

Once a newborn infant-child
Held by Mary Mother mild
Now fills our hearts and thoughts with cheer
We love the Christmas time of year

Come Saviour Jesu Christ to me
Be my miracle I see
Your magic in the air reveal
You are the love and joy I feel

Christmas night is holy for
Within our poverty is more
With less we have abundance' store
With little find the Christmas door

We open secretly and share
Our hearts awake the Christ to bear
That Christmas new becomes in us
Reality like Candlemas

And many lights begin to shine
The world o'er the stars divine
Like Bethlehem in quiet lie
In stillness God and angels nigh

Descends the Child, a miracle
Is born in us; the beautiful
Love of God in Christ we find
The meaning of all humankind.

Culver City, California
Christmas Eve
December 24, 2011

Chapter Eleven. 2009 – 2013 All Previously Unpublished Poems

Hand—To Sherry

The Sun creates the day
Fashions seasons' way
By Her golden rays
With the clouds She plays

I saw a sky of blue
Maria's avenue
Of heavenly divine hue
My thoughts became the dew

Of Jesu on the flower
Upon the gentlest hour
Before the Sun's great power
Arose, a God-great tower

Like quiet came the One
The Lord of dominion
The holy divine Son
United with the Sun

I thought—or was in dream?
This radiant bright beam
Began in me to stream
The Sun the world redeem

And all the death of night
Disappeared from sight
Replaced by purest light
Of the Sun's great might

I knew that Christ within
Did enter me again
I heard Him in the voice
Of one in whom rejoice

Did the day's refrain
Of glory and the rain

Chapter Eleven. 2009 – 2013 All Previously Unpublished Poems

Through the grave disdain
I saw the Christ remain

He told me that within
My heart I felt again
His 'I AM' balancing
My efforts, those of Man

For in the memory
Of silence beyond me
I felt the quiet tree
Of shadow, light and me

Require the clear sunbeam
Awakened from my dream
The sacred sentient stream
Of God mankind redeem

And that is future now
Upon my smiling brow
For love is every how
I see and feel my vow

I see and feel each day
A true immortal way
The way in me writes God
With His Hand and Word
I now condense in me
My future destiny.

Santa Monica, California
January 23, 2012

Chapter Eleven. 2009 – 2013 All Previously Unpublished Poems

Temple

The body is a prayer sometimes
Beyond the silhouettes in times
Where souls awaken in the night
Of the everlasting light
I always thought a poem is
A prayer in which my soul lives
For in the morning I, aware
Ascend to Sun's temporal care

Accompany me through the days
I seek the Saviour after ways
He appears to me before
My brother, sister where the door

Stands open waiting for my hand
To write my poetry in sand
The Earth is mystery and deep
Immortality of sleep

Until another friend of mine
Sitting next to me does sign
Welcome to my song of love
The body is the temple of.

February 12, 2012

Peace (3)

A measurement is peace sometimes
I felt I found it in small rhymes
Where little people wished to climb
While the exalted are sublime

The peace I sought was avenue
I walked in silence quiet blue
Until I saw another hue
Peach was peace and this I knew

Chapter Eleven. 2009 – 2013 All Previously Unpublished Poems

If you would join me, sing this song
Of mercy to the place belong
Where all God's children, weak or strong
Become a joyous union-throng

But then, in secret, I did write
The love of everlasting light
Shining beauteous in the night
Before the morning big and bright

The Sun creates the day for me
Beneath the branches of this tree
I while the hours where shadows be
Because I love the Sun to see

The Sun, my fortune, warms me good
My heart and back right where I stood
The color was like cherry wood
Lacquered and well-understood

By my heart in moments still
When I am walking on God's Will
The valley and the lovely hill
Make peaceful farmland I do till

With hoe and fertile soil as rich
As humus gathered for a ditch
Planted with sweet flowers, which
Keep blossoming where farm forks pitch

The farmhand was a lad I knew
He dressed in blue jeans, wonders too
Like seeking souls ideals' view
Found one day the Christ renew

And God was good to him, who tried
Who struggled with the wolf inside
Who knew emotion with his words
Then found true meaning in God's birds

Chapter Eleven. 2009 – 2013 All Previously Unpublished Poems

They sang his poem-songs of light
Each time the Sun in glory's might
Did him greet the morning bright
Until he died into the night

And that became his poetry
As far as distant mountains see
As near as colors paintings be
Or hearts and minds, for you and me
For peace and stillness, for those free
For peace beneath the Banyan tree.

Los Angeles
February 29, 2012

Mysteries

A river is a boat in time
Separates the sleeping mind
From the passenger awake
Who his destiny does take

Take this boat, but take it thus
That the dead remember us
Then the passage into night
Shall become the soul's pure light

Then the boat like water finds
The eternal spirit-mind
God, transport us to the shore
Of immortal soul-lore

Take us in a boat, the Dove,
In the boat of heavenly love,
In a boat of liquid light
That redeemed we in Thy sight

That we sleep in pastures green
Where the angels' dreams have been,

Chapter Eleven. 2009 – 2013 All Previously Unpublished Poems

Where the Shepherd keeps His flock
Safely in His fields like locks

Of the Golden Fleece of life
Everlasting with the wife,
With the soul of Adam pure
In whom the ages all endure

Timelessness of histories
Are the ancient Mysteries
Now renewed by Christ we see
Christ in you and Christ in me.

March 5, 2012

Home

The hand that writes pens words of song
When poets' sight in verse along

I thought I'd write soliloquy
Then in the night a lullaby
Until the morn of family
When day is born all merrily

A book of gems, a library
For reading, when the children free
Do play and roam in fantasy
Throughout the home like poetry.

March 18, 2012
Santa Monica, California

Chapter Eleven. 2009 – 2013 All Previously Unpublished Poems

Christus – An Frederik van Eeden

Jesus, hilf mir gut zu sein
Ich war kleines Kinderlein
Hatte Trost im guten Gott
Der Sein' Sohn mir ewig bot

Dann erfuhr ich rastlos hin
Übergießend Wärme bin
Nachdem sank ich in die Tief'
Dunkelheit und Kälte rief

In mir Schmerz und Traurigkeit
Ich erlebt' andre Wahrheit
Schwer das Leben, hart mit Pein
Ich war nicht mehr Kinderlein

Nachdem ich gerungen viel
So erschien mir keines Spiel
Sondern blickend Augen schön
Bruder Christi Lichtessein

Das war heil und gut und lieb
Ganz verschwand der dunkle Dieb
An sein' Stelle Christus dar
Treuer Freund auf ewig wahr.

21. März, 2012

Auferstehung – An Hans Peter van Manen

Christus bilden Künstler viel
Tätig ist des Christus Ziel
Alle Menschen 'rühr' Gefühl'
Die uns trösten und befehl'n

Zu energisch lieben und
Helfen Menschen jede Stund'
Niemand lass' allein im Stich
Los das Sonnenlicht ausbricht!

Chapter Eleven. 2009 – 2013 All Previously Unpublished Poems

Wie ein goldner Sonnaufgang
Überm Wasser weit entlang
Kommt der Christus herrlich an
Wiederkunft uns fort hintan

Alle wollen warm umarmt
Wie Novalis Trost erbarmt
Sieh' die Welt empfindet Licht
Fühlt und manchmal klar auch sieht

Was prophetisch 'kündet uns
Ist gekommen wahrhaft und
Wann im Not wir stehen da
Dann erscheint der Christus nah'

Sieh' Er unter uns wohl lebt
Liebend, tröstend all' umschwebt
Nun wir wissen nicht allein
Christus ist im Wiederschein

Wo das Leben Wärme bringt
Wo die Töne klingeling'n
Wo die Farben schön zu sehn
Wird der Christus auferstehn.

22. März 2012
Santa Monica, Kalifornien

Chapter Eleven. 2009 – 2013 All Previously Unpublished Poems

(August 5, 2012) For your birthday

….
  I am very sorry that you are having to deal with so many health issues all at once! Yet your poetry continues to flourish which is truly amazing. Thank you very much for sending them to me….

Virginia Sease

Sterben, oder Sonnenuntergang

Sterben ist eine glückliche Zeit
Geister erwachen einer Ewigkeit
Freude, wie Sterne, ist leiblos und breit
Alles wird Himmel in Vollkommenheit

Ich mag den Morgen des Neuen, der Kraft
Den Morgen des Lebens, der Lebenssaft
Doch der Untergang der Sonne ist sehr tief
Die Abenddämmerung so lieb mir rief

Und jedesmal zum Ende die Tagessonne kommt
Die Lichteinweihung uns segnend frommt
Wieder ich finde im Schmerze den Sinn
Die Bedeutung des Lebens in Ruhe bin

Und schaue gen Himmel meine Heimat, den Ort
Wo balde mich finde mit dem Vater dort
Und lege mein Bündel von Arbeit und Last
Nach Gebet und Hoffnung werde Christi Gast
Und alles wieder wird Friede und gut
Sterben wird Freude, wird Freiheit Mut!

St. John's Health Center
Santa Monica, California
Juni 18, 2012
Revised Culver City, California
Juli 27, 2012
Revised Los Angeles
Dezember 1, 2012

Chapter Eleven. 2009 – 2013 All Previously Unpublished Poems

Evening

Creation is a rainbow sometimes
I always thought my walks in rhymes
Over hills, along the cliffs
I sang my song in hieroglyphs

And then, at evening, in prayer
A different sort of, balmy air
Returns like memories of where
The world was young where now with care

I long for peace and quiet time
To rest my tired head sublime
As poets' thoughts or treasures white
The Moon reflects the Sun's clear light

And so my victory for you
Is welcome all the evening dew
Taste the honeyed clover there
Where the graveyard's stillness air.

June 18, 2012

Ein Morgenlied

Na, kleiner Schlafmütze
Na, willst Du wach?
Eben gestern hörte ich
Dein glückliches Lach'

Sei nicht so trüb, Kleiner
Komm zu mir, nah'
Lächele, Dein Papa
Liebt Dich doch ja

Leben wird Freude
Kindheit ist Spiel
Elementarwesen

Chapter Eleven. 2009 – 2013 All Previously Unpublished Poems

Tanzen, so viel'

Farbig wie Regenbogen
Ist unsre Welt
Blüten, Gemälde öffnen
Türe, sieh' quellt

Das Leben der Sonne
Mächtig und gut
Prachtvoll der Tag ist
Wohl uns der tut

So, mein liebliches
Kind, stehe auf
Grüße den Morgen
Und wach wirst Du drauf!

19. Juni 2012
Morgen

ASK

Ask me aloud
Ask me within
What I shall write
What I shall win

I shall reply
Gone for an Age
After I'm gone
Read every page

What did I write?
What did I win?
I wrote the world
I won the sun.

St. John's Health Center
Santa Monica, California
June 20, 2012

Chapter Eleven. 2009 – 2013 All Previously Unpublished Poems

Journey

Europe was true Christendom and still the Evening Land
glows with the sunset thoughts of time's dying ageing hand

The Christ appear to us again in art and science true
and in religious freedom's song where hearts are red and
blue.

O Europe fair! O Europe dear!
I love thee where my past
drank from the font of sun of life of Christ, the sacred guest

and when I feel the weight of breath and pulse of blood
again,
Europe comes to me once more and Germany of men

the German language of the saints before the Renaissance,
before the music of Baroque, Romanticism's glance

the Europe Medieval times of cultures' struggles for
individual access to Christ by freedom's door;

I knew how pilgrims' journeying, a simple peasant so
did not make my own pilgrimage *this* life my journey go

and so in continuity today the age is new
the soul in consciousness wakes up; Christ will awaken you

America, my native land, I live my life with thee
but in my youth returned once more to my dear Germany

Where I experienced my Christ full daylight consciously
forever changed to suffer pain and joy in harmony

with laws of soul in union with my inner Christ, the light
who is my strength, redeems my wrongs by conscience,
sleep and sight

Chapter Eleven. 2009 – 2013 All Previously Unpublished Poems

I love to feel; I shall endure my heart is true you see,
and Christ is my companion on this my one journey.

August 28, 2012

Seeing a Beautiful Sunset

Nature—
Thou'rt always an instance
a divine thought
made visible to us
on earth

like a poem
or a song
or a painting
we belong
a human thought
Art—
gives Thou birth.

September 17, 2012

Venus and My Child, the Poet

O joy of Christ, in me, I say
I think I thought another way
A child small did live today
In me he saw and heard what may

The child small in me was large
A spirit-Venus planet-barge
Kept opening doors of starry light
Like inner suns in coolest night

He became in me my I
As open as the starry sky
Kept twinkling beauty, love and why
I did not need a lullaby

Chapter Eleven. 2009 – 2013 All Previously Unpublished Poems

Because my I, my child big
Announced the Christ within my wig
(which is unlimited because
I'm bald, wear not the hair, the fuzz)

As open as the nighttime sky
Of spiritual transcendence nigh
Where angel-beings in processes
Higher dimensions heaven weave

With God on high all spirits white
A-flame shall dance their love tonight
For one small poet thought in song
Imagined worlds without a wrong
But only purest realms belong
Imbued an individual strong

And this his poem, written here
His vision brightly does appear
With heaven open and as near
As the earth throughout the year

This poet calls his poetry
Word-pictures each unique agree
With his heart and love, you see
Acknowledge magic mystically
Beyond the foaming moon-white sea
Shines Venus, princess-love, to me.

October 21, 2012

Sentient Soul, Mind Soul, Consciousness Soul

Sentience is another word
The soul itself in feeling heard
Like a pure and radiant bird
Sings this song in sentience' third

Soul of mind is plantlike there

Chapter Eleven. 2009 – 2013 All Previously Unpublished Poems

Thoughts in harmony we share
See awaken every where
Regular and light and clear

Soul of consciousness I know
The way in body stones repose
Depths no longer sleep and so
Wakeful self in memory shows.

Sentience, mind and consciousness
Felt and thought and known, no less
Now imparted each to us
By the God of souls: Christus.

November 21
Revised December 31, 2012

Three Songs of December 2, 2012

I. Song of Summer

Sense and sorrow, soul and sound
Stir my spirit's heart's still ground

I feel motion, feeling's found
In my voice I voice around

All the people sense with me
Life and living to be free

In a world chaos knows
My own soul weaves and goes

Pulls together like a song
Song of summer, bold and strong.

II. Peaceful

In the evening shadows fall

Chapter Eleven. 2009 – 2013 All Previously Unpublished Poems

Like a casket funeral
Like a tribute to the day
Sun is setting on Her way
To the twilight of the Gods
Planetary spheres the Word
Has renewed the Mysteries
Of the ancient elegies

For our Earth is dying and
Birth seems far and death at hand
Destinies begin to go
On the Earth their gifts bestow
All beneath the setting Sun
But I've seen the Risen One
Know the future different shall
Clear announces Christ; hear call

Now the Chosen, vision true
Have begun the future view
Step-by-step ascend they sure
Mountain God alone endure
With the Sun of humankind
Peaceful is God's human mind.

III. See

Autumn, calls the wind and rain
Cloudy will the Sun disdain
Bravely walking humankind
Hopeful thinking of the mind

Soon midwinter of the Earth
Shall again the Saviour birth
And the Christian carols old
Warm our hearts in darkness' cold

Songs of light the Child's return
Everlasting joy we learn
We, like children, small become

Chapter Eleven. 2009 – 2013 All Previously Unpublished Poems

See the heart's good inner Sun.

December 2, 2012

A Child of Light—To Cindy Hindes

A child of light I wander
In days of sun and nights
Where inner shadows happen
In sorrows grieving sight

I know I love the colors
That at the close of days
When heaven to earth descending
In sun's clear golden rays

The sunset is a sacred
Christian act so dear
The Passion of the Saviour
His crucifixion there

I feel the sunset colors
Their beauty is to me
The meaning of my inner
Heart accompany

And on the last horizon
When the sun dips down
Most tender feelings feeling
I stand on ancient ground

I join the dead and angels
In Christ I die to be
A child of heaven smiling
With love and harmony

I die the sunset knowing
I'm in good company
Depart from earth and silence

Chapter Eleven. 2009 – 2013 All Previously Unpublished Poems

To heaven's music free

Depart from earth and suffering
From sorrow, grief and pain
To join the spirits praising
God's own holy Name.

February 4, 2013
Los Angeles

Alan Lindgren

CHAPTER TWELVE

1987, 1997 – 2012

DEUTSCHE GEDICHTE

(GERMAN POEMS: A REVIEW)

TEIL EINS (PART ONE)

1987

Deutsche Gedichte

(German Poems)

Chapter Twelve. 1987 – 2012 Deutsche Gedichte (German Poems)

O Zartes Kind!

O zartes Kind!
Welch' Wunder, Schönheit
Augen groß und wäßrig
Körper weich und sanft
Durchleuchtende Haut

Empfindsames Wesen
Alles Wirkliche empfindest Du
Welch' Leben und Licht
Der Himmel Dir so nahe
Dein Schützengel
Der liebe Gott wirkt durch Dich

Wir wollen Dein Entfalten
Miterleben
Und Dir, Menschenkinde,
Wollen wir unsre schönste Liebe
schenken
Daß Du weißt
Du bist auf Erden willkommen.

Ich Habe Zwei Brüder

Ich habe zwei Brüder
Die rechte Hand und die linke Hand
Sie wirken zusammen
Sie leben zusammen
Sie schaffen zusammen
Weil sie zusammenge<u>hören</u>, ja
Ich habe zwei Brüder
Meine rechte Hand and meine linke
Hand.

Teil Eins (Part One). 1987

Licht

1.
Ich bin stumm vor Dir
Du sprichst zu mir
Du erscheinst meinen Augen
Dein Licht – aus Finsterschatten,
Wolkengrauen
Durchleuchtende helle Klarheit
Reines Licht –
Ich habe nur einzuatmen
Kein Mund – die Vögel aber singen
Dein reines Licht aussprechend
Klare Töne hervorbringend
aus den Lüften
Durch die Lüften
Deiner Licht-Taten entsprechender
Gesang.

2.
Ich verweile dort
Unter Himmelgeschichten
Zwischen Wolken, Vögeln
Tiefen Blauen, Sonnenmächten
Ein Kampf über mir, um mich herum
Und ich öffne mich vor großem Wunder
Der Offenbarungen des Lichtes –
Meine Augen aufgewacht
Und dann die Ohren
Bis ich (so erfüllt von lichtvoller,
klarer, freiender Luft)
In das enge Menschenhaus heimkehre
Weiter wundernd, staunend
Die Reinheit, Schönheit, Klarheit
des Lichtes.

Chapter Twelve. 1987 – 2012   Deutsche Gedichte   (German Poems)

Bewußt-Sein

Du siehst weder-noch
Das Gute noch das Böse
Doch spürst Du, beide Geiste

Ich sehe entweder-oder
Und spüre jedoch
Die Anwesenheit des anderen

So kann ich – in jeder Gegenwart –
Klar entscheiden
Das Gute in mir, in Dir
Zu bejahen.

Culver City, Kalifornien
Januar – März 1987

TEIL ZWEI (PART TWO)

1997 – 2000; 2002

Deutsche Gedichte

(German Poems)

Chapter Twelve. 1987 – 2012 Deutsche Gedichte (German Poems)

Der Sonne Licht strömt von oben her
Durch den Himmeln zu uns auf Erden

In Abendstimmung gnadevoll
Wir preisen Gott mit Lobgesang

Die Seele hat sich aufgetan
Nun bereitet sie sich für Schlafes Ruh'

O danke Gott für diesen Sommer Tag
Und segne uns für diese stille Nacht.

****

    O Kind!
    Schauend
           lächelnd
                    grüßend
    Mit Augen
        Mund
            und Hand
    Dein Geschenk ist
    Offenheit
        und Wunder
                und Liebe
    Durch dich
        grüßt uns
                der Vater-Gott.

1997

Teil Zwei (Part Two). 1997 – 2000; 2002

Ich würde Bücher schreiben
Von Worten bunt und treffend
Über Dingen schön und zart
Die meine Seele bewegen.

Ich würde Bücher schreiben
Von Welten tief und breit
Mit Herzenswärme drinnen
Pulsierend in der Zeit

Ich bin ein Dichter grüßend
Die ganze Welt so groß
Ich möchte Lieder singen
Aus meinem Seelenschoß.

In der Dunkelheit, vergesse nicht das Licht
In Finsternisse, der Sonne Angesicht
Die strömt so warm, die leuchtet hell
Die ist des Lebens Liebesquell'
O Sonne schön, O Sonne mein
Zum Weltenschein, bringst Du Dasein.

Das himmlische Licht strömt weit und breit
Mit einer ewigen, erfreulichen Schönheit
Von der Sonne mit Wärme und Mut
Es leuchtet klar und tut uns gut
Aus einer Quelle strahlt das Licht her
Eine Quelle der Liebe, der Morgenstern.

20. Februar 1998
Inglewood, Kalifornien

Chapter Twelve. 1987 – 2012 Deutsche Gedichte (German Poems)

Ein Liebessturm

Ich möchte gerne schlafen, tief in Dunkelheit
Mit Träumen und mit Glaube, getrostet Herrlichkeit
Ich atme ein die Lüften, und aus mein Lebensblut
Ein Liebessturm des Herbstes, mit Farben und mit Mut.

Die Menschen

Es gibt im Leben vieles, was mir offenbart
Die Menschen, ihre Arten, die Wege ihrer Fahrt
Wir treffen uns bei Tage, und träumen Nächte süß
Zusammen während Schlafe, ein Menschenbrüdergruß.

Die Farben

Die Farben mannigfaltig, der Seele schwimmen frei
Im Ätherleibeswasser, fließen allerlei
Sie mischen sich wo Lichter, strahlen sonnenklar
In Fluten strömend einfach, Leben ganz und gar.

Die Liebe

Die Mitte der Erfahrung, ist Schmerz und Freude Herz
Seelisch Fühlen-Tiefen, für Wahrheit leidend Schmerz
Ein ständig ein und aus, ein Atmen rhythmisch lebt
Und von dem Herze Liebe, haucht und lacht und schwebt.

Die Menschheit

Wir wissen Sachen üblich, die Schwächen unsrer Zeit
Die Oberfläche Lebens, Gefahren Gesamtheit
Tiefer lebt Gewissen, pulsiert die Liebe treu
Und vorwärts geht die Menschheit, mit Morgenkraft ganz neu.

Juni – Juli 1999

Teil Zwei (Part Two). 1997 – 2000; 2002

Die Mahlzeit Christi

Ich fühle wie da draußen, die Ich-Sucht gefährlich droht
Ich fühle in meiner Innenwelt, die Liebe brennt und glüht
Ich denke stark Gedanken, vom Chaos ungestört
Das Denkenslicht sich strahlet, die Töne hab' ich 'hört

Die Töne fröhlich Christi, die Töne klingen laut
Die Farben heil'ges Feuer, ich habe sie geschaut
Ich will mein Herz und Seele, mit Geist durchtränken warm
Und Mut und Freiheit langen, wie nahe und wie fern.

Die Welt bringt mir kein Frieden, Getümmel herrscht in ihr
Die Unruh' der Gespenster, gehören nicht zu mir
Die Liebe stirbt am Tage, und lebt die Nächte auf
Wir brauchen stark die Glaube, und leiden dieses Haus

Unsre Erdenwohnung, der Leibestempel und
Der Seele Freud' und Schmerzen, in Rhythmen Jahr und Stund'
Der Geist des Menschen quellet, aus Gottesgründen tief
Und segnet Herz und Seele, Er ruft uns und Er rief

Seit zwei Tausend Jahren, erweckend Menschen lieb
Er wird immer treu bleiben, Er bleibt wie auch Er blieb
Der Eine, der Geliebte, der Menschensohn, das Kind
Der hilft uns wann es regnet, im Sonnenschein, im Wind.

Der Jesu-Knabe liebet, Seine Brüder hier
Sein Herz ist süß und rein, Sein Auge leuchtet klar
Er will uns immer helfen, beten wir darum
Wir brauchen Seine Hilfe, sowie Sein Heiligtum.

Nun herrscht im Himmel droben, der Vater-Gott im Geist
Er sandte uns Seinen Sohn, Ewigkeit in Zeit
Er mag die Krankheit heilen, die Toten aufersteh'n
Er wird zu jedem kommen, damit wir vorwärtsgeh'n

Wenn an die Tür es klopfet, und Christus will herein
Essen wir das heil'ge Brot, und trinken süßen Wein

Chapter Twelve. 1987 – 2012 Deutsche Gedichte (German Poems)

Das ist die Mahlzeit Christi, damit wir leben fort
Des Lebens Sinn, Bedeutung, das Licht, das Herz, das Wort.

August 1999
Los Angeles

Da war ein Mensch, der saß und meint'
Er war mit andern ganz vereint
Und dies' Gedanke bracht' ihm Trost
Sein Herz erwärmt, er trank mit "Prost"
Dann ging er hin, und sang ein Lied
Das überbrückt' all' Unterschied
Und nun gemeinsam in der Welt
Er freute sich, sein Weg erhellt.

20. November 2000

Fünf Deutsche Gedichte vom 15. Februar 2002

1. Zwei Welten

Ich werde sprechen
Du aber redest
Ich werde schreiben
Du machst Notizen
Ich werde denken
Du aber spinnest

Ich werde atmen
Du fliegst schnell über
Ich geh' in Rhythmen
Du kannst dich nicht ruhen
Ich möchte schlafen
Du nimmst nur Pausen

Ich muss klar wachen
Du träumst die Tage
Wir sind zusammen
Erwachs'ne und Kinder

Teil Zwei (Part Two). 1997 – 2000; 2002

Zwei ganz verschied'ne
Anschauungswelten.

2. Gottes Segen

Wir Menschen meinen
Alles schnell
Vorübergehend, unruhig
Rastlose Energie

Doch die Liebe
Schweigend pulsiert
Friede bringend
Ihr Gottes Segen

Wie ein Regenbogen
Nach dem Sturme des Lebens
Bei der Wiedererscheinung
Der Sonne, ihres Lichtes

Die Sonne uns erwärmend
Das wir fühlen
Das Güte wohltuend
Christi.

3. Eines

Vor kurzem
Als ich Dir vorbei fuhr
Sah ich in Deinen Augen
Das klare Christus-Licht

Wir waren für einen Moment
Eines
Christus, Du und ich

Durch unsren Herrn
Durch unsren Bruder
Christus.

Chapter Twelve. 1987 – 2012 Deutsche Gedichte (German Poems)

4. Die Welt

Die Welt
So groß
Ergibt uns
Kleine Schönheiten
Wenn wir sie bemerken

Blumen, Vögel, Bäume
Und große Landschaften
Irdische Ebene, Bergen
Himmlische Weiten, Sonnen-Taten
Dämmerungen, Sonnenuntergänge

Licht-Taten
Farben-Gemälde
Bunte Herrlichkeiten
Erfreuliche Stimmungen
Die uns zum Lächeln bringen
Und unsren Herzen erwärmen

Stille Momente
Am Abend für Andacht
Und Nachdenken
Für Atmen
Und Fühlen
Tiefen.

5. Dein Leben

Ich bin
So spricht das Herz
Höre dieses Wort

Ich bin
So fühle ich mir selber
Ich und in mir
Mein treuer Christus

Christus

Teil Zwei (Part Two). 1997 – 2000; 2002

Vergebe mir
Meine Schulden

Ich bin
Ein Sündiger
Ich bin daran
Schuldig

Deine Luft
Atme ich
Dein Blut
Erwärmt mich
Dein Leben
Hält mich am Leben.

15. Februar 2002
Culver City, Kalifornien

Schöne Nacht

O schöne Nacht
Du bist erwacht
Und bleibst auf ewig treu

Vergessen nun
Des Tages Tun
Und Lichtes Scham und Scheu

In dieser Welt
- die Sternenzelt
Still, geheimnisvoll

Um mich herum
- mein Mund ist stumm
Klingt Sternen Dur und Moll

In Dunkelheit
Und Raumes Weit'
Erscheint das ew'ge Licht

Chapter Twelve. 1987 – 2012 Deutsche Gedichte (German Poems)

Die Sonne singt
Der Vater bringt
Uns Christi Angesicht.

29. März 2002

Hellsehen

Hellsehen
Sonne Schönheit
Lieber Christus

Himmelskrone
Herrlich strahlend
Wunderbar

Unsre Liebe
Dankbar schenken
Herz erfüllt

Nach Dir
Frühlingsfreude
Mit den Vögeln

Bis zur Sonne
Zu den Sternen
Kosmisch ist Dein
Ew'ges Leben

Mit der Erde
Ist der Atem
Ausgeatmet

Das wir unsres
Selbst in Dir
In Deinem Leben
Finden.

5. April 2002

Teil Zwei (Part Two). 1997 – 2000; 2002

Freund

Sag mir Bescheid
Das mein Kummer und Leid
Vorübergehend ist

Nimmst Du mein' Hand
Aufs Meer und aufs Land
Das ich weiß Du bist mein Freund

Wehe all' Grau
Nur Purpur und Blau
Nur Grün, Gelb und Rot sind gut

Farben sind bunt
Sie geben sich kund
Beim Licht, Wasser, Wolken und Blut

Sing mir ein Lied
Dann darfst Du Mitglied
Unter Vögel und Sänger sein

Dann bleibst Du mir treu
Und auf ewig neu
Du mein Freund und ich auch Dein.

27. Juni 2002

Frieden

Komm kleines Kind
Mit mir – und wir
Werden gehen zu Fuß zu den Fluß
Wo wir werden reden mit Fäden.

Wenn dunkel es funkeln
Die Sterne gerne
Bis Morgen Sorgen.

O Pracht der Nacht!

Chapter Twelve. 1987 – 2012 Deutsche Gedichte (German Poems)

Erwacht mit Macht;
Mein Leben wird Streben,
Mein Tod führt zum Gott;

Sein Angesicht von Licht ist
Linder für Seine Kinder,
Ganz Glanz;
In Seinen Händen enden
Die Bücher Geistsucher.

Nimm mein Sinn;
Führe mich zum Traum Baum.
In des Grafes Schlafes
Sinke zur Linke.

Mein Geist reist,
Mein Leib bleibt
Zum Glück zurück,
Meine Seele am Landrand
Den Strand fand.

Höre die Chöre
Singen, sie bringen
Frieden hernieden.

21. November 2002
Los Angeles

TEIL DREI (PART THREE)

2003 – 2007

Deutsche Gedichte

(German Poems)

Chapter Twelve. 1987 – 2012 Deutsche Gedichte (German Poems)

Wirklichkeits Glück

Ich bin
Am Rande des Lebens,
Am Strande des Meers;
Ich will
Durch Hoffnung und Streben,
Trotz Bange und Leer,

Mein Ziel
Für Selbstheit und Ich-Sein
Die Zukunft finden,
Mein Herz
Durch Liebe und Du-Dein
Mit Freunden verbinden

Wir sind
Bedeutung des Herzens
Und Wirklichkeits Glück;
Wir sind
Mit Mut Angst und Schmerzen
Genügend und Stück;

Die Welt
Mag chaotisch, kalt werden,
In Dunkelheit sein;
Der Mensch
Bezaubert Gebärden
Und funkelt gar fein.

Der Mensch
Mit Glaube und Liebe,
Mit Hoffnung und Kraft;
Der Mensch
Kann Totes beleben,
Was trocken wird Saft;

Denn Geist
Ist mystisch und zaubert,

Teil Drei (Part Three). 2003 – 2007

Liebt Freiheit und Licht;
Der Mensch
Was schmutzig schön saubert
Und hellt sein Gesicht.

22. März 2003

Lieben und Ruhen und Schlafen und Träumen

Der Liebende, Ruhende, Schlafende, Träumende
Der liebet and ruhet und schlafet und träumet
Er grüßet die Kinder, die lächeln und spielen
Er hilfet die Greisen, die wachen und hören

Der gütige, christliche Priester, der Dichter
Beweiset nach Christus, er zeiget und zeichnet
Mit Finger und Bleistift, mit Auge und Stimme
Sein Antlitz erstrahlet, erleuchtet und glänzet

Die Stimme des Priesters, des Dichters erklinget
Ertönet mit Schönheit und Klarheit und Wärme
Die Worte derselben, sie sprechen und reden
In Rhythmen und Tiefen des Fühlenden Herzens

Beschreiben Gelände, Gebirge, Natur
Vorstellen Geschichte, darstellen Szenen
Die Hände derselben erwärmen und tasten
Und zeigen die Wunden der Nageln des Kreuzes
Die Todestat Golgathas des Herrn Jesus Christus.

Geschwister, Gebrüder und Freunden und Väter
Und Mütter und Kinder zusammen gemeinsam
Unter den Sammelnden wandelt der Christus
Segnet ihr' Herzen, beruhigt ihr' Seelen

Dann schlafen die Menschen ermüdet, veraltet

Chapter Twelve. 1987 – 2012 Deutsche Gedichte (German Poems)

Und unter den Engeln, den Toten mit Christus
Verjüngern, verstärken sich, wärmen und trösten
Sie lieben und ruhen und schlafen und träumen…

10. April 2003
Los Angeles

Fünf August Abendgedichte

1. Hans Peter van Manen

Mein Sonnenfreund
Viel verdanke ich Ihnen:

Ihre Freundlichkeit
Ihre Lebensfreude
Ihre stete Interesse an dem
Was am Leben interessant ist.

Durch Sie atme ich einen Teil
Ihres sonnendurchtränkten Atems
Der aus weitrer Ferne
Zu mir, zu meinem Herzen weht.

2. Gedanken

Die Verbindung die uns über
Zeitliche and räumliche Distanzen überbrückt
Ist ein Faden
Von feiner Gedankensubstanz
Die klar leuchtet
Und die kleine Wesen feierlich spinnen.

Lichtsubstanz
Liebe genannt
Denn solche Gedanken in Seelen aufleuchten
Uns einander begrüßend
Herzlich erwärmen
Liebeslicht sei Gedanken.

Teil Drei (Part Three). 2003 – 2007

3. Abend Andacht

Rosapurpur Farbendunst
Ein Abendhauch der Liebe
Rosa und Blau des Himmels
Herrlich und andachtsvoll.

So beendet sich
Der Tag der Farben
Und die heimliche Nacht
Geister erwacht.

4. Sonnenuntergang

Am Ende des Tages
Müdigkeit die Menschen veraltet
Doch wenden sie sich
An der Sonne
Die sie durch den Tag
Begleitet hat

Und sie sehen
Schönheit
Glühendes Rot
Das sterben bedeutet
Und die Liebesnacht
Eröffnet.

5. Liebesgeburt

Rosa, Blau und Violet
Bezaubern Herzen
Zur Liebe.

Lieb bist Du Lila
Lieblich und innerlich
Herzlich und christlich
Geburt Jesu.

Zarte Maria und

Chapter Twelve. 1987 – 2012 Deutsche Gedichte (German Poems)

Zartes Kind
Des Himmels.

Westchester
23. August 2003

Einsamkeit

Einsamkeit
Da ich bin ein Teilchen hier
Ein Mensch von andren Menschen umgeben
Körperlich getrennt und individualisiert
Doch unter den andren
Das ich weiß, Ihr und ich
Wir sind die Menschheit.

Einsamkeit
Das ich durste nach Christus
Mein Bewußtsein durstet nach Christus
Brauche ich Seiner
Ich nehme Sein Leib – das Brot
Ich trinke Sein Blut – der Wein
Und zelebriere das Sacrament des Bewußtseins

Einsamkeit
Wo ich auf Erden stehe und gehe
Wo ich sehe in den Himmeln die Sonne
Bin von ihrem Lichte erwärmt und erleuchtet
Bin vom Winde berührt
Bin von der Erde unterstützt

Unter Tiere und Vögel
Pflanzen und Bäume
Steine und Felsen
Ich atme die Lüften
Und fühle mich nicht mehr einsam
Denn ich bin nicht allein.

Du, Menschenbruder

Teil Drei (Part Three). 2003 – 2007

Du, heilger Christus
Du, Freundin Natur
Bist bei mir
Und ich bin bei Dir
Und wir bauen zusammen Drei Welten:
Irdisch, Himmlisch, Menschlich.

Natur-, Geistes- und Menschenwelten
Erschaffene Wesen auf Erden
Engelwesen in den Himmeln
Menschenwesen Hand und Fuß
Auge und Ohr, Lippen und wir
Freuen uns innig und jubeln in Weltengesang –
Wir danken Euch, Welten Gottes
Wir danken Euch!

September 2003

Tendenzen

Tendenzen – das Wort im Munde
Das Wort der Aussprache
Das Wort der Dichtung.

Tendenzen – ein Moment nachdem
Nach dem anderen
Wo die Vögel fliegen
Und die Häuser sich bauen lassen
Tendenzen

Bejahung – die Hoffnung
Die Erfüllung des Wortes
Die Erfüllung der Sprache
Die Erfüllung der Dichtung.

Bejahung – wann alles sich ausgleichen läßt
Und kleine Schritte sich belauschen lassen
Und die Engel sich zur Sinfonie vorbereiten
Und die Engel die Sphärenmusik vor sich geben

Chapter Twelve. 1987 – 2012 Deutsche Gedichte (German Poems)

Und die Engel singen
Bejahung

Inzwischen liegen Bausteine
Bausteine und Arbeiter
Arbeiter die tüchtig leben und schaffen
Häuser bauend

Inzwischen erhöhen sich Wolken
Herrliche weiße Wolken
Himmlisch und gewölbt
Unter Sonnenlicht und Vögel

Inzwischen schreiben Studenten
Aufsätze für Kursen
Klassenexamen
Schulenprüfungen
Die Ferien kommen schnell.

Die Ferien – ein Weihnachtsabend
Wo das Kind eintritt
Und die Welt ganz anders wird
Denn Jesu Christ wird aufs neu geboren
Und Herzen jubeln
Denn Er ist gekommen.

22. November 2003
Los Angeles

Höret! Die Sonne – Für Gérard Klockenbring

Höret! Die Sonne
Singet im Chore
Singet ihr' Wonne
Mensch, Tier und Flore

Höret! Die Sonne
Singet durch Tage
Singet gar schöne

Teil Drei (Part Three). 2003 – 2007

Lieder im Sage

Höret! Die Sonne
Singet die Nächte
Sage und Märchen
Wahrheiten dächten

Höret! Die Sonne
Singet gar edel
Königins Herrschaft
Königins Regel

Höret! Die Sonne
Singend und sprechend
Dichtungs Gesangbuch
Weihnachten jubelnd.

28. August 2004

Einsamkeit und Licht

Einsamkeit steht trüb, darf nicht
Froh erlauben helles Licht;
Licht durchleuchtet Einsamkeit,
Strahlet in die Dunkelheit,

Schaffet Liebespoesie,
Eine sanfte Melodie,
Tönend zart durch Gegenden,
Tröstet alle Elenden

Wie die Wehmut klingt das Lied
Überbrückt all' Unterschied
Sieh! das Licht umarmt die Welt
Sonne der Nachtssternenzelt.

25. November 2004

Chapter Twelve. 1987 – 2012 Deutsche Gedichte (German Poems)

Die Liebe

Die Liebe ist der höchste Preis des Menschenlebens
Erreicht, erlebt durch Schönheits glühend, glitzernd Glanz
Wir widmen unsre Kräfte Liebesleben strebend
Und schmücken Tisch und Tür mit Liebes buntem Kranz.

Die Milde, die die Liebe in uns zart erwecket
Ist wunderschön und hold und lieb und immer treu
Wir tanzen gerne durch die Räume Liebe decket
Und wie die Mädchen schauen offen sowie scheu.

Wie süß bleibt ewig Herz der Liebe, Liebesdichtung
Wie innig und wie fromm wir fühlen da
Wo Liebe uns berührt führt in jene Richtung
Wo Bilder schön erscheinen Dichtungskunst ist hier.

Gemeinsam singen wir so dankbar und so froh
Die Sonne glänzt in lichter, himmlischen Harmonien
Wir werden fein wo früher Wilder waren roh
Und tönen Weltenhirten Frühlingsmelodien.

28. November 2004

Knabe Jesu

Die Liebe zwingt mir auf zu Dir
Zu Jesus, Kind des Menschen
Kind Gottes, Jesus-Knabe lieb
Du reichst mir Deine Händchen
Und mir zulächelst, winkend zu
Dein' Augen klar und gut
Ich fühle mich von Dir umarmt
Bekräftigt warm mit Mut

Du schläfst bald in mein' Armen ein
Und träumst von Gott und Mutter
Und alles ist gar still und süß
Wie Honig, Brot und Butter
Ich bin Dir gleich ganz zugewandt

Teil Drei (Part Three). 2003 – 2007

Mein Herz und Leib erwärmet
Denn Dein' Gestalt ist weich und warm
Und meiner Dich erbarmet

Du bist der Lieblichste der Welt
Der Schönste Menschenkinder
Und niemand in der ganzen Welt
Ist treuer, lieber, linder
Ich träume bald von Weihnachten
Von Hirten und Maria
Und Dir, Du kleiner, Jesus-Kind
Du kommst in aller Gloria

So arm und edel bist Du hier
So gut bei Dir zu sein
Du kleiner, Jesu, Du bist mein
Und ich, ja ich bin Dein.

Wenn jeder Mensch der Gegenwart
Von Dir berührt sich würde
So wäre diese große Welt
Erfüllt von Gotteswürde
Und Friede würde überall
Wie Melodien herrschen
Der gute Hirte auf dem Land'
Sein' Schafe wie in Märchen!

1./2. Dezember 2004

Tiefrote Rose, Gérard Klockenbring

Tiefrote Rose, Gérard Klockenbring
Duftest herrlich, Vogel – sing!
Himmelskind ganz neu und frisch
Blühend Weihnachten zu Tisch

Tiefrote Rose, lieber Mann
Tod hat schenkend seine Hand
Nun bist Du auf ewig jung
In den Chören Engel 'Sang.

Chapter Twelve. 1987 – 2012 Deutsche Gedichte (German Poems)

Tiefrote Rose, Gérard Klockenbring
Warm und saftig, Mut Du bringst
Christusknabe lebest Du
Weihnachtsfreude jubelst Du

Herrlich, andachtsvoll und klar
Golden scheint Dein Engelshaar
Golden leuchten Augen gut
Golden ist Dein Herz voll Mut.

Tiefrote Rose, Gérard Klockenbring
Stirbest Du des ird'schen Rings
Gebärest Du in Himmelsphär'
Ein neugesprossenes Rotneujahr.

Tiefrote Rose, lieber Mann
Gehörest Christi Friedenland
Leiden ist vergangnes Ding
Lieber Gérard Klockenbring.

1. Januar 2005
Inglewood, Kalifornien

TECHNIK

Technik – Du modernes Wesen!
Schreiben kannst du nicht, nicht lesen
Auch sprechen weder noch hören
Nur mannigfaltig stören!

Du kannst nicht denken, nicht singen
Dichten nicht, Schönheit bringen
Nicht sehen, nicht tasten
Nicht riechen, nur belasten!

Kalt bist du Technik, kalt und tot
Leblos bist du da, mehr Stein wie Brot
Keiner kann sich an dir ernähren
Du tötest das Leben, kannst nicht gebären!

Teil Drei (Part Three). 2003 – 2007

Technik – Du kannst nur programmiert werden
Ausführen leblose Gebärden
Information ist dein Inhalt und Welt
Erkenntnisse Dir entschlüpft und immer fehlt.

O Technik – künstlich bist Du und abstrahiert
Fotographisch, falsch manniert
Ohne Imagination oder Inspiration
Ohne Möglichkeiten oder Intuition!

Begrenzt bist du tote Technik
Begrenzt erscheinst du im Augenblick
Begrenzt heute wie morgen bleibst du
Begrenzt, was du nicht kannst ich tu'!

28. Mai 2005

Drei Kleine Juni Naturgedichte

1. O kleine Honigbiene

O kleine Honigbiene!
Wie zärtlich du die Blüte küsst
Voll Glück den süßen Nektar trinkst.

Trunken wirst du, kleine Biene
Und voll der Genüsse der Natur
Kehrst du nach Hause zurück
Den köstlichen Honig zu schaffen
Goldbraun und reich – die Liebe.

2. Gelbweiße Rose

Gelbweiße Rose
In den warmen Lüften zart duftend
Dem hellen Lichte eröffnend
Schön, milde und fein
Perfekt im Gleichgewicht
Harmonisch grüßend

Chapter Twelve. 1987 – 2012 Deutsche Gedichte (German Poems)

Mir die Liebe hinreichend
Ich bitte dich -
Liebe mich
Gelbweiße Rose!

3. Die Ameisen

Ameisenleben
Ameisenarbeit
Ameisenweben
Ameisenstreben

Beschäftigung
Tagestun
Kleiner Ruhm
Ameisentum!

8./9. Juni 2005

Nachtandacht

Abendstille deckt die Erde wie ein Kleid das sie umarmt
Die Sonne sinkt im Meere nach einem Tage ihrer großen Taten.

Die Nacht öffnet sich ihre Tür der Sterne, die funkeln und meinen
Der Tod sei Mysterium und Liebesboot zugleich.

Der Mond scheint wie eine Schale, rund und weiß, hell und schön
Und die Menschen träumen Schönes, Kinder des Vaters im Himmel.

O Nacht! Wie lieblich und zart bist Du!
Wie herrlich sind Deine Engelscharen, und die Sonne der Nacht
– Christus – auf immer und ewig.

Ewigkeit ist die Nacht, Ewigkeit und Treue
Und ich bin nur die Braut – der Dichter
Der Nachtgeschichten immer mit Bleistift im Buche des Lebens
dichtet.
Schönheit bist Du, O Nacht meines Herzens, Schönheit und Liebe

Teil Drei (Part Three). 2003 – 2007

Und der Traum des Vaters für Seine gläubigen Kinder in Seinem Schoße.

17. Juli 2005

Stimmen

Höret!
Die Stimmen der Kinder
Die Kinder die spielen
Die Kinder die lachen und meinen
Ihr Spiel sei Arbeit
Und Traum sei Wirklichkeit

Höret!
Die Stimmen der Dichter
Die Dichter die träumen
Die Dichter die dichten und meinen
Ihr Träumen ist wirklich
Denn sie singen ihr' Träume
In der Wirklichkeit

Höret!
Die Stimmen der Greisen
Die Greisen die sich besinnen
Die Greisen die fühlen und meinen
Ihr' Träume vergangen
Seien gegenwärtig
Denn die Zeit wird für sie ewig
Wird einfach Stimmung.

Höret!
Die Stimmen der Kinder
Der Dichter, der Greisen
Klingen auf ewig
Werden Träume und Stimmung
In der Wirklichkeit.

3./4. Dezember 2005

Chapter Twelve. 1987 – 2012 Deutsche Gedichte (German Poems)

Nachtgesang

Einst meinte ich das Leben wäre
Um so besser ohne Hindernisse
Dann aber aus meiner Arbeit gebäre
Der Dichter kleine Gedichtenüße.

Einst wollte ich ja immer ernster
Damit ich die Tiefen erobere
Fand aber da nur Schattengespenster
Wollte schmecken süße Beeren.

Einst tanzte ich mit Lust die Felder hindurch
Als die Sonne mir zulächelte ganz froh
Nun fang ich an in einem dunklen Loch
Hineinzufallen wie 'ne kranke Kuh.

Die Tage werden alt und grau und düster
Die Nächte zeigen mir ihre Schätze reich
Ich verweile in ihren Sternenlichter
So daß die Gedanken werden mild und weich.

Morgens aber muß ich wieder Sachen
Handeln und schwere Prüfungen durchstehen
Gerne würde ich an alles fröhlich lachen
Muß aber mühsam immer weiter gehen

Hart wird das Leben mir wie Spitzennägel
Die in meinem Kopfe täglich gehammert werden
Ohne Sinn ich spüre sie wie Regeln
Unveränderliche Marmorsteingebärden.

Umsonst sind alle meine Bemühungen
Nach sonnigen Träumen oder Blumen
Weggegangen sind die goldne Schmetterlinge
Die Blütenkelchen und die junge Damen.

Die Welt wird arm und schattenhaft und lahm
Wie ein Bettler oder eine Greise ist mein Fuß

Teil Drei (Part Three). 2003 – 2007

Der schmerzhaft jeden Schritt mir nahm
Und damit den warmen Bruderkuß.

Nur Eines ist mir noch geblieben
Damit ich weiter kann und will
Meine Freunde und die Mutter lieben
Mich und machen mich dann still.

Denn ohne Liebe kann man nichts und nimmer
Geht das Leben ohne Liebe weiter
Ich dichte friedevoll in meinem Zimmer
Die Liebe macht mich inniglich und heiter.

7./8. Januar 2006

Gründonnerstag

Christus – warum?
Warum, jedes Jahr
Musst Du leiden und sterben
In uns den Tod erleben?
In uns in der Unterwelt Menschenseelen –
Sünder helfen –

ICH WEIß ES SCHON
DU BIST ROT UND GRÜN
HIMMEL AUF ERDEN
GOTT WURDE MENSCH.

DU, O CHRISTUS
MUSSTEST DEN SCHWARZEN TOD KENNEN
DU, O CHRISTUS
STARBST, EIN MENSCH
UND DURCH DEINEN TOD
IST EIN GROßES WUNDER GESCHEHEN
DIE WIEDERGEBURT
DAS AUFERSTEHEN.

13. April 2006

Chapter Twelve. 1987 – 2012 Deutsche Gedichte (German Poems)

Zwei April Nachostern Sonnenuntergang Gedichte

1. Die Möven

Sonnenuntergang
Stimmung Christi
Rötlich gefärbt
Mut und Liebe

Siehe:
Christus stirbt für dich
Für dich, du Mensch
Mit gutem Willen
Und die ewigen Möven
Fliegend, gehend und stehend
– Freiheit und Schicksal des Menschen
Sind die Möven
Beim Sonnenuntergang
Christi.

2. Ein Mövenlied

Möve – siehe, du fliegst
Die Freiheit kannst du 'langen
Möve – siehe, du stehst
Das Schicksal magst du tragen

Du bist nicht dieser Welt
Der Himmel dein zu Hause
Doch findest du dein Brot
Hier unten auf dem Strande
Wie schreist du so vor Hunger
Ernährst dich für die Reise
Dann schwingst dich plötzlich auf
Nach deiner nächtlich' Weise.

Der Mittwoch nach Ostersonntag
28. April 2006

Teil Drei (Part Three). 2003 – 2007

Suchet

Kinder spielen mit Augen
Lippen küssen und saugen
Tränen gießen und fallen
Lieder laufen und lallen.

Wer das Leben verstehen
Der muß wandern und gehen
Heimat 'lassen und lernen
In den Weiten und Fernen.

Denn die Schule des Lebens
Bleibt zu Hause vergebens
Nur die Klassen der Jahre
Weisheit 'leihen, das Wahre.

Suchet Menschen und Geister
Brüder, Lehrer und Meister
Findet Christus, der Wahre
Ziel, Bedeutung der Jahre.

14. August 2006
Los Angeles

Die Lieder

Menschen sterben
Menschen erben
Erzählungen, Geschichte
Gedächtnis und Gedichte

Die Menschen lieben
Die leiden, geblieben
Wie Steine oder Lichter
Liebende und Dichter

Aber im Momente
Erdenelemente
Räume und Zeiten

Chapter Twelve. 1987 – 2012   Deutsche Gedichte   (German Poems)

Menschen begleiten

Bis nach deren Tode
Wie ein schön' Kleinode
Der Christ und Ewigkeit
Wilkommen Seeligkeit

Seelen und Geister
Werden Sterne und Meister
Mit dem Vater im Himmel
Verlassen Getümmel

Ruhe und Friede
Werden die Lieder.

19. September 2007
Los Angeles

TEIL VIER (PART FOUR)

2008; 2011 – 2012

Deutsche Gedichte

(German Poems)

Chapter Twelve. 1987 – 2012 Deutsche Gedichte (German Poems)

Ist die Kunst

Stil ist der Kunst Oberfläche, Schönheit ihr Leben und Liebe.

Meinung bedeutet ja nichts, denn die Kunst ist Gottesangesicht.

Farbe ist Fülle und Feuer, Schwarze ein Ungeheuer.

Schlaf ist mein Bruder und Freund, die Kunst gibt uns Ursprung kund.

Die Welt ist der Kunst immer rund, die Worte der Dichtung ihr Mund.

Licht ist die Liebe des Tags, Sonne der König und Pracht,

Schönheit der Stoff Wirklichkeit innerhalb Kunst und bereit

zu schaffen und tun eines Dings künstlerisch abends umrings.

Ruhe ist Friede gar still wenn man nach Gott neigt und will.

Mehr "Ist"

Kraft ist ein williger Macht, Denken 'ne Fähigkeit sacht'.

Das Denken ist philosophisch, Erkenntnis anthroposophisch.

Glaube nach Nächte wohl führt, Hoffnung des Morgens gehört.

Liebe ist Kinder der Nacht, die spielen und träumen erwacht.

Sterne sind Engel und auch Toten mit Atemweihrauch.

Gott ist der Weltall und ganz Liebe und ewiglich Glanz,

denn Er will leuchten in Dir, in Christus Er kommet, ist hier.

Christus ist einzig und gut, für uns Er gosset Sein Blut.

Sterben ist Pfad nach dem Gott des Ewigkeitsfriede gar hold.

Teil Vier (Part Four). 2008; 2011 – 2012

Süß ist der Schmerz Christi lieb, teuer Er bleibt wie Er blieb.

Engel singen Flügel und Geist, der Mensch stirbt, nach ihnen er reist.

1. Februar 2008,
21. Januar 2013

Menschenbruder

Ich finde mich
Im Äther
In meinem Innern
Im innren Herzen
In meinem Fühlen
In meinem Atem

Ich ruhe mich
Im fühlenden Denken
Das warm strahlet
Im Äther schwebend
Wie ein Hauch atmet
Mein Ich

Das Ich meines Herzens
Das warm rühret
In meinem Fühlen
Dich zart grüßend
Menschenbruder
Du, den ich liebe
Christus.

29. Juni 2011
Los Angeles

Herbstanbeginn nach Weihnachten schauend

I. Sensibelsein

Sensibelsein wird empfinden
Empfinden wird Fühlen

Chapter Twelve. 1987 – 2012 Deutsche Gedichte (German Poems)

Fühlen im Herzen
In Herzensgründen

Herzen, die fühlen
Herzen, die träumen
Herzen, die schauen
Geburt Liebe Christi

Geburt Liebe Christi
Geburt Leben Christi
Geburt Lichte Christi
Geburt Sonne Christi.

II. Sonne

Sonne meines Herzens
Scheine in Finsternisse
Lichthell und strahlend
Kraftvoll mit Wärme
Warm in die Kälte

Sonne Christi
In mir aufleuchte
Meine Seele
Erleuchtend
Mein Herz
Erwärmend.

Santa Monica, Kalifornien
23. September 2011
Culver City, Kalifornien
22. Januar 2013

Christus – An Frederik van Eeden

Jesus, hilf mir gut zu sein
Ich war kleines Kinderlein
Hatte Trost im guten Gott
Der Sein' Sohn mir ewig bot

Teil Vier (Part Four). 2008; 2011 – 2012

Dann erfuhr ich rastlos hin
Übergießend Wärme bin
Nachdem sank ich in die Tief'
Dunkelheit und Kälte rief

In mir Schmerz und Traurigkeit
Ich erlebt' andre Wahrheit
Schwer das Leben, hart mit Pein
Ich war nicht mehr Kinderlein

Nachdem ich gerungen viel
So erschien mir keines Spiel
Sondern blickend Augen schön
Bruder Christi Lichtessein

Das war heil und gut und lieb
Ganz verschwand der dunkle Dieb
An sein' Stelle Christus dar
Treuer Freund auf ewig wahr.

21. März 2012

Auferstehung – An Hans Peter van Manen

Christus bilden Künstler viel
Tätig ist des Christus Ziel
Alle Menschen 'rühr' Gefühl'
Die uns trösten und befehl'n

Zu energisch lieben und
Helfen Menschen jede Stund'
Niemand lass' allein im Stich
Los das Sonnenlicht ausbricht!

Wie ein goldner Sonnaufgang
Überm Wasser weit entlang
Kommt der Christus herrlich an
Wiederkunft uns fort hintan

Chapter Twelve. 1987 – 2012 Deutsche Gedichte (German Poems)

Alle wollen warm umarmt
Wie Novalis Trost erbarmt
Sieh' die Welt empfindet Licht
Fühlt und manchmal klar auch sieht

Was prophetisch 'kündet uns
Ist gekommen wahrhaft und
Wann im Not wir stehen da
Dann erscheint der Christus nah'

Sieh' Er unter uns wohl lebt
Liebend, tröstend all' umschwebt
Nun wir wissen nicht allein
Christus ist im Wiederschein

Wo das Leben Wärme bringt
Wo die Töne klingeling'n
Wo die Farben schön zu sehn
Wird der Christus auferstehn.

22. März 2012
Santa Monica, Kalifornien

Sterben, oder Sonnenuntergang

Sterben ist eine glückliche Zeit
Geister erwachen einer Ewigkeit
Freude, wie Sterne, ist leiblos und breit
Alles wird Himmel in Vollkommenheit
Ich mag den Morgen des Neuen, der Kraft
Den Morgen des Lebens, der Lebenssaft
Doch der Untergang der Sonne ist sehr tief
Die Abenddämmerung so lieb mir rief

Und jedesmal zum Ende die Tagessonne kommt
Die Lichteinweihung uns segnend frommt
Wieder ich finde im Schmerze den Sinn
Die Bedeutung des Lebens in Ruhe bin

Teil Vier (Part Four). 2008; 2011 – 2012

Und schaue gen Himmel meine Heimat, den Ort
Wo balde mich finde mit dem Vater dort
Und lege mein Bündel von Arbeit und Last
Nach Gebet und Hoffnung werde Christi Gast
Und alles wieder wird Friede und gut
Sterben wird Freude, wird Freiheit Mut!

St. John's Health Center
Santa Monica, California
Juni 18, 2012
Revised Culver City, California
Juli 27, 2012
Revised Los Angeles
Dezember 1, 2012

Ein Morgenlied

Na, kleiner Schlafmütze
Na, willst Du wach?
Eben gestern hörte ich
Dein glückliches Lach'

Sei nicht so trüb, Kleiner
Komm zu mir, nah'
Lächele, Dein Papa
Liebt Dich doch ja

Leben wird Freude
Kindheit ist Spiel
Elementarwesen
Tanzen, so viel'

Farbig wie Regenbogen
Ist unsre Welt
Blüten, Gemälde öffnen
Türe, sieh' quellt

Das Leben der Sonne
Mächtig und gut

Chapter Twelve. 1987 – 2012   Deutsche Gedichte   (German Poems)

Prachtvoll der Tag ist
Wohl uns der tut

So, mein liebliches
Kind, stehe auf
Grüße den Morgen
Und wach wirst Du drauf!

St. John's Health Center
Santa Monica, California
19. Juni 2012
Morgen

Alan Lindgren

About the Poet

Alan Lindgren was born in Encino, California in 1962. He is a poet by vocation, and a gifted fiction and non-fiction writer as well, with forty-six published books. Over 1,000 of his some 1,400 poems are published. More than 130 of his over 300 articles and essays have seen publication. His five biographies and an autobiography are also published. His stories and tales are published. He is a playwright with four plays published, and the published librettist to an operetta.

Mr. Lindgren's articles, fiction and poetry have appeared in *Biodynamics*, a publication of the *Bio-Dynamic Farming and Gardening Association, Inc.*, *The Correspondence*, newsletter of the Central Region of the Anthroposophical Society in America, and Highland Hall Waldorf School's newsletter *Rhythms*. His work has been used in an anthroposophical studies-in-English program and displayed at the Chicago Seminary of the Christian Community and a Christian Community church for the benefit of students, members and others.

He painted a series of watercolors in phthalo blue entitled *Study in Blue* (1999). After studying classical piano for ten years, Mr. Lindgren played as a *virtuoso* in May of 1987. On August 4, 1985, one day before his twenty-third birthday, he gave the *a cappella* solo *Were You There?*

Mr. Lindgren majored in German literature at Pomona College (1982-1984; 1985-1986) where he also studied sculpture, working primarily in *California alabaster*. His sculpture has appeared in three exhibitions. In 1984-1985 he attended the Freies Jugendseminar Stuttgart in Stuttgart, Germany, an anthroposophical arts youth seminar in the German language where he studied Rudolf Steiner's *Theosophy (Theosophie)*, clay sculpture, creative speech (speech formation) and eurythmy, among other subjects. Some of his sculptures are perfect works of art. He has eurythmy abilities. He is a student of the work of Rudolf Steiner (anthroposophy).

Mr. Lindgren worked on the bio-dynamic farm Buschberghof in Schleswig-Holstein, Germany, in 1982. In 1981-1982 he studied German privately. Through his private and college studies, and his experiences in Germany, he achieved proficiency in the language. Some of his poetry of

About the Poet

note is in German. His favorite language is German. He is a lyric poet.

As a child and youth Mr. Lindgren attended a Waldorf School (Highland Hall in Northridge, California, October 1973-1980; Green Meadow Waldorf School in Spring Valley, NY, autumn 1979). His Waldorf education is essential to his life. He participated in three Waldorf students' conferences 1979-1980 and has traveled in Europe. He loves Europe: the nature, peoples and cultures. In 1971-1972 he lived with his family in Tunisia, North Africa. Some of his dearest memories are of Tunisia.

He has had a variety of work experiences including dishwashing, waiting on tables, clerking in a drugstore, assistant teaching of small children on four occasions, gardening, student grounds work, work as a farmhand, a handyman, in a hardware store, secretarial work and production line work in a warehouse. He has tutored math and English. He is conversant in Spanish. He has done translation work from German into English.

Alongside writing, his greatest pleasures include walking, reading German, American and English literature (particularly anthroposophy, poetry and the classics), and playing and listening to live classical music. He has sung in eight choirs and has enjoyed singing since the fourth grade. He is a first tenor with a sweet voice. His favorite music is German Baroque religious—especially J.S. Bach—and all folk music.

Mr. Lindgren loves people of all ages and the animals. The warm and beautiful sun; the songs of birds; the green, blue and purple valleys, hills and mountains; the bright radiant clouds and sunlight; the colorful blossoms; and the wondrous ocean, moon and stars, speak to the poet in him. He has a special relationship to the realm of light and color. This is evinced in his love of flowers, the play of light, shadow and color in the heavens and painting. He loves the sunlight and sunsets clearly and dearly.

He is a "child of anthroposophy and of the Christian Community." His dearest friends are anthroposophists and priests. His father Arne Lindgren (1918-1994) was an anthroposophist from Sweden.

Mr. Lindgren lives and works in Los Angeles. His dear Mother lives nearby so that they can visit often.

www.ingramcontent.com/pod-product-compliance
Lightning Source LLC
Chambersburg PA
CBHW081123170426
43197CB00017B/2730